Lecture Notes in Computer Science 6652

Commenced Publication in 1973
Founding and Former Series Editors:
Gerhard Goos, Juris Hartmanis, and Jan van Lee

Alexander Romanovsky   Tullio Vardanega (Eds.)

Reliable
Software Technologies -
Ada-Europe 2011

16th Ada-Europe International Conference
on Reliable Software Technologies
Edinburgh, UK, June 20-24, 2011
Proceedings

 Springer

Volume Editors

Alexander Romanovsky
Newcastle University, School of Computing Science
Newcastle upon Tyne, NE1 7RU, UK
E-mail: alexander.romanovsky@newcastle.ac.uk

Tullio Vardanega
University of Padua, Department of Pure and Applied Mathematics
Via Trieste 63, 35121 Padua, Italy
E-mail: tullio.vardanega@math.unipd.it

ISSN 0302-9743   e-ISSN 1611-3349
ISBN 978-3-642-21337-3   e-ISBN 978-3-642-21338-0
DOI 10.1007/978-3-642-21338-0
Springer Heidelberg Dordrecht London New York

Library of Congress Control Number: Applied for

CR Subject Classification (1998): D.3, D.2, F.3, C.2, H.4, C.3

LNCS Sublibrary: SL 2 – Programming and Software Engineering

Typesetting: Camera-ready by author, data conversion by Scientific Publishing Services, Chennai, India

Printed on acid-free paper

Springer is part of Springer Science+Business Media (www.springer.com)

Preface

The 16th edition of the International Conference on Reliable Software Technologies – Ada-Europe 2011—took place in the John McIntyre Conference Centre, Edinburgh (UK). Previous editions of the conference were held in Switzerland (Montreux 1996 and Geneva 2007), United Kingdom (London 1997 and York 2005), Sweden (Uppsala 1998), Spain (Santander 1999, Palma de Mallorca 2004 and Valencia 2010), Germany (Potsdam 2000), Belgium (Leuven 2001), Austria (Vienna 2002), France (Toulouse 2003 and Brest 2009), Portugal (Porto 2006), and Italy (Venice 2008).

This year Ada-Europe was combined with the Ada Conference UK 2011 in one event, the Ada Connection, a union of two Ada events that have both been very successful in their own right. The Ada-Europe series of conferences has become established as an international forum for providers, practitioners and researchers in all aspects of reliable software technologies. The Ada Conference UK has been running in its current form since 2006 as a series of biennial one-day events, to highlight the increased relevance of Ada in safety- and security-critical systems. By combining these events, the Ada Connection provides a unique opportunity for interaction and collaboration between academics and industrial practitioners.

The Ada-Europe conference represents the main annual event promoted by Ada-Europe, in cooperation with ACM SIGAda. This third visit to the UK acknowledges the fact that the Ada community in this country is a major contributor to Ada-Europe's activities. This year the conference was organized by members of the Centre for Software Reliability (CSR) and School of Computing Science, Newcastle University (Newcastle upon Tyne, UK).

The scientific program of the conference, which feeds these proceedings, also included sessions devoted to multicore, verification, architecture and modelling, education and mixed criticality, all combined under a more general heading of reliable software technologies. This program is the result of a thorough selection process of 12 papers out of 30 submissions received from authors representing 14 countries.

The conference was enriched with the three keynote talks delivered by the invited speakers, opening the three central days of the conference:

- Peter Bernard Ladkin (University of Bielefeld CITEC and Causalis Limited), a recognized specialist in system safety, spoke about "Functional Safety of Software-Based Critical Systems."
- Pippa Moore (UK Civil Aviation Authority), an Avionic Systems Design Surveyor working with the CAA for over 14 years, gave a talk entitled "Hippocrates and DO-178B."

– Jeff O'Leary (US Federal Aviation Administration) with more than 18 years' experience in software development, systems acquisition and deployment of large-mission critical command and control systems, gave a keynote on "Assuring Software Reliability While Using Web Services and Commercial Products."

These proceedings include a paper by O'Leary based on the material he presented during the conference.

The conference program included two panels: *Programming Languages Meet Multicore* and *DO178C and Object-Orientation for Critical Systems*. The first panel discussed how the advent of multicore is shaking the very foundations of programming languages for concurrency, resource sharing, synchronization, etc. The panel was moderated by Erhard Ploedereder (University of Stuttgart) with Alan Burns (University of York), Tucker Taft (Sofcheck, Inc), and Kevin Hammond (University of St. Andrews) taking part as the panelists. The panel on *DO178C and Object-Orientation for Critical Systems* discussed how the high-integrity systems industry could reap the benefit of object orientation in their rigid and demanding development process. The panel was moderated by Tim Kelly (University of York) and involved Cyrille Comar (AdaCore), Jean-Pierre Rosen (Adalog) and Dewi Daniels (Verocel) debating pros and cons, risks and opportunities and ways to introduce elements of object orientation into safety-critical system development. The proceedings include a number of position statements.

As a forum that aims at connecting academics with the industrial knowledge and experience centered around reliable software technologies, the conference also included an exciting set of industrial presentations:

– *The Transition from MISRA C to SPARK Ada in Active Life Support*, by Alex Deas (DeepLife)
– *Ada Experience: ANSALDO Railways 'Available Safety Computer' CSD*, by Frederic Pinot (Ansaldo STS)
– *Executable UML Models for High-Integrity Development*, by Sam Moody (AWE)
– *Implementing a Software Product Line for a Complex Avionics System in Ada83*, by Frank Dordowsky (ESG Elektroniksystem)
– *Crimeville - Using Ada Inside an On-line Multi-user Game*, by Jacob Sparre (J.S. Andersen Consulting)
– *Monitorisation of Real-Time Properties of Certified Distributed Systems*, by Urueña Pascual (GMV Aerospace)
– *Debugging Mechatronic Applications Written in Ada*, by Wiljan Derks (NXP)
– *Automatic Code Generation Tools Developed in the Ada Language in a Safety-Critical Context*, by Laurent Duffau (Airbus)
– *Real-Time Management and Production Systems for Manufacturing and Energy Facilities*, by Jozef Cvirik (Ipesoft)

- *An Overview of DO-178C*, by Dewi Daniels (Verocel)
- *Building Software Tools in Ada: The Rapita Experience*, by Andrew Coombes (Rapita)
- *The Implementation of High-Integrity Data Structures*, by Phil Thornley (SPARKsure)

The conference also included a series of tutorials offering the participants an opportunity to learn particular approaches, technologies and tools, all aiming at the development of reliable software:

- *Experimenting with ParaSail: Parallel Specification and Implementation Language*, by S. Tucker Taft (SofCheck, Inc.)
- *Designing and Checking Coding Standards for Ada*, by Jean-Pierre Rosen (Adalog)
- *Programming Distributed Systems with YAMI4*, by Maciej Sobczak (Inspirel)
- *Why and How to Measure Non-functional Properties On-target*, by Ian Broster (Rapita Systems Ltd.)
- *Revamping the Software Technical Review Process*, by William Bail (The MITRE Corporation)
- *Use of Object-Oriented Technologies in High-Reliability Systems*, by Jean-Pierre Rosen (Adalog)
- *MAST: Predicting Response Times in Event-Driven Real-Time Systems*, by Michael G. Harbour (Universidad de Cantabria)
- *SPARK. The Libre Language and Toolset for High-Assurance Software*, by Roderick Chapman (Altran Praxis)
- *Distributed Programming Techniques in Ada*, by Thomas Quinot (AdaCore)

The conference program also included an invited lecture by Les Hatton, Professor of Forensic Software Engineering at Kingston University, well known for his contributions in software engineering. A paper drawn from Hatton's talk is included in these proceedings.

The conference's success heavily depends on the active and generous contribution of a number of individuals and organizations. All of them deserve our most sincere thanks. We are specially grateful to all who submitted quality contributions that enabled us to build an attractive and technically sound program. Of course we would like to thank all the attendees, who enable the conference to thrive. We want to thank the Organizing Committee for their help and support during the preparation of this event: Rod Chapman and Steve Riddle (Conference Co-chairs), Jamie Ayre (Industrial Chair), Albert Llemosí (Tutorial Chair), Joan Atkinson (Exhibition Chair), and Dirk Craeynest (Publicity Chair). The organizers are also grateful to the members of the Local Organizing Committee at Newcastle University: Claire Smith and Dee Carr.

The members of the Program and Industrial Committees did a fantastic job in providing quality reviews helping the Organizing Committee in the difficult task of eliciting the final contents of the conference. Last but not least, we wish to express our gratitude to the sponsors at the conference: AdaCore, Altran Praxis, Atego, BAE Systems, Ellidiss Software, Green Hills Software, INTECS and Rapita Systems Ltd.

June 2011   Alexander Romanovsky
                                                                   Tullio Vardanega

Organization

The 16th International Conference on Reliable Software Technologies – Ada-Europe 2011—was organized by Ada-Europe and Newcastle University (UK), in cooperation with ACM SIGAda.

Organizing Committee

Honorary Chair	John Barnes
	(John Barnes Informatics, UK)
Conference Co-chairs	Rod Chapman
	(Altran Praxis Ltd., UK)
	Steve Riddle
	(Newcastle University, UK)
Conference Program Co-chairs	Alexander Romanovsky
	(Newcastle University, UK)
	Tullio Vardanega
	(Università di Padova, Italy)
Tutorial Chair	Albert Llemosí
	(Universitat de les Illes Balears, Spain)
Industrial Chair	Jamie Ayre
	(AdaCore, France)
Exhibition Chair	Joan Atkinson
	(CSR, UK)
Publicity Chair	Dirk Craeynest
	(Aubay Belgium and K.U. Leuven, Belgium)
Financial Chair	Neil Speirs
	(Newcastle University, UK)

Program Committee

Alejandro Alonso	Franco Gasperoni	Stephen Michell
Ted Baker	Michael González	Javier Miranda
Johann Blieberger	Harbour	Daniel Moldt
Jørgen Bundgaard	José-Javier Gutiérrez	Jürgen Mottok
Bernd Burgstaller	Andrew Hately	Laurent Pautet
Alan Burns	Peter Hermann	Luís Miguel Pinho
Jon Burton	Jérôme Hugues	Erhard Plödereder
Rod Chapman	Albert Llemosí	Jorge Real
Dirk Craeynest	Franco Mazzanti	Alexander Romanovsky
Alfons Crespo	John McCormick	Bo I. Sanden
Juan A. de la Puente	Julio Medina	Sergio Sáez

Ed Schonberg
Theodor Tempelmeier
Jean-Loup Terraillon

Elena Troubitsyna
Santiago Urueña
Tullio Vardanega

Andy Wellings
Jürgen Winkler

External Reviewers

Albert Black
Lawrence Cabac

Ramn Fernndez
Alex Green

Alexei Iliasov
Hector Perez Tijero

Table of Contents

Education and Mixed Criticality

Panel: Language Paradigms for Multicore Programming

Panel: DO178C and Object-Orientation for Critical Systems

Signet Library Talk

Assuring Software Reliability While Using Web Services and Commercial Products

Jeffrey O'Leary

En-Route and Oceanic Programs, Air Traffic Organization (ATO-E)
US Federal Aviation Administration, Washington DC 20591, USA
Jeff.Oleary@FAA.Gov

Abstract. FAA's recent large Ada based En-Route Automation Modernization (ERAM) program has reintegrated many disparate system components into a modern composite architecture. The program must now deliver on its promise to facilitate the evolution of the U.S. National Airspace System (NAS) by integrating Next Generation Air Traffic Control (ATC) capabilities starting with System Wide Information Management (SWIM), Automatic Dependent Surveillance (ADS-Broadcast) and the En Route Data Communications (Data Comm). One of the major challenges is to implement and leverage more open, flexible interfaces made possible by web service technologies and to ensure reliability and security of high performance data and communications services despite increased reliance on less trusted commercial products. The paper focuses on maturity, problems and lessons learned during the development of the initial SWIM as a Service Oriented Architecture (SOA) extension to the En Route Automation Modernization ERAM System.

Keywords: FAA, Air Traffic Control, ATC, Web Technologies, High Reliability, Safety Critical, ERAM, SWIM, DataComm, ADS-B, FUSE™, Lessons Learned, SOA, SOA Security.

1 Introduction

The U.S. Federal Aviation Administration (FAA) manages sixty percent of the world's air travel. The agency depends upon large, complex and highly available and reliable software systems to manage the vast commercial and civil aviation network and to carry out the agency's mission of ensuring high capacity, efficient and extremely safe air travel for the flying public. Ada has become a strategic technology in developing and sustaining systems that require high availability and high reliability.

ERAM, developed by the Lockheed Martin Corporation provides the automation services for the En Route domain at the twenty Continental United States Air Route Traffic Control Centers (ARTCCs). The ERAM system is comprised of three environments: 1) Operational, 2) Support, and 3) Test and Training and is the backbone of the U.S. En-route Air Traffic Control system. The current total ERAM

A. Romanovsky and T. Vardanega (Eds.): Ada-Europe 2011, LNCS 6652, pp. 1–16, 2011.
© Springer-Verlag Berlin Heidelberg 2011

software size is approximately 1.45 million lines of code with more than fifty percent of the operational code written in Ada.

The Next Generation Air Transportation System (NextGen) [1] is the Federal Aviation Administration's (FAA) plan to modernize the National Airspace System (NAS) through year 2025. Through NextGen, the FAA is addressing the impact of air traffic growth by increasing NAS capacity and efficiency while simultaneously improving safety, reducing environmental impacts, and increasing user access to the NAS. NextGen consists of five major elements:

SWIM will provide a single infrastructure and information management system to deliver high quality, timely data to many users and applications. By reducing the number and types of interfaces and systems, SWIM will reduce data redundancy and better facilitate multi-user information sharing. SWIM will also enable new modes of decision making as information is more easily accessed.

ADS-B will use the Global Positioning System (GPS) satellite signals to provide air traffic controllers and pilots with much more accurate information that will help to keep aircraft safely separated in the sky and on runways. Aircraft transponders receive GPS signals and use them to determine the aircraft's precise position in the sky. This and other data is then broadcast to other aircraft and air traffic control. Once fully established, both pilots and air traffic controllers will, for the first time, see the same real-time display of air traffic, substantially improving safety. The FAA will mandate the avionics necessary for implementing ADS-B.

DataComm: Current communications between aircrew and air traffic control, and between air traffic controllers, are largely realized through voice communications. Initially, the introduction of data communications will provide an additional means of two-way communication for air traffic control clearances, instructions, advisories, flight crew requests and reports. With the majority of aircraft data link equipped, the exchange of routine controller-pilot messages and clearances via data link will enable controllers to handle more traffic. This will improve air traffic controller productivity, enhancing capacity and safety.

Next Generation Network Enabled Weather (NNEW) - Seventy percent of NAS delays are attributed to weather every year. The goal of NNEW is to cut weather-related delays at least in half. Tens of thousands of global weather observations and sensor reports from ground, airborne and space-based sources will blend into a single national weather information system, updated in real time. NNEW will provide a common weather picture across the national airspace system, and enable better air transportation decision making.

NAS voice switch (NVS) - There are currently seventeen different voice switching systems in the NAS, some in use for more than twenty years. NVS will replace these systems with a single air/ground and ground/ground voice communications system.

ERAM has already been developed and currently is in the deployment phase. Several of the En-route sites have already started using the ERAM system for air traffic services. Being the backbone of the En-route ATC System, all five major NextGen elements will need to integrate with ERAM. The author is involved with the software development of the ERAM programs and will oversee development and integration of the subsystems and components to incorporate the NextGen elements and capabilities.

2 Achieving Software Reliability

FAA's Software systems are growing in complexity and size, and new software paradigms support new forms of mix and dynamic progression of software applications. Following sections discusses the En Route systems environment and challenges inherent in software development of the web technology- based SWIM system, called ERAM SWIM.

2.1 NAS Service Criticality

The FAA defines service criticality in National Air Space Document NAS-SR-1000A [2] for each Air Traffic Control (ATC) service as

- Critical – A service that if lost would raise the risk associated with providing safe and efficient local NAS operations to an unacceptable level
- Essential – service if lost would significantly degrade ATC such as weather, General Info, Monitor & Control, System Data Recording
- Routine – service if lost would not significantly impact ATC such as Test & Training, Support

In terms of the availability, down time and switch time, numbers converts to the following –

Criticality	Availability	Down / Year	En Route	Down / Year	Switch Time
Safety Critical	0.99999	5.3 min	0.999998	1.1 min	6 sec
Efficiency Critical	0.9999	53 min	0.99998	11 min	½ -1 min
Essential	0.999	8.8 hrs	0.9998	1.8 hrs	½ -10 min
Routine	0.99	88 hrs	0.998	18 hrs	none

Fig. 1. Service Criticality, Down Time and Switch Time for En-route ATC Systems

The ERAM software implements requirements associated with each of these categories: radar data processing and display is safety critical while flight data processing is efficiency critical. The ERAM SWIM program was originally conceived as being essential, but as the SWIM program has evolved it became increasingly clear that the system or subsystem services provided would evolve as it offered opportunities to increase automation in efficiency critical flight data coordination across NAS systems. For example, the preliminary architecture for the initial En Route and Terminal portions of DataComm proposed to utilize ERAM SWIM to facilitate sharing of flight data from all twenty ERAM centers to support the logon and context management functions. This also introduced new requirements for explicit safety assurance engineering mitigation in both ERAM and ERAM SWIM. Switch time, of course, alludes to the reliability and fault tolerance strategies employed to achieve the higher availability requirements. These strategies include synchronized hot standby Address Spaces (AS), robust error detection and rapid recovery including data reconstitution redundant processor resources, and redundant network paths guaranteeing message atomicity, ordering, and integrity. Address Space (AS) is a unit of work dispatchable by the operating system. Each AS occupies its own area of memory in the processor and each AS contains one Ada main program. Reference [3] provides a good overview of the ERAM architecture; for our purposes it is sufficient to understand that reliability engineering is a prime driving consideration in the architecture and development of En Route Systems. To achieve the availability and reliability profile, the En Route program office has implemented an increasingly feature rich middleware supporting various capabilities needed to facilitate real world operations mostly supported by the FlightDeck® [4]. ERAM is the latest evolutionary step and implements a layered API-based architecture of system management and real-time monitoring capabilities. Table 1 identifies a subset of those capabilities that are vital to the reliability strategies of ERAM.

Table 1. Key ERAM Middleware FlightDeck® Features supporting RMA

Fault Tolerance features	Low-level crash and hang detection, notification to backup resources to become primary, fault data recording, and automatic restart and recovery of failed components.
Monitoring and Control features	Continuously updated, detailed status and performance data from each application, processor and network element; failure alerts and warnings; operator commands to element to restart, switch, stop, change modes (active, backup, test); monitor system security; generate detailed off-line performance and status reports; configure and control simulations.
Software Upgrade and System Maintenance features	Ability to download, load and cutover new versions of system and application software or adaptation without impacting user operations/cutover. Ability to remove and replace hardware and configure new resources
Support for data recovery, capture and debugging	Extensive reconfigurable data recording of system and application state, messages and data; off-line and on-line diagnostics, file management and state service check pointing to support application synchronization, switching and restarting even (e.g.) from complete facility power failures.

ERAM and the other major NAS systems have developed and evolved these capabilities and the software to implement them in order to achieve the Reliability, Maintainability and Availability (RMA) and system requirements. The FAA system users who monitor, control, repair and support the operational systems have developed requirements, detailed expectations, and extensive procedures for managing and certifying the operational system resources are ready and able to meet the required availability profiles and support air traffic services. The NAS systems, including ERAM, are largely custom developed, proprietary and expensive. This makes data sharing and integration across major NAS components very difficult, expensive and inefficient. To evolve the NextGen capabilities the services and data in these systems must be exposed and connected securely to the authorized systems.

3 System Wide Information Management (SWIM)

As discussed above, today's National Airspace System (NAS) comprises systems that have been developed over time for specific purposes. In general, they are connected discretely to support specific data and information exchange needs. Each of these interfaces is custom designed, developed, managed, and maintained individually at a significant cost to the FAA. The NextGen relies upon a new decision construct that will bring more data, systems, customers, and service providers into the process. Data will be needed at more places, for more purposes, in a timely manner, and in common formats and structures to ensure consistent use. The resulting decisions must be distributed to the affected parties efficiently and reliably to support timely execution.

In the past, the state of the art for connecting two systems required a fixed network connection and custom, point-to-point, application-level data interfaces. Current NAS operations depend upon these legacy information systems, but much of their data remains inaccessible to the rest of the NAS. This is an impediment to efficiency, impairs situational awareness across the NAS, and prevents optimization of ATC services. The FAA has identified a need to reduce the high degree of interdependence among systems and move away from the proliferation of unique, point-to-point application interfaces. Therefore, SWIM as envisioned will provide an open, flexible, and secure information management architecture for sharing NAS data and enabling increased common situational awareness and improved NAS agility. SWIM will implement commercial off-the-shelf hardware and software to reduce development cost and time as well as support a loosely coupled service-oriented architecture that allows for easier integration of new connections, services and systems.

The mission of the SWIM Program is to realize greater information sharing among NAS stakeholders, both FAA and non-FAA users, to support the NextGen concept of operations. This includes, but is not limited to, aeronautical information, flight data, traffic flow management data, surveillance, and weather information. To achieve this mission, SWIM's strategy is to migrate and connect NAS applications into a distributed processing environment focused on information sharing. The larger mission requires these systems to be highly scalable, robust and agile. These open architecture principles are expected to provide value by reducing costs, reducing risks, enabling new services, and extending existing services to facilitate highly coordinated NAS wide operations.

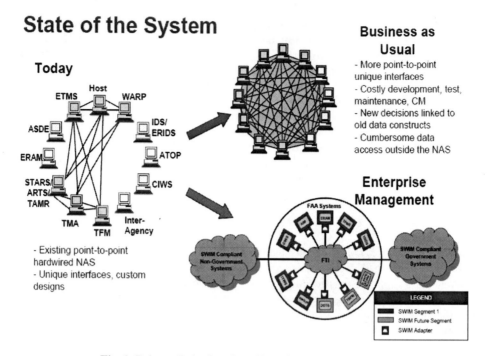

Fig. 2. Point-to-Point Interfaces Transformed by the SWIM

As indicated in Figure 2, currently numerous systems in the NAS communicate with each other using unique, custom point to point connections.

Specifically, SWIM has been under development using Service Oriented Architecture (SOA) principles in designing and specifying NAS Air Traffic Management (ATM) services. Key functional elements of the SWIM SOA are the SWIM Core Capabilities and SWIM Business services. The initial SWIM Core Capabilities are: Interface Management (Interface Specification, Interface Discovery, Schema Management, Service Invocation, SWIM Basic Profile), Messaging (reliable messaging), Security (authentication and authorization), and Enterprise Service Management (service monitoring and configuration). The SWIM Program Office specifies the standards for all SWIM Core Capabilities; however, implementation is delegated to the domain and major program offices called SWIM Implementing Programs (SIPS).

The SWIM Service Container [5] is an infrastructure component that will provide many of the needed support (hosting) capabilities. It will relieve the SWIM Implementing Program (SIP) implementers of some of the housekeeping tasks required in service delivery. It should provide connections to data, to messaging services, and to authentication/authorization services (i.e., the SWIM Core Capabilities), as well as provide logging, error handling, and other support functions. SWIM will use the Service Container as a means for achieving consistency and interoperability among diverse NAS programs and operating elements, in the absence of a centralized service infrastructure. The Service Container will be comprised of an existing product (commercial off-the-shelf (COTS) or open source software) with components configured to support SWIM specific goals such as interoperability, extensibility, and portability. The Service Container also serves as the point of enforcement for enterprise-wide SWIM policies and accelerates service implementation by providing standard, reusable common infrastructure elements. It provides access to enterprise resources and simplifies the service design and development process.

Therefore, SWIM in other words is an IT infrastructure program that will operate in the background to provide data to authorized users. SWIM will implement a Service-Oriented Architecture (SOA) in the NAS and will allow the FAA to create new system interfaces more quickly and cheaper than is possible today. It will facilitate the data-sharing that is required for NextGen. SWIM is not a set of avionics equipment or a substitute for NAS modernization programs or to replace the FAA Telecomm Infrastructure (FTI). As a matter of fact, SWIM will enable increased common situational awareness and improved NAS agility to deliver the right information to the right place at the right time.

Progress® FUSE™ Services [6], which is a middleware providing a web service stack supporting an Enterprise Service Bus (ESB) messaging framework, was selected and is now in use in several SWIM development projects. FUSE™ is an open source SOAP and REST web services platform based on Apache CXF for use in enterprise IT organizations. It is productized and supported by the FuseSource group at Progress Software. FUSE™ Services Framework service-enables new and existing systems for use in enterprise SOA infrastructure. It is a pluggable, small-footprint engine that creates high performance, secure and robust services using front-end programming APIs like JAX-WS and JAX-RS. It supports multiple transports and bindings and is extensible so developers can add bindings for additional message formats so all systems can work together without having to communicate through a centralized server. FUSE™ Services Framework is part of a family of SOA infrastructure tools that include the FUSE™ ESB (based on Apache ServiceMix), FUSE™ Message Broker and FUSE™ Mediation Router (based on Apache Camel).

Function	FUSE™ Component	Open Source Apache Project
Web Services (WS) Stack	FUSE™ Services Framework	Apache CXF
JMS Messaging	FUSE™ Message	Apache ActiveMQ
Integration Patterns (EIP)	FUSE™ Mediation Router	Apache Camel
Service Bus (ESB), OSGi Service Container	FUSE™ ESB	Apache Service Mix

Fig. 3. FUSE™ Functions Matrix

Most importantly, the FUSE™ products can be configured in a cluster type environment to support the primary/standby configuration needed for failover to achieve higher reliabilities. Specifically, the Message Broker, of Apache ActiveMQ can coordinate Master-Slave JMS message communication between applications in redundant service containers within a processor or between two processors. For ERAM SWIM the design is to establish the redundant processors into an Application Cluster LAN with two Gigabit Ethernet cables cross-mounted between the servers. EtherChannel [7] is used to combine the two connections into a single logical channel able to withstand failure in one of the connections and support high bandwidth if required. The primary/standby state information is shared through a file system on the En Route enterprise storage servers. It required extensive learning and testing, and assistance from the Progress vendor to implement this approach, however testing so far has shown that the ActiveMQ Master-Slave broker achieves almost immediate failover after detection of the failure of a primary component. As will be seen, extensive effort went into improving detection of some failures and failure modes.

Most of the SWIM programs so far, including ERAM SWIM, have selected Eclipse, a free and open source (FOSS), web service-friendly integrated development environment (IDE). The Eclipse Project (now Eclipse Foundation) was started by IBM in November 2001 with many other vendors and established in January 2004 as an independent, not-for-profit corporation, to act as the guardian for the Eclipse community. The Eclipse platform is a universal tool platform. It can handle most any type of resource (Ada, Java, C / C++, XML, HTML, even doc or text files.). The Eclipse architecture supports extensions (developed as plug-ins) that teach the platform how to work with these different kinds of resources. Hibachi Ada Development Tools project (ADT), is the Ada plug-in for Eclipse that provides extensive functionality for Ada developers, needed for the ERAM interface. For ERAM SWIM, Eclipse is supported on the developers' Windows workstations using an existing plug-in which allows Eclipse to communicate with ERAM's AIX development machines.

Maven serves a similar purpose as the Apache Ant tool which is more or less the imake equivalent for these environments. Maven (FOSS) uses a construct known as a *Project Object Model* (POM) to describe the software project being built, its dependencies on other external modules and components, and the build order. It comes with pre-defined targets for performing certain well defined tasks such as compilation of code and its packaging. Maven is also architected to support plug-ins allowing it to use any application using standard inputs. Maven dynamically downloads Java libraries and Maven plug-ins from one or more repositories. Maven provides built-in support for retrieving files from the Maven Central Repository [8] and other Maven repositories, and can upload artifacts to specific repositories after a successful build. A local cache of downloaded artifacts acts as the primary means of synchronizing the output of projects on a local system.

3.1 ERAM SWIM Architecture

The ERAM SWIM initially is developing capabilities to use this SOA web service paradigm to increase NAS wide access to flight data in support of new traffic management capabilities. As depicted in Figure 4 below, the SWIM Interface Subsystem (SIS) uses the FUSE™ ESB and infrastructure components, running on an AIX platform, to implement an OSGi service container that manifests the physical end-points and service interface. It is instantiated as a single JVM process on each of two SWIM servers which allows for load-balancing, fault-tolerance, and software maintenance. The service container also handles the inflow and outflow of management data, such as auditing, configuration, error handling, and service status. In this first phase, now in test and preparing for deployment at a single ERAM site, each SIS consists of a single service hosted in the OSGi container which will automate flight plan changes from the Traffic Flow Management System (TFMS) to mitigate severe weather or other air traffic flow initiatives [9]. TFMS will request and consume pre-departure flight plans impacted by the initiative, create a reroute amendment, and submit that back to ERAM as an update request via the SWIM Interface Service (SIS). FUSE™ Mediation router (CAMEL), Message Broker (JMS) and Services Framework (CXF) provide for SOAP/JMS messages, handle the transport mechanisms, and supports automatic failover. SIS sends the update requests (amendments) to the SWIM adapter in the appropriate ERAM using this "back-end" interface.

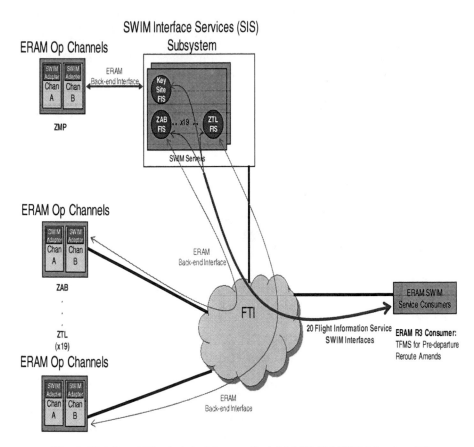

Fig. 4. High Level Physical Architecture for initial ERAM SWIM Services [9]

The SWIM adapter is a client proxy of the ERAM flight data manager (FDM) which "owns" the ERAM flight object data store. ERAM SWIM Service Consumers

(TFMS here) will communicate with the ERAM SWIM Flight Information Service (FIS) using the FAA's Telecommunications Infrastructure (FTI) routed over the existing En Route Communications Gateway (ECG). Each ERAM has an ERAM SWIM adapter component, providing the mechanism for FIS consumers to send or receive data from the ERAM core. To minimize impact on ERAM performance, the SWIM adapter - built on the ERAM Publisher FrameWork [10] - maintains a local mirror of all relevant flight data. The SWIM adapter functions as a wrapper translating the internal ERAM data representation to XML messages, publishing an XML flight object to the SWIM application database, and converting XML flight update requests back into internal ERAM binary format. Planned near-term capabilities include the ability to support terminals obtaining pre-departure flight data for local aircraft for use in uploading clearance information by DataComm in lieu of current voice procedures. Numerous other flight data "consumer" applications are in planning along with legacy replacement programs that would take advantage of the new Flight Information Service (FIS) to move away from their current custom, single-purpose interfaces. Still other services are envisioned for weather data, airspace, route and restriction status information, radar track information, etc. ERAM also becomes a consumer for other NAS system data such as Pilot Reports (PIREPs), other TFMS flow data, and ATC Tower, and Runway Visual Range (RVR) data.

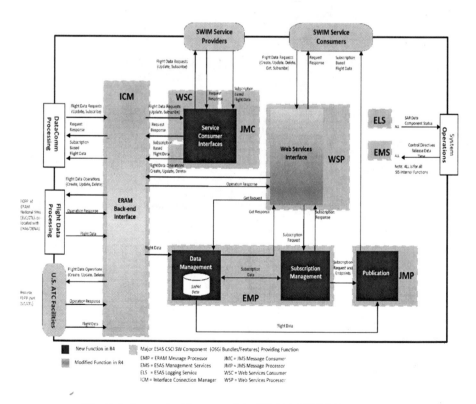

Fig. 5. Software Architecture of the ERAM-SWIM Components

The software architecture of the ERAM SWIM Application Services (ESAS) CSCI is represented in Figure 5. In addition to the update, create, delete of the initial SIS (light blue), now depicted as the ERAM Message Processor (EMP), a subscribe and publish flight data service is provided using a WSDL-based FIS interface in the Web Services Processor (WSP) component and as a JMS Message Processor (JMP) replying to subscriber requests and endpoints. WSP exposes multiple service endpoints to support load balancing and fail-over and performs authentication and authorization of service consumers.

In addition, the future ERAM service consumer interfaces are depicted as the consumer side of the WSDL-based web service (WSC) and JMS subscription service (JMC). The context of the ERAM back end interface is extended to add DataComm processing for context management and log-on services.

3.2   ERAM SWIM RMA Design Challenges

Figure 5 also explicitly depicts the System Analysis and Recording (SAR) logging service (ELS), monitor and control and software release management interfaces (EMS) providing the types of features described earlier for the ERAM FlightDeck® middleware. ERAM SWIM service element status and performance will be aggregated on the ERAM M&C consoles using the same iconography as other ERAM elements. Control commands share the same GUI and command line semantics. However, under the covers, the ERAM middleware is not there and most of these capabilities differ not only in implementation, but also their semantics and behavior which leads to a significant operator training burden and significant user acceptability risk. Even with the more limited context of the initial single service SWIM SIS a number of difficulties arose attempting to provide for similar RMA features and providing for essential service critical performance. The next phases leading to the end state architecture must be scalable to efficiency critical if, as expected, ERAM SWIM services in the future are required to meet that level (e.g. Flight Data Input Output replacement). The balance of this paper will discuss those challenges including fault detection performance, failure recovery behavior, database fault tolerance, CAS (commercially available software) and FOSS limitations and problems that even extend to the development tools.

Certainly most critical to the FAA requirements and expectations is understanding the reliability and availability of FUSE™ and other selected CAS/FOSS. ERAM's custom developed environment is carefully designed using allocated failure thresholds on each component, however vendors and licensers of many software products generally do not have or are unwilling to make failure mode and MTBF data available to support decision making. The ERAM SWIM development team therefore had to collect whatever industry available data they could, consult with company tech support personnel, and apply industry norms based on software language and size to calculate an expected failure rates for the COTS products. Table 2 shows the results of that analysis for several key products selected for the SIS software and SWIM servers.

Table 1. Calculated Failure Rates for Key ERAM SWIM CAS Products

Product	Failure Rate
FUSE™	4.785 E-06
TECTIA [11]	4.027 E-05
AIX (Includes Power VM)	1.240 E-06
ORACLE	1.376 E-06

Clearly FUSE™ presented a risk in achieving high reliability in the long run even with robust redundancy and fail-over from the Master-Slave mechanisms. Perhaps even more important to measure is the mean time to repair (MTTR) sometimes called mean time to recover. MTTR begins at the failure and includes the time to detect the failure, restart or switch processing resources, and reach steady state on the restarted application. In ERAM developed software, particularly software supporting the highest criticality services, recovery must usually complete on average within 5 to 6 seconds. To support this performance requirement, the middleware can detect the overwhelming majority of failures in 1 to 2 ms by using an OS process state change handler, complete failure handling and notify the standby address space well below 100 to 200 ms, and determine the scope and recovery action to begin restarting the failed component under 500 ms from detection, and have the restarted application redundancy restored with a complete restart of the failed element to become the standby in 2 to 5 seconds. The very rare or unlikely software hang or loop condition won't achieve this, but is detectable by a configurable heartbeat mechanism, usually set at about 6 seconds. The low probability of occurrence allows the aggregate availability requirements to be met.

However, with the FUSE™ instances on ERAM SWIM, the middleware was not there to implement these features partly to save cost and schedule, but also because the initial SWIM service simply did not justify the need for this robustness. After all, in the final analysis, SWIM is a message broker and router; for most uses it will suffice to have the consuming client set a timer on its requests and retry on another endpoint and/or the redundant service container so that the service is provided. ERAM SWIM initially therefore specifies the client/consumer retry while failure detection not detected by the ActiveMQ broker relies on a developed polling mechanism using JMX to monitor the JVM PID. The ERAM SWIM developer had to unexpectedly port and extend an ERAM low-level function to facilitate the monitoring of the poll mechanism. The resulting time for ESAS to be able to process web service requests after a single component failure on one SWIM server was established as 30 seconds, a time that will likely need to be improved upon in the future. To detect and recover broker hang conditions would be much higher and there is concern some unknown failure modes may not detectable by the system at all.

Therefore, ERAM SWIM developers had to incorporate product changes under the FUSE™/Apache license, in several processing threads. Essentially these changes provided FUSE™ components the ability to dispatch events to the monitor – basically heartbeats. The FUSE™ documentation and normal product tech support, however, was not sufficient to understand where all these beating hearts needed to go and it became necessary to engage Progress Software (Fuse™ vendor) architect level engineers as private consultants to the developers to facilitate these and other non-fatal alert features. Another key difference is that ERAM is able to make granular recovery decisions to minimize the scope of the restart, but ERAM SWIM restarts the entire service container on a node along with all of its bundles and endpoints in the event of any ESAS or CAS failure. This increases the time to restore redundant services by a small order of magnitude.

Other important differences exist in the area of commanding application resources from the M&C position. FlightDeck® has several specifically designed directives and receives an ACK from the application targeted. The system manager on SWIM relies on simple SNMP requests and has no ACK feature, so that manual configuration, maintenance, or recovery commanded actions are less certain. Likewise with status reporting, ERAM applications collect and report detailed health information on the applications resources and performance. SWIM relies on occasional polls to the major products and, ultimately SWIM application health is derived from the interfacing ERAM application which is running on FlightDeck® by monitoring the state of its communication with ESAS. In fact, all status collection and reporting for the available SWIM software elements is sent to the ERAM state service via the interfacing ERAM application which then sends the updates to the ERAM M&C for operator display and event recording.

Perhaps the biggest and most surprising challenge faced in architecture and design of ERAM SWIM has been in providing for a robust, persistent, fault-tolerant data store. Originally, SWIM expected to implement an Oracle cluster (Oracle RAC) in particular to support a publication/subscriber service prototype. Several technical problems were encountered and largely overcome. However, the procedures for reconfiguring the cluster after a new software cutover was error-prone, not consistent with current cutover design, and required administrator skills to correct if performed improperly. In addition, after a network failure in the prototype configuration, it was learned Oracle RAC will initiate a kernel panic to protect itself from shared database corruption. SWIM servers, unlike ERAM FlightDeck®, do not have capabilities to handle and recover from such a panic. Several alternative database options were evaluated which had their own limitations that made them risky for the En Route environment. The point design is now GPFS shared filed system implemented on the En Route Enterprise storage subsystem which is a redundant pair of units. ActiveMQ depends on the shared file system for queue/topic persistence and to support fail-over. While prototyping it was learned that AIX mirroring with GPFS will lead to a file system un-mount for lack of quorum when one of the two storage units is unavailable. An unplanned application had to be written to perform the mirroring instead of using the GPFS mirroring facilities which still leaves a tiny, but non zero dual failure risk.

3.3 System Safety and Security Considerations

ERAM SWIM makes some major changes which affect or relate to security. These include moving from a single service consumer to multiple consumers, expanding from a single key site to multiple ERAM SWIM sites and adding JMS inbound and outbound traffic in addition to web traffic. The inbound JMS and web traffic is externally initiated whereas the ERAM security architecture had ERAM initiating all physical and data interfaces. Key components of the security approach include:

- Transport-level encryption is used (both inbound and outbound). This is effectively HTTP/SSL for web traffic, JMS/SSL for publication traffic. The SSL exchange is two-way.

- Certificate-based authentication using x.509 credentials will be necessary to identify and authenticate users.

- Schema validation of all incoming messages

- Proxy web traffic, proxy JMS traffic.

Additionally, the credential-based access control is implemented on a per-operation, per-data element basis.

Pre-departure DataComm is architected to leverage the FIS in phase 2 of ERAM SWIM. DataComm applications are subject to safety assurance requirements of DO278 [12]. After much agency deliberation the requirement was established as AL3, but even this modest assurance level requirement requires that all developed, commercial, and FOSS products be developed to that level or the safety risk mitigated. The key challenge here is to assure flight data and message integrity in an xml and web service environment. The DataComm architecture uses ERAM SWIM as path or transport between DataComm application functionality that resides in ERAM and DataComm applications that reside on the consumer side. Since FIS does not need to do any actual flight data processing it was determined that the integrity risk could be mitigated and thus assured to an acceptable level, by implementing high integrity encryption around certain flight data. FIS will perform selection of flights and filtering (masks) of the fields of a flight object needed by each subscriber, but is constructed using the "untrusted" (per DO278) FUSE™ products. To resolve this problem, the (trusted) ERAM SWIM adapter computes robust checksums on the key protected data fields and includes the checksum as a field attribute in the SWIM XML message. FIS passes it along in the filtered data it publishes to the authorized consumer. Any consumer that requires high-integrity (such as DataComm) is then responsible to retain the attribute through its consumer web service implementation and verify field level integrity in a trusted application on the consumer side of the interface. In reality, this data integrity issue is not unique to the SWIM environment; ERAM will also be modified similarly to protect flight data integrity from CAS in the ERAM environment including AIX and the Ada Runtime. However, this significantly impacts CPU and network utilization of both ERAM and ERAM SWIM. Early prototyping verifies the increases are a tolerable tradeoff to achieve the assurance objectives while using the SWIM CAS and FOSS products.

As mentioned earlier, there is even an RMA impact from the associated development tools. Software maintainability and supportability depend on available tools. The FAA does not wish to become its own product support organization. In selecting this large number of CAS and FOSS products for ERAM SWIM, it was necessary to consider the cost and difficulty if these products later had to be replaced, and for more critical components whether the vendor or consortium managing them was capable and committed for the medium to long term. The Hibachi ADT plug in for Eclipse IDE fortunately was not actually used in this project because Ada software in the SWIM programs represented enhancements and modification of actual ERAM "owned" source code, not new features for the SWIM service environment. Therefore, all ERAM mods and additions followed the ERAM development process and used the baselined development environment. As of January 2011, Hibachi ADT is an archived project on the Eclipse Foundation web site. There appear to be no current plans to support and promote those capabilities so that had the program incorporated it would now have to evaluate its' risk and the cost to move away from it. In this CAS/FOSS collaborative environment there clearly are significant supportability risks to be managed.

4 Conclusions

ERAM SWIM developers successfully implemented initial ERAM SWIM supporting create, update, delete using Java based web services to interface with ERAM to implement a robust Flight Information Service that will be used to automate previously manual reroute procedures. Many more opportunities exist to exploit this single interface to ERAM to support sharing across the NAS. The service container will allow these services to share the interface even while maintaining independence and allowing decoupling of the internal implementation. A number of challenges were overcome; chief among them is overcoming the dearth of product documentation and support for developing high availability web services. Some of the difficulties encountered result from the institutionalization of strategies and procedures in the FAA En Route domain. The learning curve for developing high reliability web services is steep and requires significant experimenting, consulting and expert assistance, as well as analyzing the source code of the FOSS products for failure mode and implementation details not documented to the same standards that custom developed code is expected to meet. Productivity with FOSS is very high because the key functional capabilities exist already and the developers' job is to configure and harness those capabilities to meet the requirements of the particular service to be implemented.

Acknowledgements. The author wishes to thank Dr. Alok Srivastava, Technical Fellow of TASC Inc. for the initiative and the discussions, and FAA's ERAM and ERAM-SWIM Program Offices for their support. Assistance and support from the ERAM and ERAM-SWIM development team of Lockheed Martin Corporation is also highly appreciated.

References

1. FAA Next Generation Air Transportation System (NextGen),
   http://www.faa.gov/nextgen/
2. NAS SR-1000A, National Airspace System, System Requirements Specification,
   http://www.faa.gov/about/office_org/headquarters_offices/
   ato/service_units/techops/atc_facilities/cm/dcc/
   also available freely on the other websites

3. Keynote presentation - Use of Ada in Lockheed Martin for Air Traffic Management and Beyond by Judith Klein of Lockheed Martin. In: ACM SIGAda 2006 International Conference, Albuquerque, New Mexico, USA (2006)
4. Keynote presentation - An Ada Retrospective: Developing Large, Mature, and Reliable Systems by Richard Schmidt of Lockheed Martin Information Systems & Global Services. In: ACM SIGAda 2009 International Conference, Tampa Bay, Florida, USA (2009)
5. FAA SWIM Program Office Reference to the SWIM Container Infrastructure, http://www.faa.gov/about/office_org/headquarters_offices/ato/service_units/techops/atc_comms_services/swim/documentation/media/newsletters/SWIMNewsletter_EditionOneweb.pdf
6. FUSE^{TM} Source Progress Software Company, http://FUSESource.com/
7. CISCO Ether Channel, http://www.cisco.com
8. Maven – An Apache software project management and comprehension tool, http://maven.apache.org/
9. Goldstein, S., Indigo Arc LLC, Rockville Maryland USA, High Level Physical Architecture for initial ERAM SWIM Services White Paper (2009)
10. Klein, J., Sotirovski, D.: The Publisher Framework. Ada User Journal 27(4) (December 2006)
11. TECTIA Information Security COTS Solutions, http://www.tectia.com/en.iw3
12. DO 278 A Radio Technical Commission for Aeronautics (RTCA) Inc. developed Guidelines for Communications, Navigation, Surveillance, and Air Traffic Management (CNS/ATM) Systems Software Integrity Assurance, http://www.rtca.org/

Detecting High-Level Synchronization Errors in Parallel Programs

Syed Aoun Raza, Stefan Franke, and Erhard Ploedereder

Dept. of Programming Languages, University of Stuttgart
Universitaetsstrasse 38, 70569 Stuttgart, Germany
{raza,ploedere}@informatik.uni-stuttgart.de,
stefan-franke@web.de

Abstract. Synchronization errors in parallel programs are not limited to race conditions involving accesses to single variables. Absence of these errors does not guarantee that programs are error free. However, many of the remaining errors cannot be recognized without a higher level of abstraction for the communication patterns. This paper discusses two types of high-level error scenarios, namely non-atomic protection and lost-updates, and presents a static framework to detect situations where such synchronization anomalies can manifest themselves.

1 Introduction

The recent introduction of multi-core processor architecture has brought much popularity and attention to parallel programming. Nowadays, many programmers have become interested in the gains promised by parallelized programs and by multi-cores. However, simultaneous execution of threads with resources shared among them affect the speed-ups achievable by parallelization as well as the correctness of the sequential code sequences. Moreover, incorrect synchronization causes unexpected and often unacceptable results. The real limitations of exploiting multi-core architectures lie with the unexpected behavior of the parallel programs produced by thread interleaving or interference and resulting synchronization problems.

A major issue for parallel programming are race condition anomalies[1], which need to be avoided by the application of an effective synchronization strategy. Data races involving accesses to single shared variable are a well investigated issue and fall in the category of low-level access anomalies. However, application of synchronization mechanisms does not always guarantee the absence of such problems. The experience with *object-oriented languages* and their synchronization primitives provides evidence that alleviation from low-level data races alone does not guarantee program correctness on higher abstraction levels of the semantics of the applications[2]. The existing definitions of race conditions are simply not sufficient to detect higher-level race issues. New concepts and extensions of old ones are needed to uncover more erroneous situations.

In this paper we present two types of anomalies, which cover some of the higher-level race condition scenarios.

The paper is organized as follows: section 2 introduces the problem of high-level data races. Section 3 and 4 present the concepts for detecting these data races. Section 5

A. Romanovsky and T. Vardanega (Eds.): Ada-Europe 2011, LNCS 6652, pp. 17–30, 2011.

describes the implementation and section 6 presents experimental results. Related work is discussed in section 7 and section 8 concludes the paper.

2   High-Level Synchronization Errors

Synchronization errors occurring in parallel programs can result in data corruption, unintended results and eventually system failure. A higher abstraction layer enables the detection of inconsistent synchronization, even if sets of shared variables or sets of critical paths are involved. Our work targets two types of high-level synchronization anomalies. First, we discuss *non-atomic protection*, a type of anomaly that is basically identical to a high-level data race as defined by Artho et al.[2]. We extend the definitions and the associated detection mechanism further to cover nested situations and path-sensitivity. Second, we introduce an error type termed *lost-update* to cover data races occurring because of value dependencies among separate critical code segments. Both of these types will be discussed in more detail in the next sections.

3   Non-Atomic Protection

3.1   Definition and Concept

This section provides definitions and concepts for non-atomic protection faults. The following is based on high-level data races as defined by[2].

A non-atomic protection fault can occur when two concurrent threads access a set V of shared variables, which should be accessed atomically, but at least one of the threads accesses V partially several times such that those partial accesses diverge.

Artho et al. define two concepts to identify such errors, namely *view* and *view consistency*. A view expresses which fields are guarded by a lock and view consistency is defined as mutual compatibility of views between all threads. Whenever views are found to be inconsistent between threads, a non-atomic protection is being reported. Artho et al. have implemented these concepts in the form of a dynamic analysis in a run-time verification tool JPaX[3].

Our work, on the other hand, focuses on static analysis and extends the concepts accordingly. Its implementation is integrated into RCanalyser [4]. It reports a complete but conservative set of non-atomic protection faults.

In our previous work on RCanalyser we defined critical paths as those parts of a program that access shared resources and need to be executed atomically by threads. The concept of views is actually quite similar to that. Fields are accesses to shared resources and a *lock* is a way to enforce an atomic execution of a sequence of statements. A critical path $CP(l, t, \pi)$ of a thread t can then be defined as a single-entry, single exit execution path $\pi = (s_1, ...s_n)$, where s_1 locks l and s_n unlocks l.

$$CP(l, t, \pi) = \{s_j, j = 1..n | \pi \text{ an execution sequence } (s_1, ..., s_n) \wedge$$
$$\forall s_i \in \pi : s_i \in statements(t)$$
$$\wedge s_1 \text{ locks } l \wedge s_n \text{ unlocks } l$$
$$\wedge \nexists s_x \in \pi, 1 < x < n : \text{ unlocks } l\}$$

In the above definition, $statements(t)$ contains all statements reachable by a thread t. (The notion of statement refers to an intermediate level (IL) representation of the program [5], in which compound statements of the source language have been mapped to simple IL statements).

To incorporate the notion of views in RCanalyser, we use the above definition and combine it with our definition of shared memory accesses. The set of shared accesses M is defined as:

$$M = \{m | \exists s_i, s_j \in S : \exists t_i, t_j \in T : (s_i \in statements(t_i) \wedge (s_j \in statements(t_j)$$
$$\wedge (t_i \neq t_j \vee (t_i = t_j \wedge t_i \in mult\_inst)))$$
$$\wedge m \in Nonlocals$$
$$\wedge m \in (DEF(s_i) \cup USE(s_i))$$
$$\wedge m \in (DEF(s_j) \cup USE(s_j))\}$$

The set S contains all statements of the program and the set T all threads. The $mult\_inst$ indicates whether multiple instances of a thread might exist at runtime. $Nonlocals$ are variables accessed by, but not locally declared in functions (with static variables in C belonging to $Nonlocals$). The standard data-flow terms $DEF(s)$ and $USE(s)$ contain memory elements that are modified or read by statement s.

Now a view can be defined based on the statements of a critical path and shared variable accesses throughout the program. Our definition of a view is comparable to Artho's:

$$view(l, t, \pi) = \{m | m \in M : \exists s \in CP(l, t, \pi) : m \in (DEF(s) \cup USE(s))\}$$

3.2   Lockset Analysis

Our first implementation of a lockset analysis was quite similar to the flow- and context-sensitive algorithm proposed in [6]. This algorithm is endangered by an exponential runtime behaviour for special cases when several lock contexts are involved. Therefore, to avoid such behavior of the lockset algorithm, we implemented a new lockset analysis based on data-flow analysis.

Our data-flow based lockset computation is flow-, path- and context-sensitive. The computation of the information follows standard forward data-flow techniques. The algorithm traverses the program control-flow-graph to solve the data flow equations. The lock acquisition and release operations are interpreted as *Gens* and *Kills*. Further, entry- and exit-lockset information for routine bodies is mapped as *In* and *Out* sets, respectively. For a path-sensitive analysis, control joins union the results from the branches into a set of locksets, each of which is processed independently from then on. Thus a *locksetsset* results.

For each call, the called function is analyzed for each lockset in the locksetset active at the call site (the *entry-lockset*). If a previous analysis has been performed for this lockset, the cached *exit-locksetsset* is retrieved. Recursive calls are recognized and yield an empty *exit-lockset* upon first encounter. Otherwise, the function body is now analysed accordingly. At the end of analyzing a function body, the computed lock information *exit-lockset* is returned and stored in a cache to avoid future re-computations with the same entry-lockset. The function cache pairs entry-locksets and exit-locksetssets. Standard data-flow analysis techniques will iterate until the *exit-locksetssets* of recursive routines have stabilized.

The computation of shared variables and views is integrated into the lockset analysis to avoid additional traversal of the program.

Our static framework relies on several preceding analyses to get sufficient auxiliary information, i.e., points-to, control-flow and data-flow analyses. Points-to-information is required for shared variable and lock detection. A precise general points-to analysis consumes a lot of time and space, especially for larger programs. The points-to analysis we normally employ in any preceding analyses is flow- and context-insensitive (Anderson[7]). It provides us with a set of possible targets for a given pointer. If a lock variable is defined as a pointer, a flow-insensitive analysis will return all locks assigned to the variable as candidates. Based on this imprecise information, the lock of a lock-acquire statement can not be determined with adequate precision. Therefore, another feature of our lockset algorithm is the reduction of possible candidate locks returned by the points-to query. To achieve this, we implemented an inter-procedural data-flow-based search for lock pointer assignments to gather more detailed information about the value of a lock pointer at a particular acquire statement. With this, lockset analysis and view determination become more precise. The search algorithm uses the data-flow in SSA form to traverse to the most recent assignments of the lock variable. If the algorithm reaches the start of the function that contains the lock-acquire statement and finds that the lock comes from an input parameter then all callers of the function are determined and searched for an assignment of the lock. The locks thus found are then used to refine the set of candidates. In many cases a singleton is the result.

An example of such a situation can be seen in listing 1.1. The listing shows that a lock pointer is assigned twice in the code segment at point A and point B. At point C the points-to query will deliver both candidates for the view resulting in two views. It is obvious from the code segment that this information is too conservative. Our approach traverses back to the most recent assignment to the pointer and consider only that one for view generation, which reduces extra and spurious information. Consequently, the analysis produces less false positives and, in turn, reduces spurious view generation.

3.3 Path-sensitive View Analysis

The path-sensitive data-flow based lockset analysis approach discussed in 3.2 is designed to avoid exponential runtime behaviour. It enables us to easily include a path-sensitive computation of views. Path-sensitive view detection covers situations like the one illustrated in listing 1.2 correctly, which otherwise would not be detectable. The thread 1 contains three views ($\{gl.x\}$, $\{gl.x, gl.y\}$, $\{gl.y\}$) and thread 2 only one view ($\{gl.x, gl.y\}$). A path-insensitive analysis finds two views ($\{gl.x, gl.y\}$, $\{gl.y\}$) for thread 1 and therefore would not find the non-atomic protection fault.

To incorporate path-sensitive computation of views in our lockset analysis, we needed to extend the traditional approach. We define the set of views as a data-flow item, and include it in the data-flow computation along with the locks. Each decision point in the program triggers a copy of the set of current views for each branch. The current set of views is extended by a newly created view whenever a lock-acquire statement is reached.

Listing 1.1. Intra-procedural decision on possible lock

```
lockptr  l;
.......
l = l1; // Point  (A)
.......
.......

l = l2; // Point  (B)

lock(l);    // Point  (C)
   int tmp = balance;
   balance  = tmp + amount;
unlock(l);
```

Listing 1.2. Path-sensitive Viewset Analysis

Thread 1:	Thread 2:
`lock(m);`	`lock(m);`
`gl.x = 1;`	`gl.x = 25;`
`if  cond then`	`gl.y = 10;`
`    gl.y = 10;`	`unlock(m);`
`    unlock(m);`	
`    ...`	
`    lock(m);`	
`    gl.y = 1;`	
`end  if;`	
`unlock(m);`	

All views of the set are updated when a shared variable is accessed. When a lock-release statement is reached the corresponding view is finalized, stored and removed from the set of current views. It may stay active on other branches, so that path-specific views can arise and differ. At join points, the analysis unions the sets of current views of the incoming branches.

3.4 Nested Views

The basic definition of view as stated above only includes accesses to shared variables in a view. In our work, we extend this definition further to cover more complex patterns of lock acquisition and release. For example, relationships between views can provide information to improve the soundness of results. The extended definition of a view is as follows: A view expresses which shared variables are guarded by a given lock, and which locks are acquired during the execution of the critical paths associated with the view:

$$view(l,t,\pi) = \{a|(a \in M : \exists s \in CP(l,t,\pi) : m \in (DEF(s) \cup USE(s)))$$
$$\vee (a \in L : \exists s \in CP(l,t,\pi) : s \text{ locks } a)\}$$

In the above equation, L contains all locks of the program. With this extension it is possible to link a view to all views contained within that view. We call these views *child* views and the container views *parents*. The following definition describes the parent relationship:

$$parents(v) = \{v_p | v_p \in V(t) \wedge v_p \neq v \wedge lockingOperation(v) \in statements(v_p)\}$$

The parent views of a view are all views which contain the lock-acquire statement of the view. The equation contains $V(t)$, which is the set of views of thread t. In addition, $lockingOperation(v)$ returns the lock-acquire statement in v, and the set $statements(v)$ contains all statements of a view v.

Listing 1.3 illustrates a situation when ignoring the nesting of views triggers false positives. The algorithm proposed by Artho finds a non-atomic protection fault for the two views for lock l in thread 1 and the view for lock l in thread 2, but the parent views with lock m provide sufficient synchronization for the variables in this situation. The *parent-child* relationship between views defined above enables the analysis to exclude such false positives from the set of reported faults and thus to deliver more precise results. Figure 1 gives a more intuitive description of the scenario, where outer and inner views can be thought of as egg shells.

In general, a non-atomic protection fault includes three inconsistent views, two of which are from the same thread and violate the atomicity of the third view from the other thread. Whenever the two views in the first thread have a common parent view, and its generating lock is identical to the lock of the third view in the second thread or of any of its parent views, then atomicity is not violated. We define:

$$no\_nap\_error(v_1, v_2, v_3) \leftrightarrow \exists p_1 \in parents(v_1) : \exists p_2 \in parents(v_2) : p_1 = p_2$$
$$\wedge \, lock(p_1) = lock(v_3) \vee \exists p_3 \in parents(v_3) :$$
$$lock(p_1) = lock(p_3)$$

In the above equation, $lock(v)$ denotes the lock that generates the view v. This check is inserted on every non-atomic protection fault found by the basic algorithm in order to reduce the number of false positives.

Listing 1.3. Nested Views

Thread 1:	Thread 2:
lock(m);	lock(m);
lock(l);	lock(l);
gl.x = 25;	gl.x = 25;
unlock(l);	gl.y = 10;
lock(l);	unlock(l);
gl.y = 10;	unlock(m);
unlock(l);	
unlock(m);	

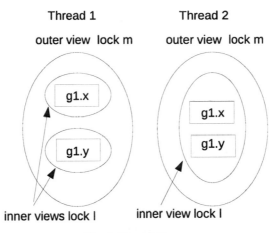

Fig. 1. Nested Views

3.5   View Generation

The view generation process is transformed into a forward data-flow problem using the following data-flow equations.

$$Gen(e) = \begin{cases} v(l,t,e) & \text{if } e \text{ is a } lockOp \text{ on } l \\ 0 & otherwise \end{cases}$$

$$Kill(e) = \begin{cases} \forall \text{ views on } l \text{ and } t & \text{if } e \text{ is a } unlockOp \text{ on } l \\ 0 & otherwise \end{cases}$$

$$In(e) = \bigcup_{x \in Pred(e)} Out(x)$$

$$Out(e) = Gen(e) \bigcup (In(e) - Kill(e))$$

The In and Out sets contain the set of active views. Each program expression (e) is processed according to its kind, i.e., whether it generates (Gen) a view or closes a view ($Kill$). If an expression e is a lock acquisition statement ($lockOp$) then a new view is created and stored in the set of already active views ($viewset$). For the purposes of view analysis, identifying the critical path by the starting expresssion e is sufficient. A lock release statement ($unlockOp$) will close ($Kill$ case) any open view for that particular lock, remove it from the set of active views and add it to the set of views of the thread ($viewset(t)$) identified by the context-sensitive information of the analysis. The computation of active views is a data-flow problem that unions the active views at control joins.

Along with the propagation of active views, the views are filled by data-flow actions. For our non-atomic update problem, we would record the variables read or written. For our second problem of lost-updates (see section 4), we also want to record the kind of access.

$$Action(e) = \begin{cases} \forall views\ v \in In(e)\ Insert(v, < x, Read >) \\ \qquad \forall\ \text{x read } in \text{ e} \\ \forall views\ v \in In(e)\ Insert(v, < x, Write >) \\ \qquad \forall\ \text{x modified } in \text{ e} \end{cases}$$

Once the DF-solution has stabilized, views can be stored as part of the description of thread t:

$$Action(e) = \begin{cases} \forall\ views\ v(t,l,*)\ in\ In(e)\ Storev(t,l,*) \\ \qquad\qquad \text{if } e \text{ is a unlockOp on } l \end{cases}$$

Similarly, the parent relationship described in section 3.4 can be computed.

$$Action(e) = \begin{cases} \forall\ views\ v\ in\ In(e)\ Insert(v, l_1) \\ \qquad\qquad \text{if } e \text{ is a lockOp on } l_1 \end{cases}$$

Any standard data-flow algorithm can be used to solve the data-flow equations and perform the additional actions. In our implementation we chose a worklist algorithm.

Our subsequent non-atomic protection detection is based on the computed views and is an extension to the high-level data race detection by Artho. The difference lies in the handling of path-sensitive view information, nested views and the translation into a static analysis.

4   Lost-Updates

Lost-Updates is a newly categorized error situation, which is detectable by an extension to the view concept.

4.1   Definition and Concept

A lost-update occurs when a value dependency exists between the reading of a shared variable in one view of a thread and the writing of the same variable in a second view of this thread, while there is a concurrent write access to the shared variable in another thread.

Listing 1.4 illustrates a situation where a lost-update fault can manifest. The functions *deposit* and *withdraw* are part of a bank account management system. There is a shared variable *balance*, which is accessed in one view of function *deposit* and in the two views of function *withdraw*. As illustrated in the code, $Thread1$ performs a *deposit* by updating the account *balance*, and $Thread2$ *withdraw*s some amount from the same account. The critical property is that there exists a value dependency between the two views in *withdraw* from the reading of the variable *balance* to its subsequent writing. The dependency is caused by the local variable *tmp*, which carries the value of *balance* from one view to the other. Whenever *deposit* and *withdraw* are called concurrently in separate threads, a lost-update can occur: *deposit* might be scheduled in between the execution of the two views in *withdraw*. The effect of the *deposit* update to the *balance* is lost.

To detect lost-updates, we further extend the definition of views and incorporate information provided by data-flow analysis. An access to a shared variable in a view now also identifies the kind of access.

Let F be the set of all shared variables of a program, f a variable of F and a the access kind read or write. The tuple (f, a) describes an access to variable f with access kind a. The set of all tuples (f, a) of a program is A. Furthermore, let $B(t, l)$ be the set of critical paths for thread t and a lock l, then each $b \in B(t, l)$ generates a view $v \in \mathcal{P}(A)$.

By using data-flow information, each write access in any view can be checked for a value dependency on the reading of the same variable in another view in the same thread. Our analysis utilizes SSA generated *def-use* information: each variable read in the examined write access is investigated for the previous write access by following the *(use)-(def)* relationship. If necessary, the variables read by this write access are analyzed in turn. The search terminates successfully if the variable originally in question is found to be read. It terminates unsuccessfully when all applicable *(use)-(def)* relationships have been examined. Successful finds are recorded for the respective variable and views. This process is repeated until all write accesses to shared variables in all views have been analyzed.In listing 1.4 *tmp* gets the value of *balance* and afterward a write into *balance* involves *tmp*. The analysis records a value dependency between the two views involving *balance*.

Listing 1.4. Lost-update example

Thread 1:	Thread 2:
| ```
void withdraw(int amount){
    lock(1);
    int tmp = balance;
    unlock(1);
    if (tmp >= amount){
        lock(1);
        balance = tmp - amount;
        unlock(1);
    }
}
``` | ```
void deposit(int amount) {
    lock(1);
    balance = balance + amount;
    unlock(1);
}
``` |

Let s be a statement in a program and the function $statement(a)$ returns the statement for the tuple $a \in A$. The function $reads(s)$ returns all read accesses that occur in statement s and the function $lastwrite(y)$ returns the last write access on a variable y by means of data-flow information. Then the described traversal of the SSA information is defined as a recursive function:

$$reads_r(s) = reads(s) \bigcup\nolimits_{x=lastwrite(reads(s))} reads_r(x)$$

Phi-nodes are handled in the same way as statements. The recursion stops when there is no read access in an assignment or an initialization. The SSA-traversal is interprocedural. Whenever the algorithm reaches the start of a function body and finds that a parameter has to be followed, all callers of that function are determined. Using this traversal we can define the set of value dependencies for lost-updates:

$$value\_dependency\_set(t) = \{(v_1, v_2, f) | v_1, v_2 \in V(t)$$
$$\wedge\, a_1 \in v_1 \wedge a_1 = (f, write)$$
$$\wedge\, a_2 \in v_2 \wedge a_2 = (f, read)$$
$$\wedge\, statement(a_2) \in reads_r(statement(a_1))\}$$

In this definition, $V(t)$ denotes the set of views generated by thread t. With the information about a value-dependency across two views in one thread, it is then possible to detect lost-updates by searching for a concurrent write access in a view in another thread. The potential lost-update fault in the example (Listing 1.4) is found in this fashion.

4.2   Algorithm

The lost-update detection is shown in algorithm 1. This fault detection phase presumes that all views and all value dependencies among them have been computed. It starts by taking all pairs of threads, views and value dependency relations. Any of the found value dependencies can result in a lost-update fault whenever a concurrent write access on the same shared variable may happen in another thread. For this reason, each view of the second thread is searched for a concurrent write access.

Algorithm 1. Lost-update detection

```
function FAULT_DETECTION(threads)
    for all pairs of threads (t₁,t₂) do
        for all vset ∈ VIEWSETS(t₁) do
            for all vd ∈ VALUE_DEP(vset) do
                sv ← SHARED_VAR(vd)
                for all view ∈ VIEWS(t₂) do
                    for all w ∈ WRITES(view, sv) do
                        REP_LOST_UPDATE(vd, view, w)
                    end for
                end for
            end for
        end for
    end for
end function
```

---

5   Implementation

The implementation is integrated into RCanalyser, which is a part of Bauhaus tool suite [5]. Bauhaus provides a strong infrastructure for static program analysis. It contains many general analyses, such as points-to, control- and data-flow analyses, which provide the basis for the implementation of the algorithms described in this paper. As illustrated in figure 2, language frontends derive an intermediate representation (IML) from program source. Many subsequent analyses operate on the IML representation, which is an *Attributed Syntax Tree* capable of representing programs from different languages e.g., C/C++, Ada and Java.

The Bauhaus tool suite contains a generic points-to analysis interface with plugable implementation of several context- and flow-insensitive algorithms e.g., Steensgaard [8], Das [9], and Anderson [7]. In RCanalyser any of these points-to analyses can be utilized to compute pointer targets. This step is necessary before the generation of control-flow information, because in the case of heavy usage of function pointers an approximation of callees would not be possible at the call-sites and control-flow graph generation may become less effective. Afterwards, a control-flow analysis is performed to obtain intra- and inter-procedural control-flow graphs of the program on which our lockset-analysis computation will be performed. Data-flow analysis and SSA generation are done, which we later use for detecting value dependencies as discussed in section 3.2.

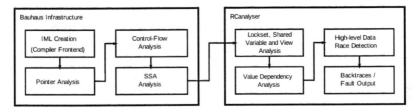

Fig. 2. Bauhaus infrastructure and RCanalyser

In the next phase a combined analysis is performed which computes the locksets, shared variables and view information. This is followed by the detection of value dependencies among multiple views of a thread with the help of SSA information. The algorithm is presented in section 4.

Once all required information is thus available, the tool proceeds with the detection of high-level synchronization errors, i.e., non-atomic protection and lost update. Non-atomic protection errors are determined by an approach similar to [2]. For lost-update detection we apply the algorithm 1.

The last step outputs the errors in the RCanalyser text-based shell. For each of the two error types we report the information needed to locate the fault in the source code. One of the most important activities is the calculation of backtraces, since we want to exactly trace a path to the erroneous expression, starting with the main program. Whenever a decision point is reached or a function call is followed, the backtrace shows this information along with source file and line number.

6   Test and Evaluation

For the test of our analysis we have selected a set of open source benchmarks of varied size. Table 1 shows all programs along with the number of lines of code, of threads, of views and of variables per view as the quantitative metrics of our analysis.

The metrics give an indication about the degree of parallelism in the analyzed programs, i.e., the maximal number of threads and the maximal number of views contained.

In addition to obtaining the shown statistics, we measured the runtime of analyses. The results are presented in table 2. All of these tests were performed on a Xeon 3GHz PC with 12 GB main memory.

Table 1. Program statistics

Program	Lines of Code	Threads	Views	Variables/View
pfscan	1K	2	11	1 – 7
aget	1K	4	4	2
retawq	15K	2	0	–
clamav	51K	5	8	1 – 53
openvpn	27K	1	0	–

Table 2. Runtime (in sec.) per functionality and program

Program	Lockset analysis	Value dependency	Viewset analysis	Backtraces
pfscan	<1	<1	<1	2
aget	<1	<1	<1	<1
retawq	29	<1	<1	1
clamav	187	<1	<1	<1
openvpn	8	<1	<1	<1

Table 3. High-level Data Races

Program	Non-atomic protection	Lost-update
pfscan	3	0
aget	0	0
retawq	0	0
clamav	0	0
openvpn	0	0

First of all, value dependency and viewset analysis are very fast for all test programs. In part, this can be attributed to the fact that the number of views and variables per view is low and thus the workload is limited. If the number of views and variables per view remains to be low in relation to the program's size, the runtime of value-dependency and viewset analysis is unlikely to become a problem. More of a problem for large programs will be the lockset analysis. Therein, it is especially the shared variable detection that takes significant time whenever use is made of points-to analysis, while the lockset analysis itself and the view detection, with all shared variable information available, was very fast in all our test cases. It should be applicable to larger code basis as well. The Backtrace algorithm is essentially of the same complexity as the lockset analysis algorithm without the shared variable detection.

In our tests on benchmark programs, we found three non-atomic protection faults in *pfscan*, but were unable to find any lost-updates. The test results are summarized in table 3.

In addition, we applied our analysis on several smaller self-written test programs which contain non-atomic protection and lost-update faults. There, all faults were reported.

7 Related Work

Several tools and techniques have been developed for analyzing multi-threaded programs for low-level data races based on static and dynamic analyses. The dynamic approach of the Eraser algorithm [10] maintains a lock set for each variable: the set of locks protecting the variable. The algorithm is also implemented in the Visual Threads tool [11] to analyze C and C++ programs. It examines a program trace for locking patterns and variable accesses in order to detect potential race conditions. The Eraser algorithm maintains a lock set for each variable: the set of locks protecting the variable. The idea of views turns this around and studies the variable association with a given lock. This notion provides the possibility to discover situations where high-level synchronization faults can occur. The original inspiration for such problematic situations was based on examples published by Artho et. al. [2], which we modified and extended to capture more scenarios, and discussed in section 3.

On the other end of the spectrum, several static analysis tools and algorithms exist to detect low-level data races in programs. Tools like RacerX [6], Jlint [12] and RCanalyser [4] all use static analysis. Theorem proving techniques are used in the ESC [13] tool which, however, requires an annotated version of the program, and does not appear to be as efficient as the Eraser algorithm in finding low-level data races.

Dynamic tools come with the advantage of delivering precise information about errors, but the analysis is of course limited to the single program execution, whereas static tools have the advantage of code coverage, but the information is less precise and may raise the degree of false positive results.

Another analysis technique is model checking, which explores all possible executions in a program. Usually model checkers use a model of the program; exceptionally, Java PathFinder, which is developed by NASA [14], checks the program directly. However, model checking techniques suffer from the state space explosion problem.

8 Conclusions

We have discussed how shared-memory concurrent programs contain data race errors on a higher-level of abstraction, which involves groups of shared variables. Absence of low-level data races ensured by proper use of synchronization mechanisms does not guarantee program correctness, however. We presented two typical synchronization errors and described concepts and implementation of an analysis for their detection. The presented static analysis is enriched with extended view consistency techniques to detect error situation, which previous techniques could not, and it reduces spurious error reporting present in other analyses. Our analysis handles nested higher-level synchronization regions and provides path-sensitive error computation. The test runs discussed in the paper have delivered positive results in reducing false positives and shown the practicability of the analysis. In the future, we plan to extend this analysis to also incorporate techniques to compute the propagation of the effects of error situations on subsequent computations of the program.

References

1. Netzer, R.H.B., Miller, B.P.: What are race conditions? some issues and formalizations. LOPLAS 1992: ACM Letters on Programming Languages and Systems 1, 74–88 (1992)
2. Artho, C., Havelund, K., Biere, A.: High-level data races. Software Testing, Verification and Reliability 13, 207–227 (2003)
3. Havelund, K., Roşu, G.: An overview of the runtime verification tool java pathexplorer. Form. Methods Syst. Des. 24, 189–215 (2004)
4. Raza, A., Vogel, G.: RCanalyser: A Flexible Framework for the Detection of Data Races in Parallel Programs. In: Kordon, F., Vardanega, T. (eds.) Ada-Europe 2008. LNCS, vol. 5026, pp. 226–239. Springer, Heidelberg (2008)
5. Raza, A., Vogel, G., Plödereder, E.: Bauhaus - A Tool Suite for Program Analysis and Reverse Engineering. In: Pinho, L.M., González Harbour, M. (eds.) Ada-Europe 2006. LNCS, vol. 4006, pp. 71–82. Springer, Heidelberg (2006)
6. Engler, D., Ashcraft, K.: RacerX: Effective, Static Detection of Race Conditions and Deadlocks. In: SOSP 2003: Proceedings of the 19th ACM Symposium on Operating Systems Principles, pp. 237–252. ACM Press, New York (2003)
7. Andersen, L.O.: Program Analysis and Specialization for the C Programming Language. PhD thesis, DIKU, University of Copenhagen (1994)
8. Steensgaard, B.: Points-to Analysis in Almost Linear Time. In: POPL 1996: Proceedings of the 23rd ACM SIGPLAN-SIGACT Symposium on Principles of Programming Languages, pp. 32–41. ACM Press, New York (1996)
9. Das, M.: Unification-based Pointer Analysis with Directional Assignments. In: PLDI 2000: Proceedings of the ACM SIGPLAN 2000, Conference on Programming Language Design and Implementation, pp. 35–46 (2000)
10. Savage, S., Burrows, M., Nelson, G., Sobalvarro, P., Anderson, T.: Eraser: A Dynamic Data Race Detector for Multi-Threaded Programs. In: SOSP 1997: Proceedings of the 16th ACM Symposium on Operating Systems Principles, pp. 27–37. ACM Press, New York (1997)
11. Harrow, J.J.: Runtime checking of multithreaded applications with visual threads. In: Havelund, K., Penix, J., Visser, W. (eds.) SPIN 2000. LNCS, vol. 1885, pp. 331–342. Springer, Heidelberg (2000)
12. Artho, C., Biere, A.: Applying static analysis to large-scale, multi-threaded java programs. In: Australian Software Engineering Conference, pp. 68–75 (2001)
13. Detlefs, D.L., Rustan, K., Leino, M., Nelson, G., Saxe, J.B.: Extended static checking. SRC Research Report 159, Compaq Systems Research Center (December 1998)
14. Visser, W., Havelund, K., Brat, G.P., Park, S.: Model checking programs. In: ASE 2000: Proceedings of the Fifteenth IEEE International Conference on Automated Software Engineering, Grenoble, France, pp. 3–12. IEEE Computer Society, Los Alamitos (2000)

Design and Implementation of a Ravenscar Extension for Multiprocessors

Fabien Chouteau and José F. Ruiz

AdaCore
46 rue d'Amsterdam, 75009 Paris, France
{chouteau,ruiz}@adacore.com

Abstract. New software architectures demand increasing processing power, and multiprocessor hardware platforms are spreading as the answer to achieve the required performance. Embedded real-time systems are also subject to this trend, but in the case of real-time high-integrity systems, the properties of reliability, predictability and analyzability are also paramount.

The Ada 2005 language defined a subset of its tasking model, the Ravenscar profile, that provides the basis for the implementation of deterministic and time analyzable applications on top of a streamlined run-time system. This Ravenscar tasking profile, originally designed for single processors, has proven remarkably useful for modelling verifiable real-time monoprocessor systems.

The forthcoming Ada 2012 language proposes a simple extension to the Ravenscar profile to support multiprocessor systems using a fully partitioned approach. The implementation of this scheme is simple, and it can be used to develop applications amenable to schedulability analysis.

This paper describes the design and implementation of a restricted run time supporting the Ravenscar tasking model on a bare board multiprocessor machine for safety-critical development.

1   Introduction

The Ravenscar model for single processors defines a deterministic and analysable tasking model which can be supported with a run-time system of reduced size and complexity. It supports accurate analysis of real-time behavior using Rate Monotonic Analysis (RMA) [13] and Response Time Analysis (RTA) [12]. In recent years, research on scheduling theory for multiprocessor systems [8,6] has paved the way to timing analysis in multiprocessor systems.

Major aspects to be dealt with in the design of a multiprocessor environment are priority handling, assignment of tasks to processors (the terms processor and CPU will be used interchangeably in this paper), communication and synchronization mechanisms, time keeping, delays, and handling of external events.

According to the allocation of priorities to tasks, there are either static off-line scheduling algorithms, or dynamic policies, where priorities are calculated at run time. Dynamic-priority scheduling algorithms for multiprocessors, such as Pfair scheduling [7], can achieve better processor utilization than static-priority ones. However, the higher complexity of dynamic algorithms, their much higher run-time overhead, and

A. Romanovsky and T. Vardanega (Eds.): Ada-Europe 2011, LNCS 6652, pp. 31–45, 2011.

their lower predictability and robustness in overload situations make them less attractive for high-integrity systems. The Ravenscar profiles follows this static approach.

In terms of relationship between tasks and processors, the spectrum goes from global scheduling, where any task can be executed on any processor at any time, to partitioned scheduling, where each task is allocated for its whole lifetime to concrete processors. The schedulability of neither approach is strictly better than the other [3] (there are task systems that are feasible using a global partitioning that cannot be scheduled in a partitioned system and vice versa). However, the partitioned approach has some interesting advantages: 1) it can rely on well-known optimal monoprocessor priority-assignment schemes and timing analysis techniques (local RMA on each CPU), and 2) the run-time support is simpler.

This partitioned approach simplifies also development and testing, and eventually certification, by the physical separation between tasks executing on different processors. This concept is the major strength of the Integrated Modular Avionics (IMA) [15] architecture and the ARINC 653 [5] standard, that enables independently-produced applications to execute together on the same hardware. Note that the proposed Ravenscar extension for multiprocessors provides limited temporal partitioning (a task allocated to a given processor cannot use execution cycles from another processor) and no memory partitioning, while ARINC 653 provides a more flexible temporal partitioning (it can provide protection for tasks executing in the same processor) plus memory partitioning. However, the Ravenscar scheduling model could be supplemented with space protection, and a more flexible temporal partitioning using execution-time clocks and timers and timing events [10].

According to the Ravenscar principles of simplicity, reliability, and predictability, fully partitioned scheduling, using static-priority policy, appears as the natural extension of the monoprocessor Ravenscar profile [4]. There are tools and techniques supporting the allocation of tasks to processors, the assignment of task's priorities, and the timing analysis of the resulting systems. The major drawback of such scheduling mechanism is that the maximum worst-case achievable utilization is a third the capacity of the platform [3]. The worst-case achievable utilization is defined as the total utilization that makes any periodic task set below this limit schedulable, while there may be a task set with a total utilization above this limit which is not schedulable.

Note that finding an optimal assignment of tasks to processors is an NP-hard bin-packing problem that needs to be solved off-line in this partitioned scheme (not by the system scheduler), although there exist heuristic algorithms, such as Rate-Monotonic-Next-Fit (RMNF) [9], Rate-Monotonic-First-Fit (RMFF) [9], and Rate-Monotonic-Best-Fit (RMBF) [14].

There exist many different communication and synchronization paradigms for multiprocessor architectures, such as semaphores, monitors, message passing, etc. Restricted protected objects are used in the Ravenscar profile for this, and they will be used the same way over multiprocessors. The underlying run-time support will have to be modified to cope with the new requirement of synchronizing tasks which are potentially operating in parallel, hence demanding extra locking mechanisms.

The provision of a common high resolution time reference and precise and deterministic absolute delays is based on the use of two different hardware timers [21]. There may be multiprocessor hardware platforms with more timers (there may even be per-processor timers), but requiring just two timers will facilitate portability to different targets.

Finally, handling of external interrupts is supported using protected procedures. Interrupt handlers could be handled by one or more CPUs in the system, but for simplicity of implementation and timing analysis the chosen approach is to allocate each interrupt to a single CPU.

This paper and the described implementation build on the ideas presented at IRTAW 2009 [17] which led to the definition of AI05-0171 [4]. The following sections will describe the specific additions to the existing monoprocessor Ravenscar profile to support multiprocessor systems using a fully partitioned approach, with each task and interrupt allocated statically to a concrete processor. This scheme can be supported by a streamlined run-time system, and applications built following this approach can apply timing analysis techniques on each processor separately (the scheduling problem for partitioned allocation is a combination of bin packing followed by single processor dispatching).

2 Definition of Ravenscar for Multiprocessors

This section provides a high-level description of the model implied by the Ravenscar extension to multiprocessors, based on the monoprocessor definition.

2.1 Task Scheduling

Scheduling is proposed as a simple extension to the monoprocessor fixed-priority preemptive scheduling algorithm supported by the Ravenscar profile, where tasks are statically allocated to processors and task migration among CPUs is not allowed. Each processor implements a preemptive fixed-priority scheduling policy with separate and disjoint ready queues. A task is only in the ready queue of one processor, and the CPU to which a task belongs is defined statically. Whenever a task running on a processor reaches a task dispatching point, it goes back to the ready queue of the same processor.

Tasks are statically allocated to processors using a new pragma (*pragma CPU*). If the pragma is not specified, the task is allocated to a default CPU.

The underlying idea is that each processor executes a statically defined set of tasks, as it would be the case for Ravenscar on a single processor.

There is a single run-time system, where the only per-processor information would be the ready and alarm queues. Some run-time data is common and shared among tasks on different processors (such as the time reference).

When internal data in the run-time system can be modified by tasks executing on different processors, we need to add inter-processor locking mechanisms (such as spin-locks or similar, see section 3.4, "Fair locks"), to guarantee mutual exclusion. The standard monoprocessor solution of disabling interrupts to guarantee that the task is not preempted before the access has been completed is not sufficient for multiprocessors.

Finally, something that must be taken into account is that the execution of a task (or an interrupt handler) in a given processor may modify another processor's ready queues (and may also force the preemption of the running task). These operations on different processors can be implemented triggering a special interrupt in the target processor, which is the one performing the actual changes in the ready queue.

2.2 Task Synchronization

The restricted library-level protected objects defined by the Ravenscar profile are used for inter- and intra-processor communication and synchronization. The same restrictions that exist in the Ravenscar profile for single processors apply to the case of a multiprocessor (a maximum of one protected entry per protected object with a simple boolean barrier using ceiling locking access).

One big advantage of monoprocessor Ravenscar is the simple and very efficient synchronization mechanism required for protected objects, where entering/exiting to/from the protected object can simply be done by just increasing/decreasing task's priorities [16].

In order to simplify timing analysis, and to allow for an efficient implementation when possible, protected objects used only by tasks within the same CPU could use the optimized monoprocessor implementation.

Protected objects for inter-processor communication would require multiprocessor synchronization mechanisms. When a task waiting on an entry queue is awaken by another tasks executing on a different processor than the waiting task, we need to use the inter-processor interrupt facility to modify the ready queues, as described in subsection 2.1, "Task Scheduling".

One possibility would have been to allocate affinities for protected objects to facilitate timing analysis of the application (not part of AI05-0171). Protected objects bound statically to a given processor (local protected objects) would never be affected by interference coming from tasks executing on other processors, as well as no interference being caused on other processors. The design of the application must take into account this fact, and static analysis (and static tools) can also help detecting the use of protected object by tasks living in different processors.

Suspension_Objects are implemented over protected objects. It may seem overkill, but given the restrictions imposed by the Ravenscar profile, protected operations are very efficient. Moreover, this allows for a generic implementation that is not dependent on the underlying support.

For the handling of shared-memory in the target multiprocessor environment (LEON3 based on SPARC V8), the standard memory model called Total Store Ordering (TSO) [19] is used. This memory model guarantees that the stores, flushes, and atomic load-stores of all processors are executed by memory serially in an order that conforms to the order in which the instructions were issued by processors. It means that memory barrier instructions are not required for consistency among different processors. The write-through caches and snooping mechanism in LEON3 guarantee memory coherency.

2.3   Interrupt Handling

The only Ravenscar-compliant mechanism to specify interrupt handlers is to attach a protected procedure. The differences in a multiprocessor system are related to mutual exclusion and assignment of interrupts to CPUs.

The mutual exclusion mechanisms for interrupt handlers will be those of the protected operations, and therefore the same considerations for intra- and inter- processor synchronization (as described in subsection 2.2, "Task Synchronization") apply.

With respect to the processors that may handle the different interrupts, multiprocessor hardware and operating systems typically allow setting and changing the affinity mask for interrupts. It means that the set of processors that may serve a given interrupt can be statically set at initialization time, or it can change dynamically. Additionally, the set can be restricted to a single processor or any number of them.

In order to simplify timing analysis, statically setting the affinity masks for interrupts is the model that fits better the Ravenscar philosophy.

Interrupts can be configured to be handled by any number of processors, and the decision of using one or more processors to handle interrupts depends on several factors. When more than one processor handle a given interrupt, a single interrupt event will be delivered to more than one processor, and hence the interrupt handler will be invoked and executed more than once (the interrupt handler will be executed concurrently on different processors). Mutual exclusion issues are handled by the underlying mechanisms, but the handler needs to take into account these multiple executions. On the one hand, it may decrease the response time, because of the highest probability of having a processor ready to handle the interrupt (not executing a highest priority activity). On the other hand, timing analysis of a system with interrupt events delivered to multiple processors is more complex, and the increased interference reduce the utilization of the system.

Setting the affinity masks of interrupts to a single processor, that may be different for each interrupt, would be the recommended approach. Allocating the interrupts to the CPUs where the tasks use them would remove the associated overhead of inter-processor synchronization.

Affinity for interrupts is not part of AI05-0171. In the current implementation this affinity is set in the startup routine, but it would be interesting to be able to use the same *pragma CPU* defined for tasks. The pragma could be attached to the definition of the protected handler.

2.4   Timing Services

In multiprocessor architectures, hardware support for timing services ranges from just a few shared hardware timers for all processors to several timers per processor.

In the reference implementation used in this paper for the LEON3 multiprocessor board [2], a single common hardware clock and a single shared hardware timer are used for all processors. It provides a common reference for all the tasks in the system, thus avoiding time drifting problems, and limits the amount of hardware resources required from the underlying platform.

Following the same approach as for the partitioned implementation of the ready queue (see subsection 2.1, "Task Scheduling"), each processor implements a separate and disjoint delay queue. Hence, a task waiting on a delay statement will be placed in the delay queue of the processor where it is allocated.

The interrupt service routines for the two hardware timers are executed in the context of a single given processor. When a timer expires, it has an effect on the ready and delay queues of potentially any processor, not only the one where the timer interrupt is handled. The timer handler may awake tasks waiting on a delay statement, or execute the protected actions associated to either timing events or execution time timers. In any of these cases, the mechanisms to exert the required actions in the different processors are the same as those described in previous subsection 2.1, "Task Scheduling", subsection 2.2, "Task Synchronization", and subsection 2.3, "Interrupt Handling"; if there is a task with an expired delay in a different processor from the one handling the interrupt then an inter-processor interrupt is triggered on the target processor, and the handler for this inter-processor interrupt will traverse the list of local expired events, executing the required actions in the local queues (an operation in a given processor cannot directly modify the queues of another processor).

3   Design and Implementation Details

This section describes the main design decisions and implementation details of a realization of the ideas described in previous sections on a bare board LEON3 multiprocessor board [2]. The LEON3 is a 32-bit processor based on the SPARC V8 architecture with support for multiprocessing configurations. The processor used was synthesized with 2 CPU cores, configured as symmetric multiprocessing (SMP).

3.1   Starting Point

GNAT Pro supports the Ravenscar tasking model on several bare board monoprocessor architectures [16], including LEON3. The idea was to extend the LEON3 monoprocessor run-time system to support the partitioned Ravenscar model defined in this paper, making it easy to choose between the monoprocessor and multiprocessor support according to the hardware platform used.

3.2   Initialization

There is some initial work that needs to be done before jumping to the user application code, which involves both the hardware initialization (registers, devices, etc.) and setting up the run-time system (internal data structures such as the different queues). To avoid race conditions problems, this initialization is performed in a monoprocessor context, by one statically designated CPU (init CPU).

The other CPUs (slave CPUs) wait in a busy loop until initialization is done. At the end of the initialization phase, the slave CPUs are released and start the execution of the first task (highest-priority task) in their ready queue.

As an exception to the partitioned approach, the init CPU has access to all the ready queues during the initialization phase, to assign tasks on the different processors during initialization time.

In multiprocessor mode, the init CPU executes the same initialization as in the previous monoprocessor implementation, the only difference being that there is a ready queue per processor.

3.3 Task Management

Tasks and their related data structures are statically created at compile time, without any use of dynamic memory. Task affinities are specified using the new *pragma CPU* (the default processor when the affinity is not specified is *CPU' First*). The compiler inserts the affinity into the Task Control Block (TCB) so the run-time system knows where to schedule the different tasks.

The ready queues (one per processor) are internally implemented as single-link priority ordered queues, in which each thread points to the next thread to execute, and there is an array of pointers containing the first task for each processor. Task affinities never change, so each task can only be on a given ready queue. Modifications to the ready queue are performed with interrupts disabled only on the affected processor, and the rest of processors can continue their normal operations unaffected (no inter-processor interference).

Tasks are scheduled according to the FIFO within priorities policy [1, D.2] on each processor, as it is the case for a monoprocessor Ravenscar system.

3.4 Synchronization

Mutual exclusion. In the monoprocessor version of the run time, the ceiling priority rules (*Locking_Policy (Ceiling_Locking)*) and the strictly preemptive priority scheduling policy (*Task_Dispatching_Policy (FIFO_Within_Priorities)*) guarantee that protected objects are always available when any task tries to use them [18] (otherwise there would be another task executing at a higher priority), and hence entering/exiting to/from the protected object can simply be done by just increasing/decreasing the task priority. Obviously, this protection no longer works with two or more processors because of the actual parallelism.

Mutual exclusion is now guaranteed by the use of an additional multiprocessor lock (see fair locks below). Access to protected objects is performed in two phases: first, the calling task raises its priority following the ceiling locking rules, and then it tries to get the fair lock. Raising the priority ensures that at most one task per CPU will try to get the lock at a given time. Tasks on different processors trying to access the protected object will wait in a busy loop.

Note that protected objects used only by tasks within the same CPU will always get access to the fair lock, so the multiprocessor overhead in this case is negligible.

Fair locks. In this multiprocessor context, multiple tasks on different CPUs may have to be synchronized, to protect access to shared data or hardware registers for example.

The well-known spin lock algorithm is not suitable for real-time systems, like the Ravenscar run-time, because of starvation risks [20, chapter 2. Existing Solutions].

On a processor with four cores, all of them fighting for the same spin-lock. There can be a situation where lock's ownership switches from core1 to core2 infinitely. In that case, core3 and core4 are in a state of starvation and will not be able to gain lock. Even if this situation is not likely to last a long period, it would be a major flaw in the predictability of the Ravenscar run-time.

Fair lock [20] is a cooperative mutual exclusion algorithm. When the owner of the lock wants to release, it will search for the next CPU waiting for the lock and transfer the control to it (scanning for waiting CPUs in a round-robin fashion). Therefore, unlike spin locks, the execution time is bounded and thus suitable for real-time systems.

In the case described earlier, the sequence of lock ownership will be:

- core1 → core2
- core2 → core3
- core3 → core4
- core4 → core1
- core1 → core2
- etc. . .

Fair locks are designed to synchronise tasks over two or more CPUs, but they must not be use by two tasks on the same CPU. This constraint is ensured by the properties of the Ravenscar profile and some protected (interrupts disabled) sections of code in the run-time .

Served entries. In the monoprocessor run-time, when a task (the `caller`) tries to call an entry whose barrier is closed, it becomes blocked. Then, another task (the `server`) will release the barrier, execute the `Entry_Body` (proxy model), and then wake up the `caller`.

The proxy model [11] implies that at the end of the execution of any protected procedure, that may change the state of the entry barrier, if there is a task waiting on the protected object's entry, then the barrier is evaluated, and if needed, the entry is executed by the task that opened the barrier on behalf of the queued task. It enhances efficiency, when both the `caller` and the `server` execute on the same processor, by avoiding unnecessary context switches. The self-service model (the `caller` executes always the code associated to the entry it calls) would be interesting for multiprocessors, as the entry could be executed in parallel by another processor, thus increasing the parallelism and reducing the worst-case blocking time. However, the proxy model is used for both the monoprocessor and multiprocessor implementation for maintainability, to reduce the difference between both cases.

Both models (proxy and self-service) require that the `server` wakes up the `caller`. If the `server` runs on a different CPU, it cannot directly wake up the task, because it would imply to modify the ready queue of the `caller` CPU, which is forbidden in the implemented partitioned approach.

In the multiprocessor implementation, if the two tasks are not on the same CPU, the `server` task will open the barrier, and execute the `Entry_Body` (the proxy model is still used). The difference with respect to the monoprocessor model is that it will put the `caller` task in a list (`Served_Entry_Call`, an array containing a list per processor), and then wake up the `caller` CPU using an inter-processor interrupt (see subsection 3.6, "Interrupt Handling"). The handling of the inter-processor interrupt in the `caller` CPU will finally insert the blocked task in the ready queue as a result of the barrier being open. Of course, if the two tasks run on the same CPU, there is no need for such mechanism, so the run-time will check it and directly wake up the `caller`.

If the `caller` task has a lower priority than the currently executing task on the `caller` CPU, the inter-processor interrupt will not be triggered, and the `caller` task will be inserted in the ready queue at the next scheduling point, without triggering the inter-processor interrupt. It may look like there could be a race condition, if the priority of the `caller` task changes just after it was checked. However, this race condition is not possible because dynamic priority changes are not allowed by the Ravenscar profile restrictions.

To ensure data consistency, the `Served_Entry_Call` lists are protected by fair locks.

3.5   Time-Keeping and Delays

Clock. The implementation of the time-keeping functionality does not differ when migrating to a multiprocessor architecture. The only detail to take into account is to choose the CPU in charge of handling the clock interrupt.

As described in [21], the requirements of having a good resolution and range with 32-bit hardware timers force us to use a hardware periodic timer to store the least significant part of the clock value, while the most significant part of the same value is stored in memory, and incremented by the clock interrupt handler.

Reading the clock (the hardware least significant part plus the most significant part in memory) is not an atomic operation, and there is the possibility of a consistency problem (race condition) if an interrupt occurs between the reading of the hardware and software components of the time. The monoprocessor implementation reads the hardware clock twice to prevent this race condition, and this method can be safely used on multiprocessor systems without introducing any kind of locking mechanism.

Alarms. The implementation of alarms in the Ravenscar run-time relies on a hardware timer. Since most systems have fewer timers than processors, this resource must be shared.

Each CPU manages its own list of alarms but one processor is in charge of the alarm interrupt (Alarm_CPU).

When the alarm interrupt is triggered, the Alarm_CPU will get the time for the next alarm on each CPU. If this time has expired, the Alarm_CPU uses an inter-processor interrupt to wake up the other CPU; otherwise, the next alarm is used to reconfigure the timer.

The CPU that receives the inter-processor interrupt will wake up all the expired alarms in its own list.

Each processor has to configure the timer itself. The CPU checks if the new alarm is before the current one and reconfigures the timer if needed. We use a fair lock to avoid race condition during this operation.

```
for CPU_Id in CPU loop

    if CPU_Id /= Current_CPU then
        Alarm_Time := Get_Next_Timeout (CPU_Id);

        if Alarm_Time <= Now then

            --  Alarm expired, wake up the CPU

            Poke_CPU (CPU_Id);

        else
            --  Check if this is the next non-expired alarm
            --  of the overall system.

            if Alarm_Time < Next_Alarm_Overall then
                Next_Alarm_Overall := Alarm_Time;
            end if;
        end if;
    end if;
end loop;

if Next_Alarm_Overall /= Time'Last then
    Update_Alarm (Next_Alarm_Overall);
end if;
```

3.6 Interrupt Handling

No modifications to the interrupt handling code are required for the multiprocessor support. However, during an interrupt, the context of the running thread is saved and the execution switches to the interrupt context (interrupt stack). If the processor does not have any task to execute, there is no context to save. To handle this case, each slave CPU will create a task with minimum stack to provide an interrupt context.

The implementation currently requires setting the affinity masks of interrupts to a single processor (different interrupts may be handled by different CPUs), which is the approach recommended in subsection 2.3, "Interrupt Handling".

Each time an event on one CPU involves a rescheduling for another CPU, the former needs a way to wake up or interrupt the latter (inter-processor interrupt). It is done by simulating an external interrupt with the LEON3 IRQ manager. Using specific registers, the run-time can trigger an interrupt on one or more CPU. Therefore, on the chosen target we can trigger an interrupt on any CPU (similar inter-processor interrupt capabilities are typically available on other multiprocessor architectures).

3.7 Sharing Code between Monoprocessors and Multiprocessors

The support for multiprocessor systems implies modifications to the previous implementation of the Ravenscar run time, and shared code between monoprocessor and multiprocessor targets.

Most of the modifications are useless in a monoprocessor context, and would lead to dead object code. For example, any call to the fair locks routines (section 3.4, "Fair locks") is a non-sense on a monoprocessor system and would reduce the performance.

To avoid this effect, and limit the impact of the multiprocessor support, the new implementation takes advantage of the compile-time optimizations provided in GNAT.

With the following construction the code will be statically optimized. The call to the *Lock* procedure will only remain if the run-time is configured to handle more than one processor.

```
if Multiprocessor then
   Fair_Locks.Lock (Any_Lock);
end if;
```

where the *Multiprocessor* condition is defined as:

```
Multiprocessor : constant Boolean := Max_Number_Of_CPUs /= 1;
```

and *Max_Number_Of_CPUs* is a parameter of the run-time representing the maximum number of CPUs available on the target system.

Therefore, multiprocessor-specific code becomes deactivated code in monoprocessor systems, which is never present in the final application binary. The same run-time sources are used for the monoprocessor and multiprocessor targets, and the only thing that needs to be modified is the constant *Max_Number_Of_CPUs*. Once the run time is recompiled, it can be used on the new target.

4 Performance

Here are presented the results of some performance tests used to measure the impact of the new implementation. The test platform is a 40MHz LEON3 FPGA.

These measurements were taken over a large number of iterations. For each of them there will be a table with the lowest values observed (Min) and the highest ones (Max).

The first three tests compare performances of the new multiprocessor implementation with the previous run-time. Since the previous implementation does not support multiprocessor systems, these tests only run tasks on one CPU.

Tests are executed on four different run-times:

- Monoprocessor : Previous implementation
- Multiprocessor (1) : New run time, configured for 1 processor
- Multiprocessor (2) : New run time, configured for 2 processors
- Multiprocessor (16) : New run time, configured for 16 processors

4.1 Measurements

Delay until + context switch.

What is measured here is the elapsed time between the last statement executed at a task dispatching point (a "delay until") until the first statement in the next running task.

Min:

run-time	time (μs)	ratio	diff (μs)
Mono	52.000	1.000	0.000
Mp (1)	48.625	0.935	-3.375
Mp (2)	70.125	1.348	18.125
Mp (16)	86.500	1.663	34.500

Max:

run-time	time (μs)	ratio	diff (μs)
Mono	64.500	1.000	0.000
Mp (1)	59.000	0.914	-5.500
Mp (2)	78.000	1.209	13.500
Mp (16)	96.000	1.488	31.500

Protected objects.

This is the time to switch from one task to another using a protected object (one task waits on an entry and the other task release it). We measure the time between opening the barrier and the first statement after the entry call in the waiting task.

Min:

run-time	time (μs)	ratio	diff (μs)
Mono	56.125	1.000	0.000
Mp (1)	50.000	0.890	-6.125
Mp (2)	83.500	1.487	27.375
Mp (16)	116.625	2.077	60.500

Max:

run-time	time (μs)	ratio	diff (μs)
Mono	72.500	1.000	0.000
Mp (1)	68.250	0.941	-4.250
Mp (2)	101.000	1.393	28.500
Mp (16)	134.250	1.851	61.750

Alarm precision.

These numbers correspond to the delay until lateness [1],D.9(13), which is the difference between the requested time of delay expiration and the resumption time actually attained by a task following an absolute time suspension.

Min:

run-time	time (μs)	ratio	diff (μs)
Mono	50.375	1.000	0.000
Mp (1)	54.875	1.089	4.500
Mp (2)	70.000	1.389	19.625
Mp (16)	105.875	2.101	55.500

Max:

run-time	time (μs)	ratio	diff (μs)
Mono	76.125	1.000	0.000
Mp (1)	76.000	0.998	-0.125
Mp (2)	95.000	1.247	18.875
Mp (16)	136.250	1.789	60.125

Alarm precision on slave CPU.

This show the overhead introduced by the alarm mechanism (section 3.5, "Alarms"), when alarms are served on slave CPUs. It is the same test as "Alarm precision", except that the test task is first assigned to the Alarm_CPU and then to a salve CPU.

Min:

Alarm on	time (μs)	ratio	diff (μs)
Alarm_CPU	70.000	1.000	0.000
Slave	87.750	1.253	17.750

Max:

Alarm on	time (μs)	ratio	diff (μs)
Alarm_CPU	95.000	1.000	0.000
Salve	132.125	1.390	37.125

4.2   Analysis

When the run-time is configured for one processor, we observe comparable performances, even a slight improvement. This is due to the optimization described earlier (subsection 3.7) and also to the improvements made on the run-time beside multiprocessor implementation.

With run-times configured for more than one CPU, the overhead looks like non-negligible, but once we consider that the measured elapsed times are very short, even a not very big difference represent a noticeable percentage. Looking at the actual time differences, we can see that they are in the range of a few tens of microseconds. For a 40MHz processor (the hardware used), the time difference represents a few hundreds of CPU instructions, which is actually a very low overhead.

5   Conclusions

This paper contains a description of a simple and natural extension to the Ravenscar model to address multiprocessor systems. The idea behind it is to take an Ada application (the whole partition in the Ada sense), and to statically allocate each task to a processor. Any given processor will then have a set of tasks, protected objects and interrupts to handle, that can be modelled and analyzed as a separate monoprocessor Ravenscar system.

A *pragma CPU* is used for task partitioning, a concept already supported by most operating systems (affinity management). The GNAT Pro compiler and run-time already implement this Ada 2012 extension.

With respect to the implementation, handling the access to shared resources (hardware and data) in a simple and efficient way is the main issue. Fair locks have been added for ensuring inter-processor mutual exclusion. Inter-processor interrupt facilities are the mechanisms typically used to enforce scheduling and dispatching operations on different processors.

Configuring the run-time support from a single CPU to any number of CPUs is a matter of simply specifying the required value for the constant *Max_Number_Of_CPUs*.

The proposed partitioned approach provides a simple and analyzable model which can be supported by a streamlined run-time system. It can be implemented directly on a bare-board machine or on top of operating systems supporting affinity assignments. The associated run time overhead remains small.

References

1. Tucker Taft, S., Duff, R.A., Brukardt, R.L., Plödereder, E., Leroy, P.: Ada 2005 Reference Manual. LNCS, vol. 4348. Springer, Heidelberg (2006)
2. Aeroflex Gaisler: LEON3 Multiprocessing CPU Core (2010),
   http://www.gaisler.com/doc/leon3_product_sheet.pdf
3. Andersson, B., Baruah, S., Jonsson, J.: Static-priority scheduling on multiprocessors. In: RTSS 2001: Proceedings of the 22nd IEEE Real-Time Systems Symposium. IEEE Computer Society, Los Alamitos (2001)
4. ARG: Pragma CPU and Ravenscar Profile. Tech. rep., ISO/IEC/JTC1/SC22/WG9 (2010),
   http://www.ada-auth.org/cgi-bin/cvsweb.cgi/ai05s/
   ai05-0171-1.txt
5. ARINC: ARINC Specification 653, Avionics Application Software Standard Interface. Aeronautical Radio, Inc. (2005)
6. Baker, T.P.: An analysis of fixed-priority schedulability on a multiprocessor. Real-Time Systems 32(1-2), 49–71 (2006)
7. Baruah, S.K., Cohen, N.K., Plaxton, C.G., Varvel, D.: Proportionate progress: A notion of fairness in resource allocation. Algorithmica 15, 600–625 (1994)
8. Carpenter, J., Funk, S., Holman, P., Srinivasan, A., Anderson, J., Baruah, S.: A categorization of real-time multiprocessor scheduling problems and algorithms. In: Handbook on Scheduling Algorithms, Methods, and Models. Chapman Hall/CRC, Boca Raton (2004)
9. Dhall, S.K., Liu, C.L.: On a real-time scheduling problem. Operations Research 26(1), 127–140 (1978)
10. Mezzetti, E., Panunzio, M., Vardanega, T.: Preservation of timing properties with the ada ravenscar profile. In: Real, J., Vardanega, T. (eds.) Ada-Europe 2010. LNCS, vol. 6106, pp. 153–166. Springer, Heidelberg (2010)
11. Giering, E.W., Mueller, F., Baker, T.P.: Implementing ada 9X features using POSIX threads: Design issues. In: Proceedings of TRI-Ada 1993, pp. 214–228 (1993)
12. Joseph, M., Pandya, P.: Finding response times in real-time systems. BCS Computer Journal 29(5), 390–395 (1986)
13. Liu, C.L., Layland, J.W.: Scheduling algorithms for multiprogramming in a hard-real-time environment. J. ACM 20(1) (1973)
14. Oh, Y., Son, H.: Tight performance bounds of heuristics for a real-time scheduling problem. Tech. rep., Department of Computer Science, University of Virginia (1993)
15. RTCA: RTCA/DO-297: Integrated Modular Avionics (IMA) Development Guidance and Certification Considerations. RTCA (August 2005)

16. Ruiz, J.F.: GNAT pro for on-board mission-critical space applications. In: Vardanega, T., Wellings, A.J. (eds.) Ada-Europe 2005. LNCS, vol. 3555, pp. 248–259. Springer, Heidelberg (2005)
17. Ruiz, J.F.: Towards a Ravenscar extension for multi-processor systems. Ada Letters 30, 86–90 (2010)
18. Shen, H., Baker, T.: A Linux kernel module implementation of restricted Ada tasking. Ada Letters XIX(2), 96–103 (1999); Proceedings of the 9th International Real-Time Ada Workshop
19. SPARC International, Inc.: The SPARC Architecture Manual (1992), version 8
20. Swaminathan, S., Stultz, J., Vogel, J.F., McKenney, P.E.: Fairlocks — a high performance fair locking scheme. In: International Conference on Parallel and Distributed Computing Systems, pp. 241–246 (2002)
21. Zamorano, J., Ruiz, J.F., la de Puente, J.A.: Implementing Ada.Real_Time.Clock and absolute delays in real-time kernels. In: Craeynest, D., Strohmeier, A. (eds.) Ada-Europe 2001. LNCS, vol. 2043, p. 317. Springer, Heidelberg (2001)

A Real-Time Framework for Multiprocessor Platforms Using Ada 2012*

Sergio Sáez, Silvia Terrasa, and Alfons Crespo

Instituto de Automática e Informática Industrial,
Universidad Politécnica de Valencia,
Camino de vera, s/n, 46022 Valencia, Spain
{ssaez,sterrasa,alfons}@disca.upv.es

Abstract. The next release of the Ada language, Ada 2012, will probably incorporate explicit support for multiprocessor execution platforms.
However, the implementation of multiprocessor scheduling approaches
over the low-level abstractions offered by Ada forces the programmer
to reconstruct complex task templates and algorithms in each new system. This work proposes to extend the previous Real-Time Utilities by
Wellings and Burns to support multiprocessor platforms and to complete
the framework with a code generation tool that translates the scheduling
analysis reports into the real-time applications code.

Keywords: Real-Time Framework, Multiprocessor Scheduling, Multiprocessor Support, Ada 2012.

1 Introduction

Real-Time and embedded systems are becoming more complex, and multiproces-
sor/multicore systems are becoming a common execution platform in these areas.
Although schedulability analysis techniques for real-time applications executing
over multiprocessor platforms are still not mature, some feasible scheduling approaches are emerging. However, to apply these techniques a flexible support at
kernel and user-space level is needed. The forthcoming release of Ada 2012 is
expected to offer explicit support for multiprocessor platforms through a comprehensive set of programming mechanisms [1].

However, the complexity of current real-time systems not only requires powerful execution platforms, but also support for different levels of criticality. This
situation gives rise to heterogeneous system workloads that mix hard, soft and
non real-time tasks. These tasks need to manage different kind of situations
as deadline misses, termination of optional parts, control of CPU budgets, etc.
Although Ada 2012 will provide powerful mechanisms to implement different
multiprocessor scheduling approaches at application level [2,3], the offered abstractions to cope with these new requirements are still low level ones. Under this

---

* This work was partially supported by the Vicerectorado de Investigación of the Univ.
Politécnica de Valencia under grant PAID-06-10-2397.

A. Romanovsky and T. Vardanega (Eds.): Ada-Europe 2011, LNCS 6652, pp. 46–60, 2011.

situation, Wellings and Burns argued in their work [4] that *there is a need for a standardized library of real-time utilities that address common real-time problems*. With the introduction of multiprocessor support and the related scheduling mechanisms, the need for a real-time standardized library avoiding the programmer to reconstruct the same algorithms and task templates on each system is exacerbated.

The main goal of this work is to make a step forward in this direction and to extend the Real-Time Utilities proposed in [4] to support the new requirements that arise in multiprocessor platforms. However, complex multiprocessor systems normally require complex analysis techniques. The results of this analysis, i.e. the *real-time analysis report*, will contain the scheduling attributes for each task in the system. These scheduling attributes could be composed by multiple task priorities, relative deadlines, release offsets and task processor migrations at specified times. Additionally, the programmer may want to handle some special events, e.g. deadline misses and execution time overruns. To translate this set of attributes into the real-time application code is an error-prone process. This work proposes to use a specific development tool that will generate the *scheduling task behavior and initialization code* on top of the new Real-Time Utilities, leaving the functional task behavior to the system programmer.

The rest of this paper is organized as follows. In section 2, the system load the new framework will support is presented. Section 3 briefly describes some multiprocessor scheduling approaches and their implementation feasibility at application-level. Section 4 outlines the previous proposal of a real-time support library and the new requirements imposed by the multiprocessor scheduling approaches. Then, section 5 presents the new components of the multiprocessor real-time framework. Finally, the code generation framework and the work conclusions are drawn in sections 6 and 7.

2   System Load Model

A real-time system is composed of a set of *tasks* that concurrently collaborate to achieve a common goal. Each real-time task can be viewed as an infinite sequence of *job* executions. Depending on the activation mechanism used to release each job the tasks are classified into aperiodic and sporadic tasks, if their jobs are released by asynchronous events such as an external interrupt from a physical device, or periodic tasks, if their jobs are released by equally spaced internal clock events.

Typically, a job performs its work in a single step without suspending itself during the execution, and therefore, a task is suspended only at the end of a job execution to wait for the next activation event. However, some kind of jobs organize the code as a sequence of well-differentiated *steps* that can be temporally spaced to achieve a given system goal. An example of such tasks is a real-time control task following the IMF model [5], that are divided into three steps or parts: an Initial part for data *sampling*, a Mandatory part for algorithm *computation* and a Final part to deliver *actuation* information. Although these steps usually share the job activation mechanism, different release offsets and priorities can be used for each step to achieve input/output jitter reduction during sampling and actuation steps.

These job steps constitute the *code units* where the programmer of the real-time system will implement the behavior of each task. However, as pointed out in [4], complex real-time system could be composed by tasks that need to detect deadline misses, execution time overruns, minimum inter-arrival violations, etc. The system behavior when these situations are detected is task-specific and it has to be implemented in different code units in the form of task control handlers. An example of this task-specific behavior could be a real-time control task with *optional* parts. These optional steps or subtasks could help to improve control performance, but they have to be cancelled if a certain deadline is missed in order to send the control action in time.

When and where a given code unit is executed is determined by the scheduler of the underlying operating system. This scheduler will use a set of *scheduling attributes* to determine which job is executed and, specially in multiprocessor platforms, which CPU will use to execute it. Some of the scheduling attributes a real-time scheduler could use are: a *release offset* after the job activation, the job *priority*, its relative *deadline*, the *CPU affinity* information, different *execution times* of the job, etc.

In a complex multiprocessor system, each job step can have a different set of scheduling attributes that could change during its execution depending on the scheduling approach used to ensure the correct execution of the whole system. The next section presents some of these scheduling approaches that can be used to schedule real-time tasks in multiprocessor platforms.

3   Multiprocessor Scheduling Approaches

In order to achieve a predictable schedule of a set of real-time tasks in a multiprocessor platform several approaches can be applied. Based on the capability of a task to migrate from one processor to another, the scheduling approach can be:

Global scheduling. All tasks can be executed on any processor and after a preemption the current job can be resumed in a different processor.

If the scheduling decisions are performed online, in a multiprocessor platform with M CPUs, the M active jobs with the highest priorities are the ones selected for execution. To ensure that online decisions will fulfil the real-time constraints of the system tasks, different off-line schedulability tests can be performed [6,7]. If the scheduling decisions are computed off-line, releases times, preemption instants and processors where tasks have to be executed are stored in a static scheduling plan.

Job partitioning. Each job activation of a given task can be executed on a different processor, but a given job cannot migrate during its execution.

The processor where each job is executed can be decided by an online global dispatcher upon the job activation, or it can be determined off-line by a scheduling analysis tool and stored in a processor plan for each task. The job execution order on each processor is determined online by its own scheduler using the scheduling attributes of each job.

Task partitioning. All job activations of a given task have to be executed in the same processor. No job migration is allowed.

The processor where a task is executed is part of the task's scheduling attributes. As in the previous approach, the order in which each job is executed on each processor is determined online by the scheduler of that processor.

In addition to these basic approaches, new techniques that mix task partitioning with task that migrate from one processor to another at specified times are already available in the literature. In this approach, known as *task splitting*, some works suggest to perform the processor migration of the split task at a given time after each job release [8] or when the job has performed a certain amount of execution [9]. It is worth noting that this approach normally requires the information about the processor migration instant to be somehow coded into the task behavior.

In the case that a task is composed by multiple job steps, specific scheduling analysis tools usually decompose these steps as different real-time subtasks [5,10]. These subtasks share the same release mechanism, typically a periodic one, and separate each job execution using a given release offset. Figure 1 depicts this decomposition of a control task. The rest of the scheduling attributes of these new tasks are established according to a given goal, e.g., to improve the overall control performance by means of input and output jitter reduction. Once the task steps are separated into different tasks, the multiprocessor scheduling approaches shown above can be combined with the control specific ones.

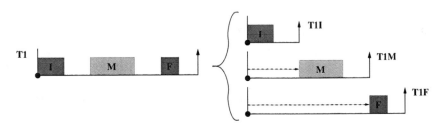

Fig. 1. Decomposition of a task with multiple job steps

Although schedulability analysis techniques that ensure the timeliness execution of the task set are not mature enough for all the scheduling approaches presented above, to offer a flexible support to easily apply the most established ones is part of the goals of this work. The next section analyzes the required functionalities a library of Real-Time Utilities has to provide to help in the applicability of these approaches and proposes a redesigned Real-Time Framework that helps to implement complex real-time systems over multiprocessor platforms.

4   New Design of Real-Time Utilities

This section analyses the current proposal of a library of Real-Time Utilities and revise the needed requirements to support the existing multiprocessor scheduling approaches presented above. This work proposes to redesign the framework presented by Wellings and Burns [4] to cope with these new requirements.

4.1   Previous Proposal of the Real-Time Utilities

The Real-Time Utilities proposed by Wellings and Burns offer a set of high-level abstractions that allow the Ada 2005 programmer to build real-time task with different release mechanisms (periodic, aperiodic and sporadic) and with different ways to manage deadline miss and execution time overrun events.

This framework organizes the support for building complex real-time systems around four kind of components:

Task State. This component encapsulates the main *code units* of a real-time task: initialization, the code to be executed on each release of a task job and specific handlers for deadline miss and execution time overrun events. Extending this component the programmer can easily build the tasks that compound the system. The task state also maintains the scheduling attributes for that task.

Release Mechanisms. This set of components provides different mechanisms to control the activation of each system task: periodic, sporadic and aperiodic tasks. However, release mechanism components also implement the support for deadline miss and execution time overrun detection and notification. As the detection and notification of these events are optional and orthogonal also with respect to the kind of release mechanism used, this gives rise to four different classes per release mechanism ($2^{\text{number of events}} \times$ number of release mechanisms). As the implementation of multiprocessor scheduling approaches explained in section 3 could require an increased number of events to be managed by the task code, this solution seems to be inadequate.

Real-Time Task. This kind of components implements the main structure of a real-time task, integrating the task state and its corresponding release mechanism. Different task templates provide support to immediately terminate a task on the occurrence of a given event. Once again, as the number of task templates depends on the number of termination events ($2^{\text{number of events}}$), this approach does not scale properly in relation to the number of such events[1].

Execution Servers. This component allows to manage group of tasks ensuring that a certain proportion of CPU time is not exceeded. As new Ada 2012 will tie group budgets to a single processor [11], this work is not going to consider this kind of components.

---

[1] Although not present in the original framework, a notifycation mechanism introduced in a later version allows to mitigate this drawback.

Although these components provide a useful set of high-level abstractions to implement real-time systems, they can be inadequate to implement multiprocessor scheduling techniques. As introduced above, scalability problems will arise if the number of events that could be managed by a given task is increased, as the number of types required to implement each release mechanism has an exponential relation with the number of events. Currently only deadline miss and execution time overrun events are managed, but the introduction of a new event will require to double the number of supporting types.

It is also important to remark that the current class hierarchy of the Real-Time Utilities is not compatible with the code generator framework proposed in this work. For example, Listing 1 shows how the periodic release mechanism M and the real-time task T have to be declared after the programmer defines and declares the final task state P. With this code structure, a code generation tool only can set up the scheduling attributes of a task in its Initialize procedure, and therefore, it has to provide a task-specific Periodic_Task_State with this procedure already implemented. When the programmer extends this new task state type to implement the task behavior its initialization code will collide with the one provided by the code generation tool. Although a possible solution to this problem could be to provide an additional Setup procedure to allocate the initialization generated code, this work proposes bellow a complete separation of scheduling and behavior task code.

Listing 1. A simple example of a periodic task using the Real-Time Utilities

```
-- with and use clauses omitted
package Periodic_Test is
  type My_State is new Periodic_Task_State with
  record
    I : Integer;
  end record;

  procedure Initialize(S: in out My_State);
  procedure Code (S: in out My_State);

  P : aliased My_State;
  M : aliased Periodic_Release(P'Access);
  T : Simple_Real_Time_Task(P'Access, M'Access, 3);
end Periodic_Test;
```

4.2   Real-Time Multiprocessor Requirements

Real-Time multiprocessor scheduling techniques presented in section 3, such global scheduling, have some implementation requirements that have to be provided by the underlying Real-Time Operating System or be implemented at user level be means of some kind of Application Defined Scheduler [12], that also requires some support from the RTOS. However, the rest of the scheduling approaches, i.e. task partitioning, job partitioning and task splitting can be implemented using the low-level constructions that will be probably available in Ada 2012. This new support at language level has already been used in several works to show these multiprocessor scheduling techniques can be feasibly implemented [3,2,13]. This section presents the requirements the new framework has to fulfill to allow the implementation of the techniques with a new set of high-level abstractions.

Previous sections have presented a task model and a set of scheduling scenarios where a task could require:

– To establish its scheduling attributes, including the CPU where each job will be executed. These scheduling attributes can be set at the task initialization to support task partitioning, they can be dynamically changed at the beginning of each job to provide job partitioning support or after a given amount of system or CPU time has elapsed to provide support for some of the task splitting techniques.
– To program and to be notified about the occurrence of a wide set of runtime events. These events could include: deadline misses, execution time overruns, mode changes, timed events using system or CPU clocks to inform about a programed task migration, etc. Some of these events could also terminate the current task job.
– To specify task release delays or offsets in order to support the decomposition of tasks with multiple steps into several subtasks.

To support these requirements a new set of components are proposed in the following section.

5   New Framework Components

Taking into account the behavioral and scalability requirements that will be desirable in a library of Real-Time Utilities to support multiprocessor platforms and automatic code generation, the original components presented in section 4.1 have been split in: *Real-Time Task State*, *Real-Time Task Sched*, *Control Mechanisms*, *Release Mechanisms* and *Real-Time Tasks*. Figure 2 shows dependencies among new packages. The details are discussed in the next sections.

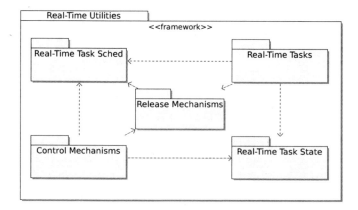

Fig. 2. Structure of new Real-Time Utilities packages

5.1   Real-Time Task Scheduling and Task State

The original Task_State tagged type provides the structure that allows the programmer to implement the code the real-time task will execute. Along with this code, the scheduling attributes of the task and the state variables associated with the real-time task are also allocated in this type or in the extended type the programmer defines to implement the task behavior.

As the scheduling attributes of a real-time task have been shown as something that different scheduling approaches can change dynamically during the task lifespan, it could be interesting to present this concept as an independent type. This will allow one to fully define the task attributes before the final task state is defined, to associate scheduling attributes to a task event, or to define arrays of attributes to implement static scheduling plans or job partitioning schemes.

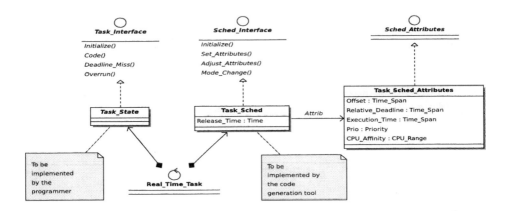

Fig. 3. Task related types

On the other hand, some multiprocessor scheduling approaches will require to implement part of the scheduler behavior in the task code, giving rise to task templates that depend on the results of the real-time analysis tool. Examples of these task templates in Ada for task splitting techniques can be found in [3] and a brief outline of a task using job partitioning in [13]. Since this work proposes to automatically generate this *scheduling task behavior* using a properly formatted real-time analysis report, it is suggested to encapsulate this code in a new Task_Sched tagged type. Although this conceptual separation of the scheduling behavior is not strictly necessary, it will prevent the programmer from accidentally overriding the scheduling code. Figure 3 shows the relations among these new types and Listing 2 sketches their basic operations.

The new tagged type Task_Sched will implement the operations to manage common scheduling situations. Example procedures shown in Listing 2 are intended to support different scheduling behaviors:

Listing 2. Task tagged types

```
package Real_Time_Task_Sched is
    ...
    type Task_Sched_Attributes is new Sched_Attributes with private;
    -- Get/Set operations omitted
    ...
    type Task_Sched is abstract new Sched_Interface with private;

    procedure Initialize (S : in out Task_Sched) is abstract;
    procedure Set_Attributes (S : in out Task_Sched) is null;
    procedure Adjust_Attributes (S : in out Task_Sched) is null;
    procedure Mode_Change(S: in out Task_Sched) is null;
    -- Get/Set operations omitted
private
    type Task_Sched_Attributes is new Sched_Attributes with
        record
            Offset            : Time_Span := Time_Span_Zero;
            Relative_Deadline : Time_Span := Time_Span_Last;
            Execution_Time    : Time_Span := Time_Span_Last;
            Prio              : Priority  := Default_Priority;
            CPU_Affinity      : CPU_Range := Not_A_Specific_CPU;
        end record;
    ...
end Real_Time_Task_Sched;
```

- **Initialize** – this code will be used by the code generation tool to initialize the task attributes and the task scheduling mechanisms.
- **Set_Attributes** – this code will be used to establish the task attributes to its original values on each job release after a task split or to establish new values in the case of job partitioning scheme.
- **Adjust_Attributes** – this code will adjust task attributes during its execution, e.g., to perform a task split or a dual priority scheme [14].
- **Mode_Change** – this is the code that specifies how the task scheduling attributes are adapted to the new execution mode.

5.2   Real-Time Task Control Mechanisms

Multiprocessor scheduling techniques will require a higher number of events to be managed by the task code. This work proposes to detach the event management from the previous version of the release mechanisms, moving this support to the new package Control_Mechanisms. This new package contains two main component, Control_Objects and Control_Events, that will collaborate to implement the *Command* design pattern [15]. Control Objects will perform the *Invoker* role, that will ask to execute the *Command* implemented by the Control Event upon some scheduling event occurs. The *Receiver* role is played by Task_State or Task_Sched types, while the *Client* role is performed by the initialization code that creates the event command and sets its receiver. Specialized versions of Control Objects will enable to trigger scheduling events under different situations:

Listing 3. Execution Time Overrun Control Event

```
...
-- Cost Overrun Event
type Cost_Overrun_Event (State: Any_Task_State;
                         Attrib:  Any_Task_Sched_Attributes;
                         Termination: Boolean) is new
   Control_Event_Using_CPU_Clock(Termination) with null record;
procedure Dispatch(E: in out Cost_Overrun_Event);
function Get_Event_Time(E: in Cost_Overrun_Event) return CPU_Time;
...
-- Cost Overrun Event
procedure Dispatch(E: in out Cost_Overrun_Event) is
begin
    E.State.Overrun;
end Dispatch;

function Get_Event_Time(E: in Cost_Overrun_Event) return CPU_Time is
begin
    return Clock + E.Attrib.Get_Execution_Time;
end Get_Event_Time;
```

- *On job release*: it will allow the job partitioning scheme to be implemented by creating a new control event that will execute Set_Attributes procedure of the Task_Sched object before a new job is released.
- *After a given amount of system time*: The use of an Ada Timing_Event will allow a task splitting based on system time to be implemented. Command

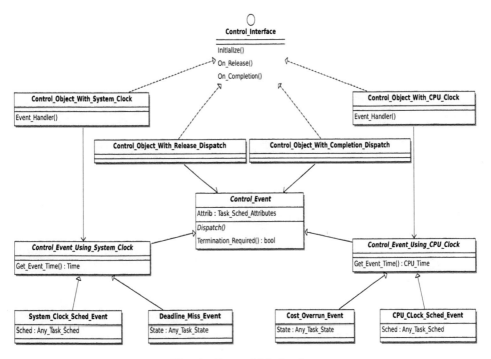

Fig. 4. Control Mechanisms

executed by the control event will invoke the Adjust_Attributes procedure of the Task_Sched object.

- *After a given amount of CPU time*: task splitting based on CPU time will use Ada Execution_Time.Timers to trigger the appropriated event. In this case, the command executed by the control event will also invokes the Adjust_Attributes procedure after the specified CPU time.
- *On job completion*: It will allow a task to execute a given procedure to respond to scheduling events that have deferred their actions until the current job completes its execution. This task procedure could change the task attributes before the next job activation occurs, e.g., the Mode_Change procedure could be used to change the priority and period of a task before reprogramming its next release event.

Listing 4. Periodic Release Mechanism

```
 1    ...
 2       protected type Periodic_Release (S: Any_Periodic_Task_Sched) is
 3           new Release_Mechanism with
 4          entry Wait_For_Next_Release;
 5          pragma Priority(System.Interrupt_Priority'Last);
 6       private
 7          procedure Release(TE : in out Timing_Event);
 8          TE : Timing_Event;
 9             ...
10       end Periodic_Release;
11    ...
12       protected body Periodic_Release is
13          entry Wait_For_Next_Release when New_Release or not Completed is
14          begin
15             if First then            -- Release mechanism initialization
16                First := False;
17                Epoch_Support.Epoch.Get_Start_Time (Next);
18                Next := Next + S.Get_Period;
19                S.Set_Release_Time (Next + S.Get_Offset);
20                TE.Set_CPU (S.Attrib.Get_CPU);
21                TE.Set_Handler (S.Get_Release_Time, Release'Access);
22                New_Release := False;
23                requeue Periodic_Release.Wait_For_Next_Release;
24             elsif New_Release then    -- Job begin
25                New_Release := False;
26                Completed  := False;
27                -- Invocation of On_Release procedures of Control Objects
28             else                      -- Job end
29                Completed := True;
30                -- Invocation of On_Complete procedures of Control Objects
31                -- TE.Set_CPU (S.Attrib.Get_CPU); --> Version with Control Objects
32                Next := Next + S.Get_Period;
33                S.Set_Release_Time (Next + S.Get_Offset);
34                TE.Set_Handler (S.Get_Release_Time, Release'Access);
35                requeue Periodic_Release.Wait_For_Next_Release;
36             end if;
37          end Wait_For_Next_Release;
38
39          procedure Release (TE : in out Timing_Event) is
40          begin
41             New_Release := True;
42             -- Set_CPU(S.Attrib.Get_CPU, T_Id); --> Version with Control Objects
43          end Release;
44       end Periodic_Release;
```

On the other hand, Control Events only have to implement the Dispatch operation that will execute the corresponding task behavior. Most of the control events are triggered by a time event and, in this case, they also have to provide the Get_Event_Time function to program that time event adequately. Listing 3 shows the implementation of *Execution Time Overrun* event.

Figure 4 depicts Control Objects and Control Events hierarchy, showing how *Deadline Miss* and *Execution Time Overrun* events along with events to support task splitting can be mapped into this new mechanism.

Control Object procedures On_Release and On_Completion, that will be invoked by the corresponding release mechanism, will allow the task to program the *Timing Event* or the *Execution Time Timer* on job release and to cancel them on job completion.

5.3   Real-Time Task Release Mechanisms

Once the control mechanisms have been introduced, the release mechanisms become simpler. Only two kind of protected types are needed per release mechanism. The first one, Release_Mechanism, remains similar to the previous version of the Real-Time Utilities with some minor changes to support CPU affinities and release offsets. Listing 4 shows the definition of Periodic_Release.

The second release mechanism, Release_Mechanism_With_Control_Objects, is almost identical to the former one but invoking On_Release and On_Completion procedures of all registered control objects each time a job is released or completed (marked as commentaries in Listing 4). It also offers the notification operations Notify_Event and Trigger_Event to add task termination support. As suggested in [13], the new Set_CPU procedures of Timing_Event and Dispatching_Domains are used to avoid unnecessary context switches when a job finishes its execution in a different CPU than the next job release is going to use, e.g, due to the application of a job partitioning or task splitting scheme (see lines 31 and 42).

Listing 5. Real-Time Task with Event Termination

```
task type Real_Time_Task_With_Event_Termination (
    S : Any_Task_State; C : Any_Task_Sched;
    R : Any_Release_Mechanism_With_Control_Objects) is
end Real_Time_Task_With_Event_Termination;
...
task body Real_Time_Task_With_Event_Termination is
    E : Any_Control_Event;
begin
    C. Initialize ; S. Initialize ;
    loop
        select
            R.Notify_Event(E);
            E.Dispatch;
        then abort
            R.Wait_For_Next_Release;
            S.Code;
        end select;
    end loop;
end Real_Time_Task_With_Event_Termination;
```

5.4   Real-Time Tasks

Finally, although the *Simple Real-Time Task* remains almost identical, the template of a *Real-Time Task With Event Termination* becomes simpler due to the new event dispatching mechanism. As it can be observed in Listing 5, the task initializes the Task Sched object, containing the automatically generated initialization code, and Task State object, containing the programmer initialization code, before starting the main loop. It is also worth noting that the Wait_For_Next_Release procedure can also be aborted to support event notification while a task job is inactive.

6   Code Generator Tool

The proposed real-time multiprocessor framework have been redesigned to better adapt its components to multiprocessor platform requirements. However, the number of small components required to implement a complex task has increased and also the relations among them. This fact gives rise to a more elaborated initialization code to set up a task scheduling infrastructure. As translating scheduling attributes to application code and interconnect the resulting components can be an error-prone process, this work suggest the use of a very simple development that generates the *scheduling task behavior and initialization* from the real-time analysis report.

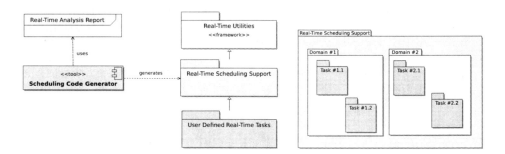

Fig. 5. Real-Time Multiprocessor Framework

The current prototype of the code generation tool has been implemented using the PHP script language[2], and the YAML language [16] to format the file with the real-time analysis report. PHP languages is used due to its agile programming style and code generaton facilites that eases the prototyping process, while YAML language selection is based on its human readability. Specific XML2YAML conversion tools can be provided to support systems specified in standard XML formats.

---

[2] Using the PHP Command-Line Interface.

A scheme of the proposed real-time multiprocessor framework is shown on the left side of the Figure 5. On the right side, it is depicted the structure of the generated code: one package per Scheduling Domain and each Task of a given domain represented by a child package. The system programmer only has to extend the specialized Task_State type provided for each task in the system and implement the task behavior in the corresponding procedures.

7 Conclusions

The complexity of modern real-time system will require the use of multiprocessor platforms. Future Ada 2012 will provide basic mechanism to support part of the scheduling approaches proposed for that platforms. However, the Ada language support provides low-level mechanisms and the programmer have to reconstruct complex task templates and algorithms on each system.

This work has extended the previous Real-Time Utilities presented in [4] to support multiprocessor platforms and to better adapt its structure to an automatic code generation framework. The multiprocessor scheduling approaches have been analyzed, and the new requirements have been taken into account in the new framework components. The resulting framework allows the programmer to center the implementation efforts only in the task behavior, letting the scheduling mechanisms to be automatically generated from the real-time analysis report. Currently, the support for multi-stepped jobs is being finished and a web site to share the real-time framework code and the development tools is being set up.

References

1. Burns, A., Wellings, A.J.: Multiprocessor systems session summary. In: 14th International Real-Time Ada Workshop (IRTAW-14) (2009)
2. Burns, A., Wellings, A.J.: Dispatching domains for multiprocessor platforms and their representation in ada. In: Real, J., Vardanega, T. (eds.) Ada-Europe 2010. LNCS, vol. 6106, pp. 41–53. Springer, Heidelberg (2010)
3. Andersson, B., Pinho, L.M.: Implementing multicore real-time scheduling algorithms based on task splitting using ada 2012. In: Real, J., Vardanega, T. (eds.) Ada-Europe 2010. LNCS, vol. 6106, pp. 54–67. Springer, Heidelberg (2010)
4. Wellings, A.J., Burns, A.: Real-Time Utilities for Ada 2005. In: Abdennahder, N., Kordon, F. (eds.) Ada-Europe 2007. LNCS, vol. 4498, pp. 1–14. Springer, Heidelberg (2007)
5. Balbastre, P., Ripoll, I., Vidal, J., Crespo, A.: A task model to reduce control delays. Journal of Real-Time Systems 27(3), 215–236 (2004)
6. Baruah, S., Fisher, N.: Global fixed-priority scheduling of arbitrary-deadline sporadic task systems. In: Rao, S., Chatterjee, M., Jayanti, P., Murthy, C.S.R., Saha, S.K. (eds.) ICDCN 2008. LNCS, vol. 4904, pp. 215–226. Springer, Heidelberg (2008)
7. Baruah, S.K., Baker, T.P.: Schedulability analysis of global EDF. Real-Time Systems 38(3), 223–235 (2008)
8. Lakshmanan, K., Rajkumar, R., Lehoczky, J.P.: Partitioned fixed-priority preemptive scheduling for multi-core processors. In: 21st Euromicro Conference on Real-Time Systems, ECRTS 2009, pp. 239–248. IEEE Computer Society, Los Alamitos (2009)

9. Kato, S., Yamasaki, N., Ishikawa, Y.: Semi-partitioned scheduling of sporadic task systems on multiprocessors. In: 21st Euromicro Conference on Real-Time Systems, ECRTS 2009, pp. 249–258. IEEE Computer Society, Los Alamitos (2009)
10. Hong, S., Hu, X.S., Lemmon, M.: Reducing delay jitter of real-time control tasks through adaptive deadline adjustments. In: Euromicro Conference on Real-Time Systems, ECRTS 2010, pp. 229–238. IEEE Computer Society, Los Alamitos (2010)
11. Ada 2005 Issues. AI05-0169-1/06: Defining group budgets for multiprocessor platforms. (2010) Version: 1.7. Status: Amendment 2012
12. Aldea, M., Miranda, J., González Harbour, M.: Implementing an Application-Defined Scheduling framework for Ada tasking. In: Llamosí, A., Strohmeier, A. (eds.) Ada-Europe 2004. LNCS, vol. 3063, pp. 283–296. Springer, Heidelberg (2004)
13. Sáez, S., Crespo, A.: Preliminary multiprocessor support of Ada 2012 in GNU/Linux systems. In: Real, J., Vardanega, T. (eds.) Ada-Europe 2010. LNCS, vol. 6106, pp. 68–82. Springer, Heidelberg (2010)
14. Burns, A., Wellings, A.J.: Dual priority assignment: A practical method for increasing processor utilisation. In: 5th Euromicro Workshop on Real-Time Systems, pp. 48–55. IEEE Computer Society, Los Alamitos (1993)
15. Gamma, E., Helm, R., Johnson, R.E., Vlissides, J.: Design Patterns: Elements of Reusable Object-Oriented Software. Addison-Wesley, Reading (1995)
16. Ben-Kiki, O., Evans, C., Ingerson, B.: YAML ain't markup language (YAML) (tm) version 1.2. Technical report, YAML.org (September 2009)

The SQALE Quality and Analysis Models for Assessing the Quality of Ada Source Code

Thierry Coq[1] and Jean-Pierre Rosen[2]

[1] DNV France, Paris, France
thierry.coq@dnv.com, http://www.dnv.com
[2] Adalog, Issy-les-Moulineaux, France
rosen@adalog.fr, http://www.adalog.fr

Abstract. This article presents the quality and analysis model of the SQALE assessment method of software source code. It explains how an Ada quality model compliant to SQALE is implemented and the results of its application to selected software, and how the use of Ada reduces the quality debt unlike many other technologies.

1 Introduction

Det Norske Veritas (DNV) is a not-for-profit organization specialized in risk management. As such, we are conducting research in the measurement of software quality (qualimetry). We discovered that the analysis model, and more precisely the rules used for aggregating raw measures, is a key factor for the effective implementation of qualimetry. This paper introduces the analysis model of the SQALE (Software Quality Assessment Based on Lifecycle Expectations) method to assess the quality of software and in particular software source code. A detailed view of SQALE has been presented in our white paper [1]. The quality model of SQALE and its application to real-time or embedded software has been described in [2]. Its particular strength resides in its compliance to the representation clause [3]. The SQALE method is open source and freely available [4]. Several tool vendors provide implementations for various languages such as C, C++, Java and Cobol. We explain in this paper how the SQALE for Ada quality model is developed in compliance with the SQALE requirements, how the basic Ada metric and quality measurements tools can be used. Finally a few results of applying SQALE for Ada are described and analyzed, putting in evidence the small quality debt incurred in the selected projects.

2 The SQALE Analysis Model

Before describing in detail the implementation of the SQALE model for Ada, the quality model of the SQALE method will be briefly presented. The quality model of the SQALE method expresses the requirements applicable to the software and its source code over its life cycle. In the same manner that the activities linked to making the software and in particular its source code, follow a clear

A. Romanovsky and T. Vardanega (Eds.): Ada-Europe 2011, LNCS 6652, pp. 61–74, 2011.
© Springer-Verlag Berlin Heidelberg 2011

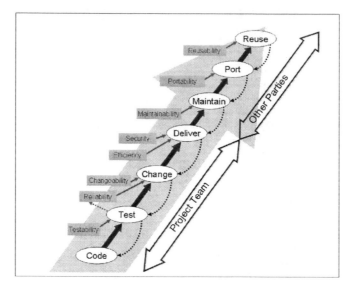

Fig. 1. Dependencies between Activities and Quality Characteristics

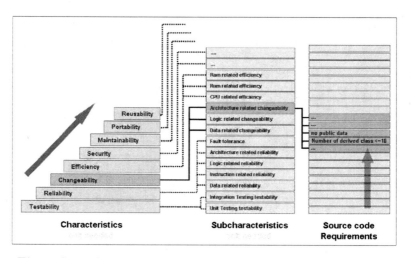

Fig. 2. Some details of Level 2 and 3 of the SQALE Quality Model

chronology the requirements applicable to the source code appear in a same order. The approach and the structure of the SQALE quality model has been detailed elsewhere [1] and are summarized in figures 1 and 2.

The generic SQALE model is derived according to the implementation technologies (design and source code languages) and the tailoring needs of the project. As stated in [1], the quality model is a requirements model. The way it is built ensures the quality targets a total absence of non compliances. As written by Ph. Crosby [5], assessing a software source code is therefore similar to measuring the distance which separates it from its quality target. To measure this distance, the concept of remediation index has been defined and implemented in the SQALE analysis model. An index is associated to each component of the software source code (for example, a file, a module or a class). The index represents the remediation effort which would be necessary to correct the non compliances detected in the component, versus the model requirements. Since the remediation index represents a work effort, the consolidation of the indices is a simple addition of uniform information, which is compliant with the representation condition and a critical advantage of our model. A component index is computed by the addition of the indices of its elements.

A characteristic index is computed by the addition of the base indices of its sub-characteristics. A sub-characteristic index is computed by the addition of the indices of its control points. Base indices are computed by rules which comply with the following principles:

- A base index takes into account the unit remediation effort to correct the non-compliance. In practice, this effort mostly depends on the type of non-compliance. For example correcting a presentation defect (bad indentation, dead code) does not have the same unit effort cost as correcting an active code defect (which implies the creation and execution of new unit tests, possible new integration and regression tests).
- A base index also considers the number of non-compliances. For example, a file which has three methods which need to be broken down into smaller methods because of complexity will have an index three times as high as a file which has only one complex method, all other things being equal.

Base indices are aggregated either by the artifact where the non-compliance has been identified, or by the relevant (sub-)characteristic. In the end, the remediation indices provide a means to measure and compare non compliances of very different origins and very different types. Coding rule violation non-compliances, threshold violations for a metric or the presence of an antipattern non-compliance can be compared using their relative impact on the index.

The standard measure set of SQALE has more than 30 control points and the extended set more than 60. A few examples of base measures are explained in more detail, to show how each complies with the conditions explained above:

- A well-known issue contributing to reduced testability is an excessive cyclomatic complexity for a given operation (procedure or function) in the code. The default threshold for excessive complexity in SQALE is 15. Any operation having a V(G) over 15 will be counted as one violation, and the count is cumulative per class and file in order to apply the representation condition. This measure is mostly independent of the programming language, each language has an equivalent.
- A contributor to reliability measurement is the absence of dynamic memory allocation (for real-time software) or a balanced use of allocation and deallocation instructions (malloc and freemem in C for example). Each violation of this rule increments the count by one, again for each class and file.

- A contributor changeability measurement can be obtained by computing the number of operations (methods) per class (excluding getters and setters) and checking it is beneath a threshold, fixed in SQALE at 30.
- A contributor to maintainability measurement is obtained by measuring the comment ratio, for each file. If it is below SQALEs default threshold of 25%, a violation is counted.
- Finally, for real-time software, the presence of dead code and commented-out code is also counted as a contributor against maintainability.

Of course, the various examples presented above have different remediation indices. The SQALE method uses the organizations remediation indices built using historical data from the projects. If it is not possible, a Delphi analysis [6] or AHP [7] may be used with the project and the SQALE experts to define expert-based remediation indices.

In the above examples, the thresholds provided are examples in a particular context, the SQALE method providing conservative defaults if needed. Many authors (f.e.: [8,9,10,11,12]) have proposed individual check points and thresholds that can be used in SQALE, provided the representation clause is satisfied [3].

The SQALE quality and analysis models have been used to perform many assessments of software source code, of various application domains and sizes. The same layered and generic quality model has been used to assess Cobol, Java, embedded Ada, C or C++ source code. For Java, C++ and Ada, the quality model contains object-oriented metrics to assess Testability, Changeability and Reusability. The quality model also provides control points to detect the absence of antipatterns such as those identified by Brown [13]. The indices are computed based on the average remediation efforts estimated by the development team. The index thresholds providing a rating in five levels (from "poor" to "excellent") are established by the application managers.

3   The SQALE for Ada Quality Model

Making a SQALE Ada quality model requires defining the requirements for the Ada language. Some requirements can be reused as-is from the SQALE default quality model, such as the maximum cyclomatic complexity for subprograms, or the absence of copy/paste (for 100 tokens). Other requirements such as the one for comments can be applied to Ada, but with a lower bound (and a maximum) due to the inherently more readable nature of the language.

Other requirements are not applicable as they are enforced by the compiler. The most notable of those is the requirement for a directed acyclic hierarchical dependency graph between units of compilation: cyclic dependencies between packages are prohibited by the language.

Some requirements related to object-oriented concepts are more difficult to analyze in the dual nature of the Ada language and have to be adapted to the language. For example, the stability requirement is computed on the efferent and afferent coupling of packages, not objects. The final list of selected requirements, for our SQALE Ada Quality Model covers most characteristics and subcharacteristics of the SQALE model.

A drawback of the model is the lack of efficiency requirements. SQALE requirements in other languages require the absence of certain statements or library functions likely to cause inefficiencies. A first analysis has not uncovered the equivalent in the Ada language. Other efficiency requirements need to be set up, related to the two sub-characteristics: CPU performance, memory (RAM) performance. One requirement was identified related to the absence of dead code in the source, and linked to the memory (ROM) performance subcharacteristic. The final SQALE Ada Quality Model is presented in table 1. The reusability requirement is based on the stability principle, where the dependency graph and the stability are computed to determine the actual reusability. If a less stable package is reused by a more stable one, then it is a violation of the model (for both packages). The stability is computed as the ratio of using packages over

Table 1. The SQALE for Ada Default Quality Model

No	Characteristic	Sub-Characteristic	Generic Requirement Description	Ada Requirement
1	Testability	Unit testability	Acceptable number of parameters in a call (NOP)	NOP $\leq$ 5
2	Testability	Unit testability	Acceptable number of test paths in a module (V(G))	$V(G) \leq 15$
3	Testability	Unit testability	Tolerable number of test paths in a module (v(G))	$V(G) \leq 60$
4	Testability	Unit testability	Acceptable number of different called modules from a module (FANOUT)	Efferent coupling $\leq$ 20
5	Testability	Unit testability	Acceptable duplication within a module (CPRR100)	Number of CPRR100 violations
6	Testability	Unit testability	All code paths within a module are reachable	All code is reachable
7	Testability	Unit testability	All modules are reachable	All modules are reachable
8	Testability	Unit testability	No module calling itself recursively	No recursion
9	Testability	Integration testability	Acceptable coupling between objects (CBO)	$CBO \leq 7$
10	Testability	Integration testability	No public data within classes	No directly accessed globals, all public (tagged) types are private.
11	Testability	Integration testability	Acceptable number of direct declared required files	With count < 50
16	Reliability	Data reliability	All types are safely converted	No unchecked conversions
17	Reliability	Data reliability	No use of unitialized variables	No use of unitialized variables
19	Reliability	Logic reliability	One single point of exit per module	No multiple exits
25	Reliability	Statement reliability	Reproducible floating point computations	No equality comparison between reals
27	Reliability	Statement reliability	No ambiguous statement execution order	No operator precedence order ambiguity
28	Reliability	Synchronization related reliability	Shared resources are used in protected scope	No shared variables used in several contexts
34	Reliability	Architecture reliability	Standardized error and exception handling	No exception propagates to other languages
38	Changeability	Architecture changeability	No different elements with the same name	No local hiding
39	Changeability	Architecture changeability	Acceptable number of class methods (NOM)	NOM (public) $\leq$ 60 (for a package)?
42	Changeability	Data changeability	No explicit constants directly used in the code (except 0,1...)	No literals in expressions or statements
43	Changeability	Data changeability	All objects are declared at smallest scope	No unnecessary use or with clause, no reduceable scope
45	Efficiency	RAM efficiency	No unused variable, parameter or constant in code	No unused variable, parameter or constant in code
48	Efficiency	ROM efficiency	All statements are useful	No simplifiable statements
51	Maintainability	Readability	Acceptable File size	LSLOC < 2000
58	Maintainability	Readability	Capitalization rules are followed for code elements.	Casing
59	Maintainability	Readability	Rules for identifying types, variables and other code elements are followed.	Check the project's naming rules are applied. (To be adjusted to the project)
60	Maintainability	Understandability	Acceptable minimum level of comments	Comments density $\geq$10% (needs to take into account verbose FOSS headers)
61	Maintainability	Understandability	Acceptable maximum level of comments	Comments density $\leq$35% (needs to take into account verbose FOSS headers)
64	Maintainability	Understandability	No unstructured statements (goto, break outside a switch...) (eV(G))	$eV(G) \leq 1$
66	Reusability	Stability	The SDP (Stability Dependency Principle) is applied	The less stable package is not used by the more stable package[1]

the total of the using and used packages. If a package does not use any other packages, it has a stability of one.

Unlike tool-based quality models, the SQALE Ada Quality model is based on defining the objectives and requirements first, then finding or building the tools needed to implement it, creating the tools check points from the requirements.

In addition to the quality model, an analysis model was defined for the Ada language. Each requirement was assigned a remediation factor, based on the estimated work units required to correct the defect.

The remediation factors are defined by the following table, and mapped to the quality model.

Table 2. The SQALE Ada remediation factors

Non-Compliance Type Name	Description	Remediation Factor	Sample
Type0	Undefined	0	Not applicable
Type1	Fixable by automated tool, no risk	0.01	Change in capitalization
Type2	Manual remediation, but no impact on compilation	0.1	Add comments
Type3	Local impact, need only unit testing	1	Replace an instruction by another
Type4	Medium impact, need integration testing	5	Split a big function in two
Type5	Large impact, need a complete validation	20	Architectural change

Table 3. The effort scale per source line for each type of package

Package Type	Work Unit per Line
Package Specification (.ads)	1
Package Body (.adb)	0.1

In addition, in order to compute index densities, the size of the packages (in source lines of code) was used as a rough estimate of the number of work units to produce the package from scratch, if it were entirely rewritten.

For example, a typical package with 15 lines of specification and 250 lines of body rates 15 + 25 or 40 work units in this model. The justification for this choice is based on the authors experience of using Ada as a specification language where the structure of the packages is as important as the implementation.

This number can then be compared with the indices obtained, either in total or for a given characteristic, and the file rated using the rating scale described in table 4. For example, a package with 25 work units and a remediation index of 30 would be rated as "E", very bad (rating of 1.2 in the interval $]1, +\infty[$) . The same with a remediation index of 7 would be rated as a "C", medium (rating

Table 4. The SQALE Ada rating thresholds

Class Name	Class Letter	Rating Interval	Color
Excellent	A	[0, 0.03]	green
Good	B	]0.03, 0.1]	light green
Medium	C	]0.1, 0.3]	yellow
Bad	D	]0.3, 1]	orange
Very Bad	E	]1, +∞[	red

of 0.28 in the interval]0.1, 0.3]). Of course, where available in organizations, a better estimation model may be used to assign more precise remediation and work effort factors in the analysis model.

Once the quality and the analysis models are defined, the tools implementing these models may be selected and implemented where missing.

4   Implementing SQALE for Ada Quality Model

The first step of the method consists in building the non-compliance table from the source code. The choice of an appropriate set of tools for this is fundamental to the method, since the significance of the results depends strongly on the accuracy and reliability of the measurement tool. For example, simple text processing tools like Unix's "grep", are too sensitive to presentation issues to be used [15].

The generic SQALE quality model [4] identifies more than 66 points of measurements, and no single tool is able to measure all of the derived checkpoints. Developing a custom tool for SQALE is not feasible, given the limited time and budget allotted to the Ada implementation. However, using a limited number of tools and some "glue" processing, we were able to implement the method for Ada. These checkpoints are close to programming rules: they are places in the source code where undesirable features are used (goto, multiple loop exits), or where a certain limit is exceeded (number of parameters, cyclomatic complexity).

The requirements are designed independently of any programming language. An interesting property of Ada is that, among the 66 requirements, 17, which correspond to features that are best avoided, are actually forbidden by the language definition (and thus automatically enforced).

Our main checking tool is Adalog's AdaControl [14]. The choice of AdaControl was motivated by several reasons:

- Since it is an ASIS [21] tool, its analysis on the language is based on the same technology as the compiler, thus increasing the confidence that the tool processes the language correctly.
- It has a rich set of rules. Out of the remaining 49 requirements, 22 had checkpoints that were provided right out of the box.
- It can output its results in CSV format, making them directly loadable in a spreadsheet program for further analysis.
- Moreover, since AdaControl is free software and easily extendable [15,16,17], more checkpoints can be added at will.

AdaControl is oriented towards finding occurrences of various constructs, more than actually measuring mathematical or statistical properties of the source. For rules that were of this second kind (number of paths, cyclomatic complexity, fan-out), we used AdaCore's Gnatmetric tool. Gnatmetric is also ASIS based and free software.

PMD-CPD[18] is also used to compute the copy/paste non compliances. In addition, a little post-processing was used to compute some of the complex checkpoints, glue the results together and build the indices. Table 5 summarizes the tool set used.

Table 5. The SQALE Ada tool set

Tool	Usage
AdaControl	Most check-points
Gnatmetric	Volumetry, comments
PMD-CPD	Copy/Paste detection
Specific tooling	Stability, dependencies, Index assembly

5   Some Results of SQALE for Ada

Two open-source projects are used to present SQALE for Ada: AdaControl[14] and Ada Web Server (AWS)[19,20]. The data presented here are for illustration purposes and does not constitute an endorsement or rejection of either project.

5.1   SQALE for Ada Applied to AdaControl

Naturally we used AdaControl as an example of applying SQALE to an Ada project. AdaControl is free software: the source code is readily available, and our results can be published, unlike most industrial applications of SQALE which are performed on confidential software.

In this analysis, we analyzed the AdaControl as a whole, and computed the indices for the three parts: AdaControl itself, the ASIS framework, and the GNAT packages used. Showing the indices for the 3 different parts allows us to show how each part has unique properties. Each SQALE analysis first provides size measurements as in figure 3:

The total line code is around 230 KLoc, evenly distributed between the three parts of the application. This is a rather low range of the application size for SQALE, which can target the 0.1 40 million lines of code range. It is an ideal example, however to demonstrate the usefulness of SQALE.

Once the indices and the densities have been computed, it is possible to use the aggregated indices and compare the index densities, as in figure 4. The total quality index for the AdaControl application is 2930 work units, where the GNAT library takes 1474, the ASIS library 1109 and the AdaControl specific part 347. The absolute numbers are difficult to compare, so the index densities are computed over the sum of the lines of code, resulting in a quality index density of 40, 20 and 10 for each KLoc of code for the GNAT library, the ASIS

Volumetry	GNAT	ASIS	AdaControl	Total
Total number of lines	74 550	99 248	56 282	230 080
Total number of source lines	38 860	48 105	36 810	123 775
Total number of source files	64	131	183	378
Sum of cyclomatic complexity (v(G))	5 523	7 079	4 766	17 368
Total number of methods or functions	-	-	-	-

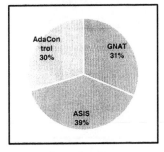 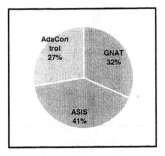

Distribution of source lines   Distribution of cyclomatic complexity

Fig. 3. Volume indicators for the AdaControl software

Code Type	GNAT	ASIS	AdaControl
Sum of Indexes	2 469	3 709	2 297
Σ Index/ Σ V(G)	0.45	0.52	0.48

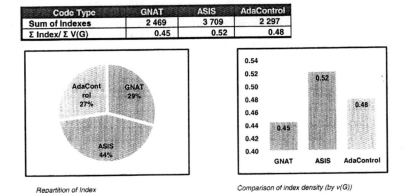

Repartition of Index   Comparison of index density (by v(G))

Fig. 4. The indices and index densities for the three parts of AdaControl

library and the AdaControl specific part, respectively. For an industrial analysis, where the parts could be delivered by different teams, this figure could be used to benchmark the quality results of each team, against expected quality targets.

There is another way to look at the results, especially from a project managers point of view, which has a limited budget for the improvement of the quality of the software. Which defects should be corrected first? Figures 5 and 6 present a vivid picture demonstrating where the major benefits could be obtained.

The GNAT library actually has a limited testability issue and the ASIS framework has a higher index, as well as a higher index density. Improving the ASIS framework would increase the overall quality of this application and is a major result of the SQALE analysis.

TESTABILITY	GNAT	ASIS	AdaControl
Unit level Testability	175	725	460
Integration level Testability	-	-	34
TOTAL	175	725	494

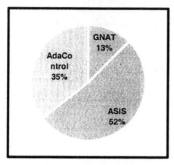

Repartition of Index

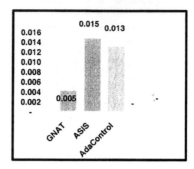

Fig. 5. The testability indices and index densities

RELIABILITY	GNAT	ASIS	AdaControl
Data related Robustness	-	-	-
Instruction related Robustness	-	-	-
Logic related Robustness	1 062	276	19
Architecture related Robustness	-	-	-
Fault Tolerance	-	-	-
Exception Handling	-	-	-
TOTAL	1 062	276	19

Fig. 6. The reliability indices and index densities

The reliability indices computed by the SQALE method are mostly linked to the GNAT library, and within the indices, related to the use of global unprotected data. If some quality budget remains, it might be useful for the maintainers to review and protect the global variables published by the GNAT library. Fully half of the indices have been analyzed by just reviewing the first two characteristics of the SQALE model. A careful project manager may not need to look further for quality increases until these issues have been solved. The SQALE pyramid provides the same indication in a clear picture: 1731 work units out 2930 are assigned to the testability and reliability characteristics. The actual amount of files to be modified is extremely low, mostly below 10%. In addition, since the

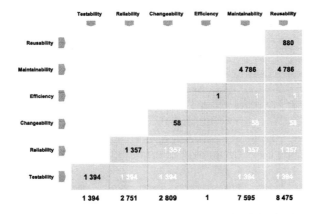

Fig. 7. The SQALE pyramid for AdaControl

copy/paste requirement is in the testability characteristic, the low values we see here indicate a low copy/paste problem, which is often not the case in industrial SQALE analyses.

5.2   SQALE for Ada Applied to Ada Web Server

Ada Web Server (AWS) is a framework to provide complete web based applications. It can be embedded in an Ada application to provide web services. See [19] for more information. AWS itself reuses other libraries available within the Ada community, such as XMLAda, a SSL library. It contains a well-defined

Volumetry	AWS	XMLAda	SSL	Templates	Total
Total number of lines	69 112	51 498	709	11 275	132 594
Total number of source lines	37 773	37 286	459	7 059	82 577
Total number of source files	275	196	2	21	494
Sum of cyclomatic complexity (v(G))	3 461	3 410	-	509	7 380
Total number of methods or functions	-	-	-	-	-

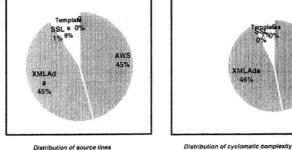

Distribution of source lines   Distribution of cyclomatic complexity

Fig. 8. Application of SQALE to another Ada framework: Ada Web Server (AWS)

"templates parser" module to separate web design from the code. For our analysis, we decided to rate each part separately.

The overall size of the framework and its parts is shown in figure 8 below. With 132 KLOC, this framework is smaller than the AdaControl application. The 7000 cyclomatic complexity sum is consistent with the size. The "templates parser" module is a small component of AWS, while XMLAda is roughly equivalent to the rest of the code base. Figure 9 below shows the SQALE pyramid for AWS. Testability and reliability indices are quite correct, whereas some work might still be useful on the maintainability and reusability characteristics. The final quotation shows little need for improving the AWS packages for

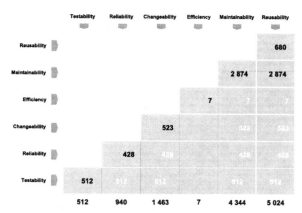

Fig. 9. The SQALE pyramid for AWS

testability, while maintainability might be an issue for some of the packages. Most of the remediation in the maintainability characteristic is related to the requirement "eV(G) $\leq$ 1" and needs more investigation. Again, as for AdaControl and contrary to common industrial practice, there is little need for copy/paste refactoring.

6   Future Work

The validity of the SQALE model is based on its focusing on the quality requirements first, then drilling down into the sub-characteristics and how the requirements are implemented by the tools as check points. As described above, the efficiency characteristic is lacking requirements for Ada. Additional research can therefore identify requirements, or if that proves too difficult, identify why in the Ada language such an endeavor is difficult. Additional reusability requirements would also be very useful. Once SQALE starts to be used, the Ada community will be able to review the various SQALE requirements and fine-tune them for its specific needs.

Building a SQALE quality model for Ada has proved surprisingly easy, especially compared to other languages. SQALE has always been intended as a method for checking software quality, not only source code quality. SQALE for Ada might be the right quality model to extend SQALE and start using requirements for other software artifacts such as requirements or design models, test cases and test results (using coverage and dynamic analysis tools). Particularly, being able to measure design at an early stage may result in SQALE being used as early predictor of final quality.

7   Conclusion

This paper proposes a quality model and an analysis model for measuring the quality of applications using the Ada language, based on the SQALE method. It also describes a set of tools for implementing the checkpoints and computing the resulting indices, index densities and ratings according to the SQALE method. These indices are computed to estimate the remaining technical debt, or work effort remaining in the application from quality non-compliances.

Two examples of the application of the SQALE method are described, to the AdaControl tool itself, and to the Ada Web Server framework. Both demonstrate the value of measuring the software, pinpointing testability, reliability and maintainability issues that, once corrected, will raise the quality of the software by more than half.

Finally, since the indices of the SQALE method are independent of the target language, once computed, the results provided demonstrate the low quality debt remaining in an Ada application, quality debt which can be comparably estimated in other applications in other languages. SQALE for Ada can be one of the benchmark tools to help promote the use of Ada.

References

1. Letouzey, J.-L., Coq, T.: The SQALE Models for assessing the quality of software source code, DNV Paris, white paper (September 2009)
2. Letouzey, J.-L., Coq, T.: The SQALE Models for Assessing the Quality of Real Time Source Code, ERTSS 2010, Toulouse (September 2010)
3. Letouzey, J.-L., Coq, T.: The SQALE Analysis Model - An Analysis Model Compliant with the Representation Condition for Assessing the Quality of Software Source Code. In: VALID 2010, Nice (August 2010)
4. http://www.sqale.org
5. Crosby, P.B.: Quality is free: the art of making quality certain. McGraw-Hill, New-York (1979) ISBN 0-07-014512-1
6. Linstone, H.A., Turoff, M.: The Delphi Method: Techniques and Applications. Adison-Wesley, Reading (1975)
7. Saaty, T.L.: Fundamentals of Decision Making and Priority Theory. RWS Publications, Pittsburgh (2001)
8. McCall, J.A., Richards, P.K., Walters, G.F.: Factors in Software Quality. The National Technical Information Service 1(2,3) (1977)
9. Boehm, B.W., Brown, J.R., Kaspar, H., Lipow, M., McLeod, G., Merrit, M.: Characteristics of Software Quality. North Holland, Amsterdam (1978)

10. McCabe, T., Watson, A.H.: Structured Testing: A Testing Methodology using the Cyclomatic Complexity Metric, National Institute of Standards and Technology, Special Publication 500-235 (1996)
11. Chidamber, S.R., Kemerer, C.F.: A Metrics Suite for Object Oriented Design. IEEE Transactions on Software Engineering 20(6), 476–493 (1994)
12. Fenton, N.E., Pfleeger, S.L.: Software Metrics: A rigourous & Practical Approach, 2nd edn. PWS Publishing Company, Boston (1997) ISBN 053495425-1
13. Brown, et al.: Anti patterns: refactoring software, architectures and projects in crisis. John Wiley, Chichester (1998) ISBN 978-0-471-19713
14. http://www.adalog.fr/adacontrol2.htm
15. Rosen, J.-P.: AdaControl: a free ASIS based tool, presentation at FOSDEM, Brussels, Belgium (February 2006)
16. Rosen, J.-P.: On the benefits for industrials of sponsoring free software development. Ada User Journal 26(4) (December 2005)
17. Jemli, M., Rosen, J.-P.: A Methodology for Avoiding Known Compiler Problems Using Static Analysis. In: Proceedings of the ACM SIGAda Annual International Conference (SIGAda 2010), October 24-28. ACM Press, ACM order number 825100, Fairfax (2010)
18. PMD-CPD site, http://pmd.sourceforge.net/cpd.html
19. Ada Web Server site, http://libre.adacore.com/aws/
20. Rosen, J.-P.: Developing a Web server in Ada with AWS. Ada User Journal 25(3) (September 2004)
21. ISO/IEC 15291:1999. Information technology Programming languages Ada Semantic Interface Specification (ASIS)

Adapting ACATS to the Ahven Testing Framework

Dan Eilers[1] and Tero Koskinen[2]

[1] Irvine Compiler Corp.
http://www.irvine.com
dan@irvine.com
[2] tero.koskinen@iki.fi

Abstract. The Ada Conformity Assessment Test Suite (ACATS) includes thousands of individual executable test programs, but no test driver or tools for grading the output. We show how ACATS can be adapted to work with the Ahven testing framework, resulting in a single easy-to-build executable program that combines the executable ACATS tests, runs them in order, and grades and summarizes the test results. Our goal is a highly portable and automated ACATS driver, and as a side benefit we obtain a somewhat more stressful test capability for Ada compilation systems.

Keywords: ACATS, Ahven, testing framework, test harness, test automation, conformance, conformance testing, Ada, compiler.

1 Introduction

The Ada Conformity Assessment Test Suite (ACATS) [1] is a publicly available test suite intended to check Ada compilers for conformance with the Ada [2] standard. It is derived from the original Ada Compiler Validation Capability (ACVC) sponsored by the former Ada Joint Program Office (AJPO).

Although ACATS is intended to be relatively straightforward to use, it requires much more effort than simply typing a few commands and waiting for the results. This is partly because there is no supplied test driver nor any tools for grading the output. ACATS users are expected to develop their own driver scripts and analysis tools, which presents a high barrier to use, especially for those who are accustomed to downloading and building large software packages with a single command. We look to automated testing frameworks as a solution.

Testing frameworks for Ada have become popular relatively recently, notably including Ahven [3,4] developed by Tero Koskinen (co-author of this paper) and AUnit [6] developed by Ed Falis. Both frameworks were inspired by the JUnit testing framework for Java, and both are open source Ada packages in the Debian GNU/Linux distribution [5,7]. These frameworks work by combining a collection of individual test procedures into a single executable program, where they are

A. Romanovsky and T. Vardanega (Eds.): Ada-Europe 2011, LNCS 6652, pp. 75–88, 2011.

run in order and graded, with a summary of the results produced at the end. A single "Ada make" command suffices to build the combined test program, with no need for unportable shell scripts. We focus on the Ahven framework because it avoids the need to write a test wrapper for each individual ACATS test.

Combining ACATS test programs is something that the ACATS User's Guide envisions for efficiency reasons. However, our concern is not efficiency. Instead we are concerned with automating the process in a portable manner. And as a side benefit, combining the tests creates the possibility of exposing runtime errors that might otherwise have gone undetected.

ACATS includes both "positive" and "negative" tests. That is, tests that are intended to compile and run successfully, and those with errors that are intended to be rejected by the compiler. We have found that the positive tests are well suited for automation using Ahven. The negative tests, however, are not. Negative tests pose grading difficulties because they typically have multiple intentional errors per test. The grader must verify that the compiler has detected each of those, without rejecting any legal constructs. Negative tests are also not suitable for testing frameworks such as Ahven that expect to successfully compile and run each test case. So this paper is concerned only with the positive tests.

Fortunately, the positive ACATS tests are both the easiest to grade as well as the most interesting, for users who are especially concerned with correctness of compiled Ada code, since negative tests do not exercise the dynamic semantics, optimization, and code generation phases of the compiler. Users who may have modified the compiler's run-time system, or who are using an unusual set of compiler switches would also benefit most from the positive tests. Some previous language test suites, such as those for Cobol and Fortran did not even include any negative tests [12]. There are however occasional cases where negative tests can have value with regard to preventing incorrectly compiled code, such as where a negative test enforces a language rule designed to prohibit a dangerous combination of features.

We envision Ahven being used with ACATS primarily for informal compiler testing, particularly by those who have never used ACATS before because they considered it too much trouble. So we are not bothered by a few unusual tests that may require omission or special handling. We believe that the minor ACATS test modifications we describe would be beneficial to incorporate into a future version of the test suite, and are happy to make them available upon request.

Section 2 describes ACATS and existing scripting capabilities; Section 3 describes Ahven and how it can be integrated with ACATS; Section 4 describes some elaboration issues requiring test modification; Section 5 describes how using a framework can make ACATS more effective; Section 6 compares Ahven with AUnit; and Section 7 gives the conclusions.

2   Background and Related Work

I've written the following simple routine, which may separate the "man-compilers" from the "boy-compilers". *Donald Knuth*

Unfortunately, Ada compiler conformance testing is not as simple as Knuth's clever 10-line test program for Algol 60 compilers [8]. But perhaps his novel idea of a single executable test program is not as far-fetched as it might seem.

For Ada, we have the ACATS test suite, which was designed from the beginning to include thousands of individual test programs, intending to provide a comprehensive conformance assessment [9]. Composing a test suite from many tests has obvious advantages. It produces meaningful results for partially conforming compilers, and it simplifies analysis of failing tests. But such a large collection of tests requires some sort of test harness and automated grading tools in order to be cost effective.

ACATS does not come with a modern testing framework such as Ahven or AUnit. This comes as no surprise, since ACATS and the ACVC before it predate such frameworks. The ACATS User's Guide [10] was written with the expectation that users of the suite would use custom-developed shell scripts to compile, run, and grade the positive tests. Ideally, such scripts would be provided with ACATS. But it is difficult if not impossible to create portable shell scripts that would work with any potential compiler on any potential operating system.

A significant milestone in ACATS automation was a shell script developed by Laurent Guerby for running and grading the ACATS positive tests using the gcc Ada compiler. This script was incorporated into the testsuite of gcc 3.4 and later [11, Section 2.3.4]. It has provided various individuals and organizations who rehost and/or retarget the gcc Ada compiler with an effective means of demonstrating that the compiler and run-time system are working properly. It also provides a fully automated compiler test capability for system administrators, compiler testers, and end users who download and build the gcc Ada compiler from source code. Most such users would not be using ACATS if it were not fully automated.

The shell scripts used by the gcc testsuite rely on textual analysis of the ACATS output, using the "Expect" tool. Although the shell interpreter and the Expect tool are both widely available, our goal is to have a more portable pure Ada solution that eliminates any textual analysis by hooking directly into the ACATS grading mechanism. We also wish to have a compiler-independent solution.

2.1   Nature of the ACATS Tests

The ACATS positive tests are supplied in a directory structure organized by chapter of the Ada Reference Manual. Some tests have multiple compilation units in the same file, and some tests have multiple compilation units spread across several files. Each test, and each compilation unit within a test, generally has a unique name, so all such tests could conceivably be compiled into the same Ada environment without interference.

The ACATS User's Guide specifies that the tests should be compiled and run in the order given, but generally the tests are independent of each other, and the order of compilation and execution doesn't matter. So a compilation system's "make" facility for automatically determining compilation order would normally be effective. In fact, the gcc testsuite mentioned earlier uses gnatmake to determine compilation order for tests with multiple files.

There are a few tests for RM Chapter 10 that include multiple compilation units with the same name, for the purpose of testing that a later compiled unit properly replaces a previously compiled unit with the same name. These tests can be handled by submitting their source files to the compilation system in alphabetical order, except for test *ca14028e* which may require special handling.

Most ACATS tests are self-contained. However, there are approximately fifty support packages, referred to as foundation code, that are used by multiple tests. Sharing code between bundled tests presents an issue of package elaboration as discussed below.

There are a few *Text_IO* tests in RM Annex A that interfere with each other, such as when one test calls *Set_Input* to change the default input file, without restoring it, causing a later test to fail. The affected tests are *ce3806a*, *ce3806b*, *ce3706d*, *ce3605c*, *ce3405c*, *ce3202a*, *ce3411c*, *ce3413c*. We have not yet identified the best solution for these tests.

The ACATS tests generally don't use command-line arguments, which would prevent them from being bundled. One exception is test *cxaf001* which may require special handling.

2.2   Bundling Test Programs

The ACATS User's Guide was written with the expectation that the tests will normally be compiled and run individually. But Section 5.5.3 specifically describes the possibility of bundling multiple tests into a single executable for efficiency reasons.

> 5.5.3 Bundling Test Programs
>
> In some situations, the usual test processing sequence may require an unacceptable amount of time. For example, running tests on an embedded target may impose significant overhead time to download individual tests. In these cases, executable tests may be bundled into aggregates of multiple tests. A set of bundled tests will have a driver that calls each test in turn; ACATS tests will then be called procedures rather than main procedures. No source changes in the tests are allowed when bundling; that is, the only allowed change is the method of calling the test.
>
> All bundles must be approved by the ACAL (and, if necessary, the ACAA) to qualify for a conformity assessment. It is the responsibility of the user to identify the tests to be bundled and to write a driver for them.

Bundling of test programs is facilitated in Ada by the lack of any syntactic distinction between an Ada main program and an Ada subprogram. In Pascal or

Fortran, for example, the main program uses the **program** keyword to distinguish it from ordinary subprograms. Similarly, in C and C++, the main program is distinguished by its name, *main*. Java is more like Ada, in that any Java class can be treated as the main program.

So bundling of existing Ada test programs requires no changes to the tests. Given three test programs, *P1,P2,P3*, we can simply do:

```
with P1, P2, P3;
procedure Main_Driver is
begin
   P1;
   P2;
   P3;
end;
```

An obvious drawback of this solution is that if an unexpected exception is propagated out of one of the earlier tests, the remaining tests will not be run. This can be solved by adding a begin-end block with an exception handler around each call. But that starts to get messy. If we want to add protection from infinitely looping tests, it gets even messier. Keeping track of pass/fail statistics makes it messier still. We would probably want to do some refactoring, to isolate all the per-test support code in one location, which is exactly what a testing framework is all about.

Caution Regarding Undistinguished Main Programs. Although Ada's undistinguished main programs are useful for test bundling, they can surprise the unwary in other situations. An Ada main program can call itself recursively, either directly or indirectly, just like any other Ada subprogram. So the storage for the main's local variables will likely be stack based rather than being statically allocated. This raises the possibility of stack overflow when the main program includes large array variables on systems with fixed stack limits. For similar reasons, a subprogram nested in the main program may use static links to reference the main's local variables, rather than global references, affecting the nested subprogram's low-level calling signature.

An additional surprise is that in order to prevent dangling pointer references, Ada has the notion of accessibility levels, where library subprograms are considered to be one level deeper than library packages. Ada 95 had a rule (later repealed in Ada 2005) preventing type extension of tagged types at a deeper accessibility level than the parent type (RM95 3.9.1(3)). This rule disallowed extending a library-level tagged type inside the main subprogram, just like any other library subprogram [13, Section 15.1].

2.3   Hooks for Attaching ACATS Tests to a Testing Framework

ACATS tests generally have a standard structure. Section 4.6 of the ACATS Users Guide shows:

Executable tests (class A, C, D, and E) generally use the following format:

```
with Report;
procedure Testname is
   <declarations>
begin
   Report.Test ("Testname", "Description ...");
   ...
   <test situation yielding result>
   if Post_Condition /= Correct_Value then
      Report.Failed ("Reason");
   end if;
   ...
   Report.Result;
end Testname;
```

There is a package *Report*, which is common to all tests. At the beginning of each test, there is a call to *Report.Test*. In the body of each test there are one or more possible calls to *Report.Failed*, whenever an error is detected. At the end of each test there is a call to *Report.Result*. A test is considered to pass if there were no calls to *Report.Failed* before the call to *Report.Result*.

This *Report* package is convenient for our purposes, since it provides the necessary hooks to integrate a testing framework simply by making minor modifications to the *Report* package body, without needing to make any modifications to the tests, in general. The exceptional cases are noted below.

3   Integration with Ahven

Where the primary concern in OO is encapsulation, the primary concern in data-driven programming is writing as little fixed code as possible [14].
Eric S. Raymond

We have three main goals for integration of ACATS with a testing framework. The first is to avoid modifications to the tests, except in a few cases where necessary. This is easily accomplished by adding a call to *Ahven.Fail* in the ACATS *Report* package body, in procedure *Result*, when a test is determined to have failed.

ACATS actually categorizes test results into four states, passed, failed, not-applicable, and tentatively-passed. This presents an issue of how the not-applicable and tentatively-passed states should be mapped to Ahven pass-fail states. Normally, these are considered as passing. Alternatively, their results could be highlighted for hand analysis by treating them as failing, using the message parameter to *Ahven.Fail* to record the details.

The second goal is that the test driver should be hierarchical, reflecting the directory structure of ACATS, where tests are grouped by RM chapter. Ahven

supports arbitrarily deep test-suite hierarchies, although only two levels are used
for ACATS.

The third goal is to keep the test driver as simple as possible. Ideally, the
test driver will be data driven, using a framework-independent Ada aggregate,
with one line in the aggregate per test. In particular, we want to avoid having
to perform multiple operations in the driver for each test. We also want to avoid
having to write a wrapper subprogram for each test.

3.1   Framework-Independent Representation of Tests

Suppose for example we have six tests, $P1, P2, P3, Q1, Q2, Q3$, partitioned into two
groups, P and Q, of three tests each.

We would like to define a type *One_Test*, which is a record containing the necessary information about each test, consisting of an access to the test procedure,
and an access to the test name. Then we can declare type *Suite_Type*, which is
an array of *One_Test*. For example:

```
package Test_Suite is

   type Proc_Access is access procedure;
   type One_Test is record
      Proc: Proc_Access;
      Name: access String;
   end record;
   type Suite_Type is array(Natural range <>) of One_Test;

   generic
      Suite_Name: String;
      Suite_Array: Suite_Type;
   package Suites is
   end Suites;

   function "+"(S: String) return access String;
end Test_Suite;

package body Test_Suite is

   function "+"(S: String) return access String is
   begin
      return new String'(S);
   end;
end Test_Suite;
```

This example includes a generic package *Suites*, which can be instantiated
with the name of a test suite, and an array aggregate providing the data for
each test in the suite. So we would define *P_Suite* as:

```
with P1, P2, P3;
with Test_Suite; use Test_Suite;
package P_Suite is new Test_Suite.Suites(
     Suite_Name => "P",
     Suite_Array => (
         (P1'access, +"P1"),
         (P2'access, +"P2"),
         (P3'access, +"P3")));
```

And *Q_Suite* would similarly be defined as:

```
with Q1, Q2, Q3;
with Test_Suite; use Test_Suite;
package Q_Suite is new Test_Suite.Suites(
     Suite_Name => "Q",
     Suite_Array => (
         (Q1'access, +"Q1"),
         (Q2'access, +"Q2"),
         (Q3'access, +"Q3")));
```

This example meets our goal of defining each test suite with an aggregate containing one line per test.

3.2   Connecting with Ahven

Now that we have a framework-independent way of representing our set of tests, we can write some glue code to connect our *Test_Suite* package to Ahven.

In Ahven, each sub-suite of individual tests is created by deriving a new controlled type from *Test_Case*, and overriding its *Initialize* routine. Inside *Initialize*, the sub-suite's name is specified by calling *Set_Name*. Then each test in the sub-suite is registered by calling *Add_Test_Routine*, passing an access to the test, and the name of the test. Outside of *Initialize*, a framework is created by calling *Create_Suite*, and each sub-suite is added to the framework by calling *Add_Test*. The framework, which now includes all of the tests in all of the sub-suites, is run, graded, and summarized by calling *Run*.

The glue code is as follows:

```
with Ahven.Framework;
with Test_Suite;
generic
   S : Ahven.Framework.Test_Suite_Access;
   with package The_Suite is new Test_Suite.Suites(<>);
package One_Suite is
   type Test is new Ahven.Framework.Test_Case with null record;
   procedure Initialize (T: in out Test);
end One_Suite;
```

```
package body One_Suite is

   procedure Initialize (T: in out Test) is
   begin
      T.Set_Name(The_Suite.Suite_name);
      for I in The_Suite.Suite_Array'range loop
        T.Add_Test_Routine(
           Ahven.Framework.Simple_Test_Routine_Access(
                The_Suite.Suite_Array(I).Proc),
           The_Suite.Suite_Array(I).Name.all);
      end loop;
   end;

begin
   Ahven.Framework.Add_Test (S.all, new Test);
end One_Suite;

with P_Suite;
with Q_Suite;
with One_Suite;
with Ahven.Framework;
package All_Suites is
   S : Ahven.Framework.Test_Suite_Access :=
      Ahven.Framework.Create_Suite ("all tests");

   package Suite_P is new One_Suite(S, P_Suite);
   package Suite_Q is new One_Suite(S, Q_Suite);
end All_Suites;

with All_Suites; use All_Suites;
with Ahven.Text_Runner;
with Ahven.Framework;
procedure Main_Driver is
begin
   Ahven.Text_Runner.Run (S);
   Ahven.Framework.Release_Suite (S);
end Main_Driver;
```

The result of running *Main_Driver* will be the output from each of the individual tests, followed by an Ahven summary report such as the one below. The right-hand column shows the execution time taken for each test.

```
Passed :  6
 all tests:
 P:
  P1                                 PASS       0.00000s
```

P2	PASS	0.00000s
P3	PASS	0.00000s
Q:		
Q1	PASS	0.00000s
Q2	PASS	0.00000s
Q3	PASS	0.00018s

Now we can simply replace the *P_Suite* and *Q_Suite* shown above in package *All_Suites* with one suite for each subdirectory in ACATS, which is organized by chapter in the Ada RM. This achieves our goal of a single program that will run, grade, and summarize all executable ACATS tests. Since this program includes a with-clause for each individual ACATS test, it is easy to build, with just a single "Ada make" command.

4   Elaboration Issues in Shared ACATS Support Code

There are however some technical details to resolve before we can declare success. As noted above, some ACATS tests depend on shared foundation packages. When such packages use package elaboration to initialize their variables, we must ensure that the shared package is properly re-initialized before running the next test that depends on it.

There are three such foundation packages, along with the tests that depend on them, that need modification.

Specifically, foundation package *f390a00* includes the declaration

```
Display_Count_For : Display_Counters := (others => 0);
```

This package is shared between three tests, *c390a011*, *c390a022*, and *c390a031*.

Foundation package *f393a00* includes the declaration

```
Finger : Natural := 0;
```

This package is shared between four tests, *c393a02*, *c393a03*, *c393a05*, and *c393a06*.

Foundation package *fb40a00* includes the declarations

```
AlphaNumeric_Count,
Non_AlphaNumeric_Count : Natural := 0;
```

This package is shared between four tests, *cb40a01*, *cb40a021*, *cb40a031*, and *cb40a04*.

In each case there is no existing means for reinitializing the variables, so we propose to add a new initialization procedure to each of these three foundation packages, and add a call to these new procedures at the beginning of each of these eleven dependent test cases.

4.1   Shared Support Package TCTouch

There is a special shared support package, *TCTouch*, which is used by more than 40 tests. It verifies that each test performs particular actions in a particular order. It includes the declaration

```
Finger : Natural := 0;
```

Happily, there does exist an initialization procedure *Flush* that resets variable *Finger* to zero. Unfortunately, most tests that use package *TCTouch* do not call Flush. Instead they simply rely on the default initialization. We must ensure that *Flush* is called at the start of every test that uses package *TCTouch*. This could be done with a small change to 40+ tests. Alternatively we could ensure that *Flush* is called before every test, whether it needs to be or not, by inserting one call in procedure *Test* of the ACATS *Report* package.

With *Flush* called at the start of every test, we must also ensure that there are no cases where calls are made to procedure *Touch* in package *TCTouch* during initialization of the test's local variables. This affects two tests, *c393001* and *c761013*.

Test *c393001* includes the declarations

```
Short : C393001_1.Breaker'Class -- Basic_Breaker
        := C393001_2.Construct( C393001_2.V440, C393001_2.A5 );
Sharp : C393001_1.Breaker'Class -- Ground_Fault
        := C393001_3.Construct( C393001_2.V110, C393001_2.A1 );
Shock : C393001_1.Breaker'Class -- Special_Breaker
        := C393001_4.Construct( C393001_2.V12,  C393001_2.A100 );
```

These calls to *Construct* during initialization result in calls to *TCTouch.Touch*. So we need to move these three declarations into a newly created declare block in this test's main procedure, just after the call to *Report.Test*, to delay their effect.

Test *c761013* includes the declaration

```
Outer : Ctrl;
```

where *Ctrl* is a controlled type with an initialization procedure that calls *TCTouch.Touch*. So we need to move this declaration, and also procedure *Subtest_3*, which references it, to a newly created declare block in this test's main procedure, just after the call to *Report.Test*, to delay its initialization.

A more subtle issue is that we must ensure that no calls are made to *TCTouch.Touch* during the library package elaboration of any test. This is because test bundling causes the elaboration of all library packages to be done before any individual test is started. It would defeat our attempt to reinitialize package *TCTouch* before every test if calls were being made to *Touch* from the combined elaboration code of multiple tests.

This issue affects one test, *c3a2001*, which includes the library package elaboration code:

```
Short : C393001_1.Breaker'Class  -- Basic_Breaker
        := C393001_2.Construct( C393001_2.V440, C393001_2.A5 );
Sharp : C393001_1.Breaker'Class  -- Ground_Fault
        := C393001_3.Construct( C393001_2.V110, C393001_2.A1 );
Shock : C393001_1.Breaker'Class  -- Special_Breaker
        := C393001_4.Construct( C393001_2.V12,  C393001_2.A100 );
```

These calls to *Construct* during elaboration result in calls to *TCTouch. Touch*. So we need to move them into a newly created initialization procedure in package *C3A2001_5*, which we call just after the call to *Report. Test*, to delay their effect.

4.2   Tests with Unusual Organization

Test *cd5003a* is organized somewhat differently than usual. It calls *Report. Test* and *Report.Failed* in the initialization code of a library package, rather than in the test's main procedure. It is not difficult to reorganize this test into the usual format, without affecting its objective, by replacing the package elaboration code with a newly created procedure called from the main procedure. Such reorganization is necessary in order to avoid calling the *Report* package during any test's elaboration, since test bundling has the effect of combining elaboration code for all tests.

There are six tests, *c761001*, *c761010*, *c94004a*, *c94004b*, *c94004c*, and *c94005a* that call *Report.Result* as part the library unit finalization. There are four tests, *c39006f3m*, *ca5004a*, *ca5006a*, and *ca5004b2m* that call *Report. Test* in library package initialization. These tests may require special handling.

5   Bundling As a Compilation System Stressor

Bundling of tests offers a nice side benefit of increasing the stress on a compilation system, thereby maximizing the benefit of the test suite to find anomalies in the compilation system. In particular, bundling has the potential to uncover cases where the state of the run-time system at the completion of one test isn't pristine enough to run the next test. Bundling all ACATS positive tests into a single executable program also has the potential to uncover capacity issues or capacity-related performance issues in the various tools, such as the library system, compilation-order tool, linker, debugger, etc.

5.1   Repeatability and Ordering of Tests

Using a testing framework makes it trivial to stress the compilation system even further, by executing tests multiple times within the same program, to ensure repeatability. Most ACATS tests can be restarted, but a preliminary investigation suggests that some tests may require minor modifications.

Frameworks also have the potential to easily alter the order in which the tests are run. Doing so may expose subtle compiler or run-time system anomalies that might not otherwise show up.

5.2 Making Positive Tests Out of Negative Tests

We have ignored the negative tests, but Robert Eachus has suggested [15] that by removing the errors from the negative tests, we would be left with useful tests which could be treated as additional positive tests. Preliminary investigation shows this to be feasible and worthwhile, although substantial manual effort is required.

6 Ahven vs. AUnit

AUnit is quite similar to Ahven, but the way tests are registered is slightly different. Ahven accepts a parameterless test procedure, where AUnit does not. In procedure *Initialize* above, we have:

```
Ahven.Framework.Simple_Test_Routine_Access(
    The_Suite.Suite_Array(I).Proc),
```

where *The_Suite.Suite_Arr(I).Proc* designates the actual parameterless ACATS test procedure. AUnit registration requires writing a wrapper procedure for each test, which includes a parameter of type *AUnit.Test_Cases.Test_Case'Class*.

Ada does not seem to have a way of automating creation of these wrapper procedures that AUnit requires, given our array aggregate of access to parameterless procedures. Ada does allow procedures to be created dynamically using generics, but such procedures would be at the wrong accessibility level. Ada also allows procedures to be created dynamically using allocators to protected records containing a protected procedure. But AUnit does not allow registering protected procedures.

7 Conclusions

We have shown the ability to integrate the Ahven testing framework with the ACATS test suite, providing a portable test driver. This is done with only minor modifications to the ACATS test suite. The test driver is data driven, with one line of test description per test using a framework-independent Ada aggregate, organized by RM chapter. The resulting single program is easy to build using "Ada make", and it automatically runs the tests and grades and summarizes the results. Combining tests has the side benefit of providing a more stressful test of the compilation system. Improving the cost/benefit ratio of running ACATS may increase the usage of this valuable resource.

Acknowledgments. The authors would like to thank the anonymous referees for their helpful comments.

References

1. Brukardt, R.L.: Ada Conformity Assessment Test Suite (ACATS),
   http://www.ada-auth.org/acats.html
2. Taft, S.T., Duff, R.A., Brukardt, R.L., Plödereder, E., Leroy, P.: Ada 2005 Reference Manual. LNCS, vol. 4348. Springer, Heidelberg (2006)
3. Koskinen, T.: Ahven developer, http://sourceforge.net/projects/ahven
4. Koskinen, T.: Ahven 1.8 announcement on comp.lang.ada newsgroup reprinted in Ada User Journal. Ada Europe 31(3), 159–161 (2010)
5. Buerki, R., Rueegsegger, A.-K.: Ahven package maintainers in Debian GNU/Linux, http://packages.debian.org/ahven
6. Falis, E.: AUnit developer, http://libre.adacore.com/libre/tools/aunit
7. Leake, S.: LibAunit package maintainer in Debian GNU/Linux, http://packages.debian.org/libaunit
8. Knuth, D.E.: "Man or boy?". ALGOL Bulletin 17, 7 (1964); 19, 8–9 (January 1965), Reprinted as ch. 6 of Selected Papers on Computer Languages. Center for the Study of Language and Information, Stanford, California (2003)
9. Goodenough, J.B.: The Ada Compiler Validation Capability. Computer 13(6), 57–64 (1981), doi:10.1109/C-M.1981.220496
10. Brukardt, R.L.: Ada Conformity Assessment Test Suite (ACATS) User's Guide, Version 3.0 (2008),
    http://www.ada-auth.org/acats-files/3.0/docs/ACATS-UG.PDF
11. Brenta, L., Leake, S.: Debian Ada Policy. 5th edn (May 29, 2010),
    http://people.debian.org/~lbrenta/debian-ada-policy.html
12. Oliver, P.: Experiences in Building and Using Compiler Validation Systems. In: Proc. of AFIPS Conf., NCC, vol. 48, pp. 1051–1057 (1979)
13. English, J.: Ada 95: The Craft of Object-Oriented Programming (2001),
    http://www.it.bton.ac.uk/staff/je/adacraft
14. Raymond, E.S.: The Art of Unix Programming. Pearson Education, Inc., London (2004)
15. Eachus, R.: Personal communication (May 2010)

Model-Based Analysis and Design of Real-Time Distributed Systems with Ada and the UML Profile for MARTE[*]

Julio L. Medina and Alvaro Garcia Cuesta

Departamento de Electrónica y Computadores, Universidad de Cantabria,
39005-Santander, Spain
{julio.medina,alvaro.garciacuesta}@unican.es

Abstract. This paper considers the design of hard real-time distributed systems. It uses a model-based approach whose specification is made using UML, a high level standard modelling language. This work describes a tool-aided methodology to enable the assembly and transformation of such design intended models into schedulability analysis models. These analysis models are suitable for the verification of the timing properties of a fully described system in a real-time situation. The description of a real-time situation includes also the knowledge of the load the system is expected to support. In order to annotate the required non-functional properties, and to state other real-time enabling features, the UML profile for Modelling and Analysis of Real-Time and Embedded systems (MARTE), a recent modelling standard of the OMG, has been used. The methodology proposed brings several methodological guidelines to get in tune the generation of Ada applications described by the high level application modelling concepts provided by MARTE, with its corresponding schedulability analysis models. The tool associated to this methodology generates as an output the concrete analysis models used by the MAST set of tools, it invokes MAST, and also recovers the output results back into the high level design UML models.

Keywords: Ada, embedded systems, MARTE, MDA, MDE, modelling, OMG standards, real-time, schedulability analysis, UML.

1 Introduction

Model-based software development is one of the most promising software engineering approaches, since having reusable, configurable, and composable models may help significantly in the separation of concerns, the increase of development efficiency, and even enhancing the quality of the software at large.

---

[*] This work has been funded by the European Union under contracts, FP7/NoE/214373 (ArtistDesign), and FP7/CSA/224330 (ADAMS); and by the Spanish Government under grants TSI-020400-2009-108 (ITEA2-EVOLVE), and TIN2008-06766-C03-03 (RT-MODEL). This work reflects only the author's views; the EU is not liable for any use that may be made of the information contained herein.

A. Romanovsky and T. Vardanega (Eds.): Ada-Europe 2011, LNCS 6652, pp. 89–102, 2011.
© Springer-Verlag Berlin Heidelberg 2011

For applications with real-time requirements, a model-based methodology can additionally help to ease the process of building their temporal behaviour analysis models. These models usually constitute the basis of the real-time design and the schedulability analysis validation processes. With that purpose, the designer of a software (or even hardware) component must generate, in synchrony with the models used to generate the component's code (or the hardware specification), an additional parameterisable model. This other model must be suitable for the timing validation of the system resulting out of the usage of that component in the composition as a whole. The analysis model for each component abstracts away implementation details but retains the timing behaviour of all the actions it performs. In particular it needs to include all the scheduling, synchronization and resources information that is necessary to predict the real-time qualities of the applications in which it might be integrated. In the approach that we present here, these analysis models are to be automatically derived from high level software design models annotated with a minimum set of real-time features. The input data are taken from the requirements of the application in which they are to be used. In analogy to the generation of the application's code as a composition of the code of its constituent components, the analyst, or application designer, can also compose the set of real-time sub-models, and build the complete real-time analysis model of the application. This strategy helps the designer to get rid of the tedious and error prone task of building in one piece the complete reactive model of the application.

A discussion of the process followed for the design of the real-time characteristics of an application in a strict component-based development methodology may by found in [1]. This paper explores the semantics of the modelling elements provided by MARTE [3] in both sides of its principal concerns: analysis and design. It also exploits them with the aim of enabling the automatic extraction of analysis models from high level design models. This task is feasible provided the design space is restricted to those constructs that are safely implementable by specific analysable patterns described in Ada. From a model based engineering perspective, those Ada patterns serve the purpose of conducting the code generation consistently with the schedulability analysis capabilities associated to the design modelling constructs used.

The rest of the paper is organized as follows: Section 2 presents the rational for the modelling approach and visits some related work. Section 3 describes the modelling and extraction tools used for the generation of the output MAST analysis models [2]. Section 4 gives guidelines for the construction of high level application design UML models that can be transformed in an automated way in the respective schedulability analysis models. Section 5 presents our initial experiences with the analysis models for an example application. Finally we draw some conclusions and outline future work.

2 The Approach

The UML Profile for MARTE [3] brings a large number of modelling constructs and concepts that may be used for realizing schedulability analysis in a variety of ways. This effort has been driven by the goal to enable, thanks to those modelling constructs, (1) early V&V and (2) the iterative use of the models created. These requirements are key elements of any development process that aims to reduce integration costs while assuring predictability.

In order to cope with complexity, to manage the risks associated to the research and the development of tools efforts, and also to make better use of the modelling resources offered by MARTE, the complete problem has been divided in two challenging but achievable research steps. Fig. 1 illustrates these two challenges in the context of the model processing paradigm. The picture shows a re-visited version of the approach followed in a previous work [4]. Now we consider separate representations of both: the design and the analysis models in UML, and use the MARTE standard for them.

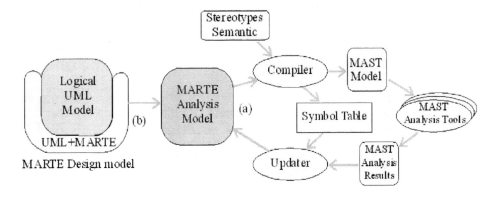

Fig. 1. The Model processing paradigm in the design and analysis approach

The first step addressed by our research effort (a) comprises the definition and manipulation of what we will denominate the "analysis models". This effort is described in Section 3 and includes two modules; one (Compiler) that extracts the MAST models, and another (Updater) that recovers analysis results back into the UML models.

The second part of this effort (b) is the specification and automation of those modelling constructs related to what we call the "design models". These models are usually entered by hand in the UML tool. Instead, the analysis models can be obtained either through model transformation from the design models, or entered by hand.

The proposed methodology extends the regular UML description of a system with a design model which includes some particular MARTE modelling elements describing specific real-time features. These constructs must be sufficient to generate the analysis model. An analysis model defines an additional view of a particular situation of the system that is subject to real-time requirements and expresses:

- the computational capacity of the hardware and software resources that constitute the platform,
- the processing requirements and synchronization artefacts that are relevant for evaluating the timing behaviour of the execution of the logical operations, and
- the real-time situations to be evaluated, which include the workload and the timing requirements to be met.

From another point of view, this method also helps to support the design of applications in terms of composable parts. As far as their granularity is concern, these parts are closer to the concept of real-time objects than to the CBSE (Component-based Software Engineering) interpretation of components. In a fully component-based approach, the creation of the analysis models would have to be made as a combination of structural elements plus the recursive inclusion of their behaviour invocations following their precise deployment. In a model-driven approach, this later strong form of composability is in a higher level of abstraction, but still may benefit from the approach described here in order to assess a variety of non-functional properties, in our case its timing properties by means of schedulability analysis.

In order to constrain the design space to the patterns that may be analysed by the currently available schedulability analysis techniques, the models of computation implicit in the high level application modelling constructs offered by MARTE are restricted to those that have been studied in our previous work [4]. This implies the use of Ada platforms with both the Real-Time System as well as the Distributed Systems annexes of the Ada standard.

Considering some related work it is relevant to mention a similar effort that has been proposed as a result of the ASSERT project [5]. Though the solutions provided there disregard the semantics framework of the design models in the MARTE standard (by using an ad-hoc profile), and commit for single processor systems, it is a very relevant effort that shows the main formalisms and the technical and industrial trends in place. Our approach differs in several aspects, first (1) the analysis models are also expressed using UML plus the MARTE standard so that they may be used for additional transformations not only to MAST but to other tools if necessary. Then (2) the constraints over the design model are not restricted specifically to the Ravenscar profile but to those of the finally used techniques, which in our case are the offset based holistic analysis techniques used for distributed systems. Finally, (3) as already mentioned the formalism to express the model of computation with the real-time features is the corresponding high level application modelling chapter of the MARTE standard itself.

Considering the conversion from MARTE to schedulability analysis tools in particular, there are some other efforts to mention. The closest in style and modelling capabilities is the RSA plugin to perform schedulability analysis with RapidRMA [8]. The version of this tool that is available shows some limitations: it supports scheduling analysis for mono-processors, with periodic and sporadic events (through sporadic servers). It does not provide support for multi-processors and distributed systems. RapidRMA and IBM RSA are not integrated through the GUI. Moreover, there is no automatic launch of RapidRMA after the input files are generated. It requires a manual operation. The current implementation does not offer any feedback capabilities from RapidRMA to the UML modelling tool. All the analysis results can be exploited within the tool only. Similar limitations plus a lack in modelling guidance is provided by the tool in [9], which aims to represent Cheddar models with MARTE. That document shows how MARTE concepts can be matched to those used in Cheddar in order to do analysis on models and proposes model transformation solutions using ATL.

3 Analysis Models

The first, and so far sufficiently solved problem, has been the definition/selection of which and how elements in MARTE are to be used in the creation of schedulability analysis models. These elements are the basis for the tool that has been developed for the generation of MAST analysis models taken from UML+MARTE annotated analysis models. Following previous research efforts [6], MARTE provides concepts to structure the analysis models using three main categories: The platform resources (a), the elements describing the logical behaviour of the system constituent parts (b), and finally the real-time situations to be analysed (c). The precise mapping from MARTE to MAST elements may be easier to see by inspecting the code, nevertheless here we summarize a condensed view of the MARTE elements proposed for their use in each of these three main categories.

Table 1. Modelling elements in MARTE used for the creation of MAST schedulability analysis models

Platform Resources	Behavioural Models	Real-Time Situations
GaResourcesPlatform SaExecHost * SaCommHost * SaSharedResource * SchedulableResource *	GaWorkloadBehavior GaScenario SaStep * SaCommStep	SaAnalysisContext * GaWorkloadEvent * Allocate Allocated Assign SaEndToEndFlow * SaSchedObs GaLatencyObs *
* Elements used in the marte2mast extraction tool in its current version.		

In the tool that has been provided for the generation of MAST models from UML+MARTE models, the platform elements and the logical (software) components are modelled as a set of structural elements with stereotypes annotated on them. Fig. 2 shows an example of the usage of these elements in the modelling of a tele-operated robot distributed application.

The stereotype annotations shown there represent the timing models of their respective operation software entities. The timing properties (i.e. the worst case execution time) for each of them appear in the properties tab of the tool corresponding to the SaAtep stereotype used. The class "Drivers" models the overheads due to the sending and reception of messages; it is used to represent in SAM the modelling elements called "drivers" in MAST. The elements used for modelling the platform include nodes, networks, tasks, channels, and operations that will be invoked as part of the internal platform behaviours.

The end-to-end flows that described execution scenarios are modelled using sequence charts or activity diagrams. Fig. 3 shows an example of the usage of these elements in the modelling of a tele-operated robot distributed end-to-end flow. Some steps in the flow are shown directly in the activity as stereotyped actions, others are statically defined somewhere else in the model but are modelled in the flow as invoked subUsages of the shown actions. These internal steps are not visible in the diagram but are retrieved by the tool recursively.

The full example is available in the web page of the tool: http://mast.unican.es/umlmast/marte2mast. There the reader can find the specification of the example application as well as the models used for its analysis. These are delivered in the form of an eclipse workspace containing all the models.

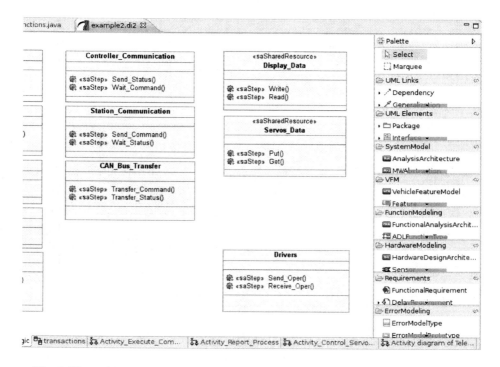

Fig. 2. View of the tool showing structural modelling elements for schedulability analysis

In summary, in the current version of this tool, the elements taken from MARTE to generate the MAST analysis models are:

```
> Processing_Resource  <=  SaExecHost, SaCommHost
> Scheduler  <=  SaExecHost, SaCommHost
> Scheduling Servers  <=  SchedulableResource
> Shared_Resource  <=  SaSharedResource
> Operations  <=  SaStep  <=  Sequence/activity Diagram
   plus subUsages (ordered list of called operations)
> Transactions  <=  Sequence/Activity Diagram +
   GaWorkloadEvent + GaLatencyObs
```

This effort has been implemented using the Eclipse technologies provided by PapyrusUML as graphical tool, the UML2 plugin as model repository, and the Acceleo plugin for the extraction of text from the UML2 models plus a significant number of Java functions. The code used as well as the scripts created are shared as open source. The current version supports the modelling of end-to-end-flows by means of activity diagrams and the composition of independently characterized timed behaviours. It also includes the invocation of the MAST tools from the eclipse environment and the recovery of the results back in the UML model. It may be downloaded from `http://mast.unican.es/umlmast/marte2mast`.

The high level algorithm to do the extraction of the MAST model is easy to identify following the script in `marte2mast.mtl`. Here you may see a summary of it:

1) Processing Resources and Schedulers take their attributes from:
   Classes with stereotype 'SaExecHost' or 'SaCommHost'
2) Scheduling Servers in processors and networks take their attributes from:
   Classes with stereotype 'SchedulableResource' and 'GaCommChannel'
3) Shared Resources (critical sections) take their attributes from:
   Classes with stereotype 'SaSharedResource'
4) The real time situation is taken from:
   A Class with the stereotype 'SaAnalysisContext'
5) Finally the Transactions in it are extracted from:
   Activities with the stereotype 'SaEndtoEndFlow'

A recursive strategy is used for retrieving composed operations and assigning them to the appropriate MAST activity-handlers. There are two ways of expressing these composed operations. One is static and is based in the use of the recursive capabilities of the subUsage association of the SaStep modelling element. This association is inherited from ResourceUsage. Fig. 4 shows the implementation model of this modelling construct in an extract from the MARTE GRM UML view.

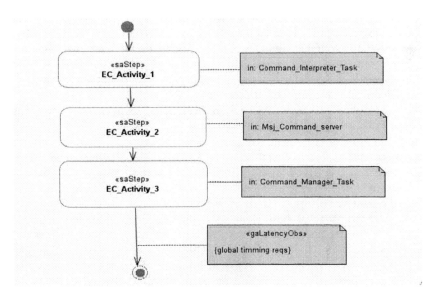

Fig. 3. View of the tool showing structural modelling elements for schedulability analysis

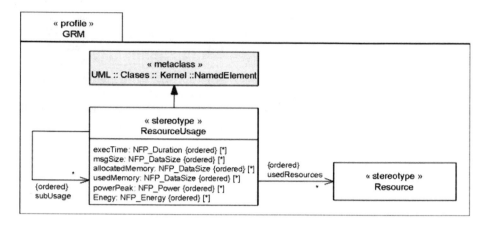

Fig. 4. The list of subUsages, a recursive mechanism to model composite operations. Extract of the model of the GRM::ResourceUsage, ancestor of SAM::SaStep.

The other way of modelling composed operations is based on the activity diagrams that are internal to the actions (as well as any internally called operation) that are placed in the activities used for representing the flows. The corresponding extracting code is implemented in java and may be seen in the source code file `ActivityFunctions.java`

4   Design Models

The second challenge is the definition of the elements in UML+MARTE to be used in early V&V design models in such a way that they can be used for the double purpose of constructing development (implementation) oriented models or even code directly while, at the same time, their respective analysis models may be generated through simple and as much as possible automated model transformation mechanisms.

For this purpose the natural candidates in MARTE are the fundamental modelling constructs described in the HLAM (High Level Application Modelling) chapter: RtUnit and PpUnit.

The RtUnit modelling element is the basic building block for handling concurrency in the design and analysis of real-time applications. The PpUnit is the modelling element used for specifying mutual exclusion between concurrent units and the adequate protection protocols in the access to passive shared resources, for avoiding unbounded priority inversion.

The key for the usage of these elements is the enabling of simple mechanisms to keep in synch the two specialized views that are elaborated as transformations from the design models built with them: the code generation and the platform configuration on the one side, and the corresponding schedulability or even performance analysis models on the other side. In order to get that semantic alignment we propose a methodology founded in a small number of modelling rules for the usage of RtUnits and PpUnits, and some directions for the generation of the subsequent implementation and analysis models.

In order to accomplish the objective of setting up the basis for an iterative development process, the driving forces for the definition of the methodology have been the easiness to iterate over modelling intents, and a design space exploration strategy to introduce analysis results back in the design constraints.

For the purpose of this methodology we will consider all the requirements as applicable to a generic unit of design called module. A module in this sense represents a fraction of the system. It is to be mapped to the equivalent abstraction/encapsulation entities defined for coping with complexity on the concrete design methodology used by the industrial practitioners in the field targeted. This results natural when considering them as independent subsystems, but it is applicable also to other composition mechanisms like loosely coupled software/hardware components, or physical concurrent units.

The modelling rules to be applied are the basis for the combined purpose of a design & analysis methodology and are complemented with guidelines for specific phases and concrete concerns.

The description of the RtUnits and PpUnits and their precise semantics are made in the domain view of HLAM chapter and the Appendix F of MARTE [3] respectively. The set of rules is worded considering the semantics described in the domain description contained in Appendix F but using the nomenclature of the attributes available in the stereotypes of the corresponding UML representation.

Early V&V assumes that at the time of analysis there are still a number of decisions about aspects like the platforms or specific interface technologies that have not been taken yet. To be able to assess the viability of the system without this information, some default values will be filled in the analysis & design models.

The set of rules for the use of UML with the HLAM modelling elements of MARTE needs to restrict the design space to get models that may be analysed by schedulability analysis with the available techniques. This way it formulates the basis for modelling at any stage of the development process. This initial set of rules is the following:

1) Real concurrency is handled by RtUnits at processing resource level, each node by them represented may in turn handle several schedulable resources by means of a regular scheduler.
2) Each RtUnit may have up to one schedulable resource on it, and all its behaviours, which may be called from other RtUnits, run under the scheduling parameters associated to that schedulable resource. In case the RtUnit has no schedulable resource, its behaviours run under the scheduling parameters of the calling RtUnit.
3) All the RtUnits deployed in a processing resource are handled by the same scheduler and use the same (or fully compatible) scheduling policy.
4) Each RtUnit whose isMain attribute is set to true, implies the presence of an execution host where the main service of the RtUnit is deployed.
5) The attribute srPoolPolicy holds the value infiniteWait.
6) ExecKind of PpUnits is ImmediatRemote.
7) All services use the same priority scheme: ImmediateCeiling or PriorityInheritance.

8) The ConcurrencyPolicy of PpUnit is "Guarded". [The concurrency policy of the kind Concurrent might be enabled in order to have the writer/reader ConcurrencyKind available but this behaviour requires additional capabilities from the analysis techniques so in principle it is discouraged].
9) Behaviours of RtUnits stereotyped as RtServices are those that may be called from others.

Additional rules that apply in specific phases of the development process are:

10) The platform models of the execution hosts are derived from the RtFeatures of RtUnits with the attribute isMain set to true. The basic assumption is that a main is the starting of the full piece of software running on a concrete node. The scheduling policy of the scheduler is derived from the one used for this main. Consistently the range of priorities (in the case in which this is the policy chosen) will be set to be greater than the number of RtUnits (with their isMain attribute to false) with which the main RtUnit has any sort of interaction.
11) The rules for analysis platform models will be refined after practising with the MAST default values (using initially no context switch time for example).
12) The links between services define the steps in the end-to-end-flows.
13) The parameters of the Analysis Context modelling element will be used to define the variations in the analysis due to refinements in the design.
14) Results will be placed back in design models by means of RtFeatures Specifications and the parameters of AnalysisContexts.
15) The iterative nature of the models used for design space exploration will be handled by specializing/using the configuration stereotype, described in the Modal Behaviour section of the CoreElements chapter of MARTE.

The tooling support for enforcing and helping to assess the usage of these rules is not yet formalized and embedded in the version of the eclipse plugin that may be downloaded at the time this paper is submitted, but it is part of our future (actually ongoing) work.

Considering the transformation of design to analysis models the procedure most difficult to automate is the definition of the real-time situations and the extraction of the precise scenarios to take into account. The key aspect to consider in order to extract the necessary execution scenarios is the manner in which the behaviours are expressed.

For passive RtUnits or for those whose behaviours are expressed as activities (by means of activity diagrams), the end-to-end flows may be composed by creating and combining the resource usage (GRM part of MARTE) that represents the operations/services of the objects involved. These are expressed in our design model as classes with the SaStep stereotype (which inherits from ResourceUsage). The precedence or control flow dependencies between them are expressed as transitions between actions inside the activities. These transitions correspond to the simple precedence relationships among the steps (as described in GQAM model of MARTE) and are the place to express also the latency or jitter constraints, see the gaLatencyObs stereotype in Fig. 3.

For the RtUnits whose behaviours are expressed as state machines, the scenarios may be extracted by assuming the order in which the independent external events that trigger the transitions of the state machine are expected to occur. An analysisContext represents a particular real-time situation. For each end-to-end-flow in the analysisContext the composition of such ordered list of event-occurrences would need in any case the specification of at least one additional diagram per end-to-end flow. Then it might be worth asking the designer for the composition and description of the high level services conforming the end-to-end flows instead of the ordered list of event-occurrences that triggers the state machine. Additional efforts would have to be required from the designer in case the state machines have concurrent states or involve several active objects.

The easier mechanism to automate the extraction of elements from the design models to be included in the analysis context of the real-time situation to analyse is the use of a collaboration whose parts are the RtUnits and PpUnits to include.

4.1   Real-Time Design Model of the Basic Ada Structures

Even though the modelling and schedulability analysis methodology presented is language independent and is useful for modelling a wide range of real-time applications, the semantics of the high-level modelling constructs defined is particularly suitable to represent systems conceived and coded in Ada [7]. Similar topics have been described in detailed in our previous work [4] but we now wish to re-visit some of the aspects that are relevant for the discussion herein in the light of the HLAM-MARTE modelling constructs.

The RT-design-model has the structure of the Ada application: The RTUnit instances may model the real-time behaviour of packages and tagged types, which are the basic structural elements of an Ada architecture:

- Each object describes the real-time model of all the procedures and functions included in a package or Ada class.
- Each object declares all other inner objects (package, protected object, task, etc.) that are relevant to model its real-time behaviour. It also preserves in the model declarations the same visibility and scope of the original Ada structures.

An object only models the code included in the logical structure that it describes. It does not include the models of other packages or modules on which it is dependent.

The RT-design-model includes the concurrency introduced by Ada tasks: An active RTUnit model an Ada task. Each task component instance has implicitly an aggregated SchedulableResource, which is associated with the processor where the component instance is allocated. Synchronization between tasks is only allowed in the invocation of RTServices belonging to active RTUnits. The model implicitly handles the overhead due to the context switching between tasks.

The RT-design-model includes the contention in the access to protected objects: A PpUnit models the real-time behaviour of an Ada protected object. It implicitly models the mutual exclusion in the execution of the operations declared in its interface, the evaluation of the guarding conditions of its entries, the priority changes implied by the execution of its operations under the priority ceiling locking policy, and also the possible delay while waiting for the guard to become true. Even though the methodology that we propose is not able to model all the possible synchronization schemes that can be coded using protected entries with guarding conditions in Ada, it does allow to describe the usual synchronization patterns that are used in real-time applications. Therefore, protected object-based synchronization mechanisms like handling of hardware interrupts, periodic and asynchronous task activation, waiting for multiple events, or message queues, can be modelled in an accurate and quantitative way. Please refer to [4] for a detailed description of the patterns that may be supported.

The RtService operations involved in the declaration of a PpUnit are implicitly modelled with mutual exclusion between them, by attaching an implicit shared resource to them. Each operation in this component implicitly locks and unlocks the shared resource before and after the operation activities.

The RT-design-model shall include the real-time communication between Ada distributed partitions: MARTE does not support explicitly in a particular construct all the data that is necessary to analyze the remote access to the APC (Asynchronous Procedure Call) and RPC (Remote Procedure Call) procedures of a Remote Call Interface (RCI), as described in Annex E of the Ada standard. It is possible to determine whether an invocation is local or remote but additional modelling constructs will be necessary to handle information for the marshalling of messages, their transmission through the network, their management by the local and remote dispatchers and the un-marshalling of messages, in order to be able to manage it automatically by the tools.

5   Practical Experience

In order to try in practical terms the modelling methodology and particularly the analysis capabilities in it, the implemented tool has been used over an example application that has been already used in previous works. So the analysis model corresponding to the Teleoperated_Robot example [6] has been introduced in UML using PapyrusUML, and the stereotypes provided by its UML MARTE Profile.

To help the reader to reproduce the modelling and analysis experience, the installation procedure to follow, and a video with usage hints, as well as a workspace for eclipse with all the files used may be downloaded from http://mast.unican.es/umlmast/marte2mast.

For the habitual users of MAST the most relevant issues found in the modelling of distributed applications like the already traditional Teleoperated_robot are related to the lack of the "driver" concept in MARTE. This is solved by inserting the corresponding overhead end-to-end flows (formerly called transactions in MAST). These transactions model the overhead due to the insertion and recovering of messages into and from the network respectively. For this reason the results in the MAST graphical results viewer show 7 instead of 3 transactions. Fig. 5 shows a snapshot of these results.

The Eclipse plugin includes an option to run the MAST set of analysis tools directly from Eclipse and finally recover the results back into the UML model. These results are annotated in the attributes of the corresponding stereotypes in the UML model. For example the system slack is recovered in the slack attribute of the

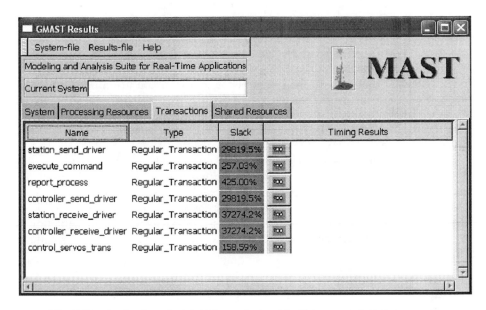

Fig. 5. Results for the schedulability analysis of the Teleoperated_Robot example

analysisContext stereotype, and for the response time of each step the attribute respT of the SaStep stereotypes is used. The response time of each End-to-end-Flow is the one stored in the last SaStep of the flow.

The UML model having all this values may be stored in the same file. In this case each new analysis result value is appended to the ordered list of values of the attribute. To identify the analysis to which the results correspond, the field "mode" of each new value is set to the "mode" field defined in the AnalisysContext at the time of launching the analysis. Alternatively the "updated" version on the UML model may be stored in a new file on disk. This way the original model may be either used again in a different analysis essay, or used to iterate searching in an optimization loop.

6   Conclusions and Future Work

Considering the prospects of the OMG´s UML Profile for MARTE as a modelling standard for analysis tools interoperability, it seems reasonable to look for model based strategies that link it with modelling intensive activities. And a clear semantics for the High level application modelling is the basis for automating the process of having timing analysis results quickly in the development life cycle.

The extraction of MAST analysis models from the UML+MARTE schedulability analysis specific models is a first demonstrable step in the direction pointed out by this effort and comprises the construction of analysis models from separated composable modelling descriptions using the specific constructs brought by the SAM chapter of MARTE, which is consistent with MAST and the previous efforts in this direction [4].

From the real-time and embedded systems research community perspective, this effort constitutes a step to get the effective exploitation of the capabilities of the available analysis and verification techniques, which despite the efforts in dissemination, have not yet reached an audience large enough to reward the many years of work in the field.

The modelling strategy and tools proposed in this work are just a first step in this direction; a significant work remains to be done in order to have a fully automated process. The validation of the rules and their automation by means of a model validator and the necessary transformations are part of our ongoing work and will be addressed in the near future.

The re-visit to former work made for the consistent modelling and analysis of Ada applications, in the light of the previous UML formalizations of the MAST model, has been a driving force in the adjustment of the high level application modelling of MARTE for this purpose. Nevertheless some lacks in the standard have been identified whose resolution requires either formal extensions to it or the definition of additional methodological guidelines, in particular for the case of remote procedures invocation.

References

[1] López, P., Drake, J.M., Medina, J.L.: Enabling Model-Driven Schedulability Analysis in the Development of Distributed Component-Based Real-Time Applications. In: Proceedings of 35th Euromicro Conference on Software Engineering and Advanced Applications, Component-based Software Engineering Track, Patras, Greece, pp. 109–112. IEEE, Los Alamitos (August 2009) ISBN 978-0-7695-3784-9

[2] González Harbour, M., Gutiérrez, J.J., Palencia, J.C., Drake, J.M.: MAST: Modeling and Analysis Suite for Real-Time Applications In: Proc. of the Euromicro Conference on Real-Time Systems (June 2001)

[3] Object Management Group, UML Profile for Modeling and Analysis of Real-Time and Embedded systems (MARTE) version 1.0, OMG doc. formal/2009-11-02 (2009)

[4] Gutierrez, J.J., Drake, J.M., González Harbour, M., Medina, J.L.: Modeling and Schedulability Analysis in the Development of Real-Time and Distributed Ada Systems. ACM Ada Letters XXII(4) (2002)

[5] Mazzini, S., Puri, S., Vardanega, T.: An MDE Methodology for the Development of High-Integrity Real-Time Systems. In: DATE 2009, Nice, France, April 20-24, p. 1154 (2009)

[6] Medina, J.L., González Harbour, M., Drake, J.M.: Mast Real-Time: A Graphic UML Tool for Modeling Object-Oriented Real-Time Systems. In: Proc of the 22nd IEEE Real-Time System Symposium (RTSS 2001), pp. 245–256 (2001), IST project COMPARE: Componentbased approach for real-time and embedded systems, http://www.ist-compare.org

[7] Tucker Taft, S., Duff, R.A., Brukardt, R.L., Plödereder, E., Leroy, P., et al.: Ada 2005 Reference Manual. LNCS, vol. 4348, pp. 43–48. Springer, Heidelberg (2006)

[8] Demathieu, S., Rioux, L.: MARTE to RapidRMA. Thales Report/Technical Document number 61565273 305 6, http://www.omgwiki.org/marte/node/31

[9] Maes, E., Vienne, N.: MARTE to Cheddar Transformation using ATL. Thales Report/Technical Documents number 61565546-179 and 61565546 108, http://beru.univbrest.fr/~singhoff/cheddar/contribs/examples_of_use/thales_rt/MARTE2CheddarTransformationRules.pdf

Developing Dependable Software-Intensive Systems: AADL vs. EAST-ADL*

Andreas Johnsen and Kristina Lundqvist

School of Innovation, Design and Engineering
Mälardalen University
Västerås, Sweden
{andreas.johnsen,kristina.lundqvist}@mdh.se

Abstract. Dependable software-intensive systems, such as embedded systems for avionics and vehicles are often developed under severe quality, schedule and budget constraints. As the size and complexity of these systems dramatically increases, the architecture design phase becomes more and more significant in order to meet these constraints. The use of Architecture Description Languages (ADLs) provides an important basis for mutual communication, analysis and evaluation activities. Hence, selecting an ADL suitable for such activities is of great importance. In this paper we compare and investigate the two ADLs – AADL and EAST-ADL. The level of support provided to developers of dependable software-intensive systems is compared, and several critical areas of the ADLs are highlighted. Results of using an extended comparison framework showed many similarities, but also one clear distinction between the languages regarding the perspectives and the levels of abstraction in which systems are modeled.

Keywords: Dependable systems, Software-intensive systems, AADL, EAST-ADL, Architecture description languages.

1 Introduction

One of the most critical phases in the development process of software-intensive systems is the architecture design phase. The architecture specification represents a set of design-decisions, which are analyzed and evaluated to ensure conformance with the system requirements. The efficiency and effectiveness of the evaluation method is largely dependent on the type of artifact being evaluated. Hence, the means used to design architectures of dependable software-intensive systems are critical to ensure quality of the system. Architecture Description Languages (ADLs) have been developed as means for designing systems' architecture.

Software-intensive systems are systems where software interacts with sensors, actuators, devices, other systems and people [1]. Examples of such systems are

---

* This work was partially supported by the Swedish Research Council (VR), and Mälardalen Real-Time Research Centre (MRTC)/Mälardalen University.

A. Romanovsky and T. Vardanega (Eds.): Ada-Europe 2011, LNCS 6652, pp. 103–117, 2011.

embedded systems for vehicles, medical equipment and avionics. What these systems have in common is that they often operate in dynamic, time- and safety-critical environments where the components embedded within the systems are heterogeneous and have to meet real-time constraints. Two widely used ADLs within both industry and the research community are the Architecture Analysis and Design Language (AADL) [2], developed by the Society of Automotive Engineers (SAE), and the Electronics Architecture and Software Technology - Architecture Description Language (EAST-ADL) [3], initially developed by the Embedded Architecture and Software Tools - Embedded Electronic Architecture (EAST-EEA) project in the Information Technology for European Advancement (ITEA) programme and further refined by the Advancing Traffic Efficiency and Safety through Software Technology (ATESST and ATESST2) projects[4]. EAST-ADL was developed specifically for automotive systems, and AADL was initially developed for Avionics but now targets all large-scale software-intensive embedded systems and systems of systems, such as, aircraft, motorized vehicles, autonomous systems, and medical devices.

In this paper, we investigate these two ADLs and compare the level of support they provide developers to ensure correctness of software-intensive systems. An ADL should support activities – or tools performing activities – such as analysis, V&V, model checking (formal verification), code generation/synthesis, etc., by providing multiple perspectives with well defined semantics. At the same time, an ADL should support understandability and communication among stakeholders, by providing multiple levels of abstraction [5]. Generally, ADLs do not support both parts [6], which is critical for dependable systems since both parts contribute to systems' correctness.

The comparison is performed by applying an extension of Medvidovic and Taylor's "classification and comparison framework for software architecture description languages" [6]. In order to be able to compare AADL and EAST-ADL, Medvidovic and Taylor's framework is expanded with aspects of hardware architectures and typical quality attributes of software-intensive systems, which are timing and dependability.

The extended framework will be presented in Section 2, before overviews of the languages under comparison is given in Section 3. The results of applying the ADLs to the extended framework are presented in Section 4, which is followed by conclusions in Section 5.

2   The Comparison Framework

Medvidovic and Taylor developed a framework [6] for classification and comparison of software ADLs. In this paper, we extend their framework with hardware architecture aspects and vital quality-attributes of software-intensive systems. The new framework consists of, as in the original framework, a set of building blocks and their features (depicted in Table 1) that an ADL should provide. The main building blocks are **components**, **connectors** and **configurations**, where these components, in order to interchange architectural information, must have

Table 1. ADL Building Blocks (bold), their Features (italic) and vital quality-attributes

ADL: Building Blocks and Features
Components
Interface, Types, Semantics, Requirements, Evolution, Non-functional properties
Connectors
Interface, Types, Semantics, Requirements, Evolution, Non-functional properties
Configurations
Understandability, Compositionality, Refinement and traceability, Heterogeneity, Scalability, Evolution, Requirements, Non-functional properties
ADL: Vital Quality Attributes
Dependability
Timing

interfaces. Connectors are the interactions within the architecture whereas configurations define how each building block is combined to form an architecture description.

Architectures of software-intensive systems can be represented by these building blocks, which are abstractions of architectural elements. The framework developed by Medvidovic and Taylor restricts these building blocks to be abstractions of architectural elements of software. The extensions are reflected in the defined restrictions (given in section 2.1, 2.2, 2.3) of what the building blocks are abstractions of, which are: architectural elements of software, architectural elements of hardware and architectural elements of software mapped on hardware.

Within following subsections, an overview of each architecture building block, their features and the vital quality attributes is given.

2.1   Building Block: Component

Components are abstractions of main hardware/execution platform-units, computational software-units or composition of software and hardware-units. Computational software units refer to procedures/functions as well as entire applications. Main hardware/execution platform-units refer to complex hardware that may be associated with software to complete its functionality. Examples of such units are: sensors, actuators, processors, memories and communication links such as buses. Composition of software and hardware units refer to systems where computational software units are mapped to main hardware/execution platform units (e.g. flight control system, GPS system, electronic cruise control system, etc.). Components interact through their *interfaces* which are logical points of interactions between a component and its environment. An interface of a component describes the services a component provides and requires. The behavior model of a component, which here is referred to as component *semantics*, is an important feature of a component since it describes requirements and provides information for analysis and V&V activities. Components that are encapsulated within a certain subset of semantics and properties are here referred to as a component *type*, which can be instantiated several times within an architecture. Component types facilitates the ability to understand and analyze architectures since instances of a component type have common properties. Types are most often created by extensible type systems within ADLs, but built-in component types should also be provided. Components should be able to be modeled with external and internal properties specifying unacceptable borders, which we here refer to as component *requirements*. Furthermore, an ADL should provide modeling of *non-functional properties* (e.g. reliability, safety, performance, etc.) associated with components for V&V, simulation and analysis purposes. In order to control evolution of components within a system, i.e., modifications of component properties, the language should be able to support the *evolution* of the system. An ADL can support the evolution by supporting subtyping of component types as well as refinement of component features.

2.2   Building Block: Connector

Connectors are abstractions of interactions, where the method to interact may be of simple or highly complex nature. The nature may exclusively consist of software (e.g. data flows, control flows, function calls and access to data), hardware (e.g. wires) or a combination of the two (e.g. bus system). Connectors may have *interfaces*, specifying interaction points which components or connectors can be connected to. The behavior models of connectors which specify interaction protocols, are here referred to as connectors *semantics*. Similar to component semantics, connector semantics provide information for analysis and V&V activities, where the information is based on interconnection and communication requirements/properties. Connectors that are encapsulated within a subset of connector semantics and properties are here referred to as a connector *type*. These types are provided, similar to component types, by ADLs to facilitate modeling and understandability by reusable building blocks. Connector *requirements* assert interaction protocol properties by describing unacceptable borders. Connectors should also be able to be modeled with *non-functional properties*, which can not be derived from the connector semantics. As these interaction protocol properties are modified according to the *evolution*, ADLs should be able to support this evolution through subtyping and refinement of connector features.

2.3   Building Block: Configuration

ADL configurations define how each building block (components and connectors) is combined to form an architecture describing correct component connections, component communications, interface compatibility and that the combined semantics of the whole system result in correct system behavior. Since a system architecture partly serves as a mutual communication blueprint among stakeholders, the *understandability* of specifications is of great importance. An ADL specification should describe the topological system with understandable syntax or/and graphical notions, where an architecture configuration can be understandable without knowing components' and connectors' architectural details. Closely related to the under-standability of an architecture configuration is the architecture *compositionality*. In order to provide an understandable architecture configuration, it is important to be able to describe the system at different abstraction levels, by abstracting away un-interesting details when concerning specific perspectives of the system. Such views can be provided by ADLs that have the capability to model a system hierarchically, where an architecture configuration may be contained within a higher abstracted component. As ADLs provide means for architectural description at different lev-els of abstraction, it is important to have *traceability* throughout the *refinement* of properties and relationships, from high levels of abstraction to the concrete system, in order to bridge the gaps between them. Since ADLs partly are used to facilitate development of large, complex and often highly heterogeneous systems, it is impor-tant that ADLs can meet these *heterogeneity* and *scalability* problems by providing possibilities to specify components and connectors described by external formal languages, and to be able to handle large and growing systems. *Evolvability*, which is closely related to scalability, does not only concern ADLs ability to accommodate to new architectural building-blocks to be added, but does also concern how ADLs can accommodate to incomplete architectural specifications, since it is unfeasible to make all design decisions at once. *Requirements* and *non-functional properties* of architectural configurations are not specific to individual components or connec-tors, but may be extracted from or are depended upon component- or connector-specific requirements and non-functional properties.

2.4   Vital Quality Attributes

Software-intensive systems are of highly complex nature with numerous criti-cal quality-attributes. What software-intensive systems have in common is that they often are operating in safety-critical and time-critical environments. Con-sequently, two of the most important quality-attributes are dependability and timing. Even though one of the fundamental results of architecture-based devel-opment is increased dependability, as a result of abstracting complex systems to understandable and manageable blueprints, an ADL for software-intensive systems should explicitly provide means for dependability modeling. An ADL should facilitate safety- and reliability-analysis, such as for example, provide means for error modeling, reliability modeling, hazard analysis, risk analysis, and structures of requirements. Another critical aspect of software-intensive sys-tems is timing since these systems often have to meet real-time constraints. An ADL should provide means to support modeling and analysis of timing require-ments and properties, such as for example, end-to-end timing (sensor to actuator timing), latency, task execution time and deadlines.

3   ADLs Under Comparison

We present an overview of both ADLs in order to provide a basis for the com-parison in section 4.

3.1   Overview of AADL

AADL (1.0) [7] [8] was released and published as a Society of Automotive Engineers (SAE) Standard AS5506 [2] in 2004. It is a textual and graphical language used to model, specify and analyze software- and hardware-architectures of real-time embedded systems. The AADL language is based on a component-connector paradigm that describes components, component interfaces and the interaction (connections) between components. Hence, the language captures functional properties of the system, such as input and output through component interfaces, as well as structural properties through configurations of components and connectors. Furthermore, means to describe quality attributes are also provided. A system is modeled as a hierarchy of components where components that represent the application software are mapped onto the components that represent the hardware platform. A component is modeled by a component type and a component implementation. The component type specifies the external interfaces of the component in which other components can interact through, while the component implementation specifies the internal view of a component, such as subcomponents and their connections, and must be coupled to a component type.

Although a new version of AADL (AADLv2) [9] was published in 2009, the survey is restricted to the version of the language released in 2004.

3.2   Overview of EAST-ADL

The EAST-ADL [3] [10] is a domain-specific ADL for modeling and development of automotive electronic systems, where the language has modeling possibilities to specify software components, hardware components, features, requirements, variability and annotations to support analysis of the system. The language supports modeling of electronic systems at four different conceptual abstraction levels, namely: Vehicle level, Analysis level, Design level and the Implementation level. These abstraction levels reflect the amount of details in the architecture where abstract features and functions modeled in higher abstraction levels are realized to software and hardware components modeled in lower abstraction levels. The language provides a complete traceability through the different abstraction levels. The basic vehicle features (e.g. wipers and breaks) of the electronic systems are captured at the Vehicle level, the highest level of abstraction. These features are refined in related functions at the Analysis level by abstract elements representing software functions and devices interacting with the vehicle environment. The Design level represents a realization of the functionalities depicted at the analysis level, where the level allows further decomposition or restructuring of software functions and preliminary allocation of software elements. Specified devices are realized at this level into hardware architectures, such as sensors and actuators, including software for signal transformations. The lowest level of abstraction, the Implementation level is defined by using the Automotive Open System Architecture (AUTOSAR) standard[11].

4   AADL vs. EAST-ADL

AADL and EAST-ADL are compared according to the comparison framework given in section 2, where each architectural building block, their features and vital quality-attributes are analyzed and discussed based on the AADL standard specification [2] and the EAST-ADL standard specification [3].

4.1   Modeling of Components

Both AADL and EAST-ADL support modeling of all three component categories (i.e. computational software, main hardware/execution platform and composition of software and hardware). EAST-ADL refer these components to *features*, *functions* or *components*, depending on which conceptual abstraction level is considered whereas AADL exclusively refer to *components*.

Interface. AADL support modeling of five different types of component interfaces, or *component features* as referred to in the AADL standard. The different types of component interfaces are: *ports*, *data access*, *bus access*, *subprogram* or *parameter*. Ports are interaction points of software components for transfer of typed data and events. Data access interfaces are used to connect software components to static data whereas bus access interfaces are used to interconnect hardware components through bus components (built-in component types are depicted in the "types" section). Subprogram components may be used as interfaces of data components, representing methods that can be called by thread components. Parameters are interaction points of subprogram components for transfer of data. EAST-ADL on the other hand provides modeling of different interfaces, depending on which conceptual abstraction layer is being modeled. At the functional analysis level and the functional design level it is possible to model interfaces such as *client-server ports* and *flow ports*. Client and server ports are interaction points for communication between clients and servers, i.e. operations are required or provided by *client ports* and *server ports*. *Flow ports* are directional interaction points for exchange of data which is specified by associated data-types. The hardware design architecture, modeled at the design level, provides *pin* interfaces in which hardware elements can be connected to electrical sources, sinks and ground.

Types. The AADL language provides ten types of built-in component abstractions: *process, thread, thread group, data, subprogram, processor, memory, bus, device* and *system*. Note that a bus component represents an entity that interconnects hardware components (processor, memory, device and bus components) for exchange of data and control according to some communication protocol, and thus, it could be argued to be a connector type. Families of related components may also be modeled in the AADL language by an extension system where a component extending an antecedent component will inherit its antecedent characteristics, which can be refined or modified. EAST-ADL has built-in component types which encapsulate semantics and properties in relation to a certain abstraction level, in contrast to AADL which types encapsulate semantics and properties in relation to the concrete component that is abstracted by the language. For example, at the vehicle level, it is only possible to model *feature* components, and at the analysis level, it is only possible to model *function* and *device* components, where the encapsulated semantics and properties of these types are abstract. As the abstraction level decreases, the types are getting more concrete. For example, at the design level, it is possible to model hardware components of *sensor* or *actuator* type, and at the implementation level it is possible to realize (by using AUTOSAR) design level functions into software components types. The EAST-ADL language provides modeling of component types where occurrences of such instances, in a modeling artifact, are called typed *prototypes*. Modeling by these typing systems is provided at every abstraction level, except at the vehicle level. The EAST-ADL language does also provide modeling of *variability models*, which has similarities with modeling of component types but with a difference of the conceptual usage. The main conceptual usage of variability models is to facilitate controllability of product lines, and not mainly to facilitate understandability and analyzability. The variability management is provided at all the different conceptual abstraction levels, where related components can be merged to a component (which can be seen as a component type) with variability properties, meaning that the aspect of such a component can vary to another closely related aspect.

Semantics. Both AADL and EAST-ADL provide specification of components' behavior, but with some limitations which can be exceeded by language annexes and integrated tools. For example, the AADL language is extended with a *behavioral annex* [12], which provides modeling of components' behavior by using automata theory whereas the EAST-ADL language has traceability to behavior models based on external notations such as Simulink [4]. Both core languages provide sufficient modeling of behavior and functionality through modeling of component modes and triggers based on data, events or timing, for exchange of modes.

Requirements. The AADL language provides modeling of requirements through the generic *property* annotation, which does not only provide modeling of requirements, but also modeling of a component's functional properties (component semantics) as well as non-functional properties. Component properties can be specified with either the *component types* or the *component implementations*, to distinguish internal and external requirements of a component. The AADL language provides built-in properties (requirements) and possibilities to define new properties. EAST-ADL, on the other hand, treats requirements as separate entities that are associated to the target EAST-ADL element with a specific association, according to principles of SysML [13]. The concept of the requirement modeling is to provide an interface between OEMs (original equipment manufacturer) and suppliers.

Evolution. AADL provides means for structural evolution through its component extension system, where an instance of a component type can be used to type other components. Since AADL is built on a paradigm where a system is modeled as a hierarchy of components, its nature provides means for refinements of component features across different levels of abstraction. EAST-ADL does not allow modeling of component subtypes, because the EAST-ADL domain model (metamodel) only describes component types and their prototypes (type instances). However, EAST-ADL provides means for refinement across different level of abstraction, but with a hierarchical difference compared to AADL. Even though starting from a high abstraction level, AADL specifies components that are abstractions of concrete implementation components (e.g. a system component with sensors, processes and actuators as subcomponents), which then can be refined with other abstracted components (e.g. thread components), modeled inside components. EAST-ADL, on the other hand, starts with specification of components that are abstractions of features and functions (which themselves are abstractions), which can be decomposed in a lower abstraction by specifying these features and functions by using more concrete building blocks (components). EAST-ADL's terminology defines this as each abstraction layer realizes its antecedent layer.

Non-functional properties. Both languages provide modeling of built-in non-functional properties of components, as well as means for specifying new non-functional properties. For example, for AADL components, there are built-in non-functional properties such as execution time, latency, throughput, startup deadline and write-time. For EAST-ADL components, there are properties such as safety, timing (e.g. execution time and latency), development cost, cable length and power consumption in addition to low-level properties represented through AUTOSAR elements. As can be seen by the presented built-in non-functional properties, EAST-ADL has properties of importance to higher levels of organizations compared to AADL.

4.2   Modeling of Connectors

Neither of EAST-ADL or AADL model connectors explicitly, instead connections are modeled "in-line" with the components, i.e. connectors are not first-class entities. Modeling of connectors within AADL and EAST-ADL basically consist of describing which component interfaces are connected. Connectors between software components are left out completely in the AUTOSAR language since the modeling concept is built on standardized component interfaces interacting through an abstract component called the Virtual Functional Bus (VFB).

Interface. EAST-ADL and AADL connectors do not have interfaces.

Types. EAST-ADL and AADL provides built-in connector types which encapsulates properties and semantics of a connector. Each connector type can be used to connect one or several types of component interfaces. For example, in AADL there is a *data access connection* connector type which can be used to connect *data access* interfaces, and in EAST-ADL there is a *FunctionConnector* connector type which can be used to connect *FunctionFlowPorts* or *ClientServer-Ports*. AADL does also provide modeling of abstract information paths through

Components	AADL	EAST-ADL
Interface	Data/event ports, component accesses, subprograms and parameters	Flow ports, client-server ports, power ports and hardware pins
Types	Process, thread, thread group, data, subprogram, processor, memory, bus, device and system	Feature, analysis function, functional device, design function, basic software function, local device manager, hardware function, hardware component, sensor, node, actuator and power supply
Semantics	Component modes and Behavioral annex	Function modes
Requirements	Through property annotations of component types/implementations and through specified interfaces, semantics and subcomponents	Through models of requirements and constraints, and though specified interfaces and semantics
Evolution	Subtyping through extension system and refinement through refine annotations	No subtyping and refinement through realize associations between abstraction levels
N-F properties	Through property annotations of component types/implementations	Through requirements and constraint models
Connectors		
Interface	None	None
Types	Port connection, component access connection, subprogram call and parameter connection	Feature link, function connector, hardware connector
Semantics	No explicit support	No explicit support
Requirements	Through associated property annotations	Through requirement and constraint models
Evolution	None	None
N-F properties	Through associated property annotations	Through requirement and constraint models

Fig. 1. Modeling of Components and Connectors

a system, called AADL *flows*, to support control- and data-flow analysis such as end-to-end timing, reliability, resource management and latency.

Semantics. Semantics of AADL connections are defined by the type of the connection, types of components involved, as well as properties specified with the connections where the properties can be used to specify communication protocols. EAST-ADL connector types have predefined semantics, where means to specify additional semantics is not provided by the language.

Requirements. Modeling of requirements on connections is feasible in AADL through property statements, which is conceptually similar as with modeling requirements of AADL components. The same conclusion goes for EAST-ADL, where modeling of requirements on connectors is similar as on components.

Evolution. As both languages do not treat connectors as first-class entities, which can not be typed or reused, they do not provide means for controlling their evolution.

Non-functional properties. Modeling of non-functional properties of connectors is supported by both languages, similarly as with modeling of non-functional properties of components.

4.3 Modeling of Configurations

Architectural configurations can be modeled and expressed syntactically and/or graphically by the AADL language whereas in EAST-ADL configurations are modeled and expressed according to the UML-based metamodel. Modeling of a system configuration that may vary to another system configuration is provided by both languages, through their modes modeling features.

Understandability. Understandability of an AADL system configuration depends on which way it is expressed (syntactically or graphically). The graphical perspective provides a view of the system configuration that is easily understood. If a more detailed view is preferred, the syntactical model offers this, consequently with difficulties to perceive the whole system at once. Since there are precise relationships between a graphical and a syntactical configuration, both can be used simultaneous to enhance understandability. The understandability of EAST-ADL configurations depends upon which abstraction level is being viewed, since each level provides a complete configuration of the system with respect to the concerns of the level. Each abstraction level is modeled according to the metamodel, where mappings between elements among two neighbor abstraction levels are expressed by *realization* relationships, which provides means for expressing all the configurations at once.

Compositionality. Both languages support hierarchical description of systems at different levels of abstractions, however with a difference which we already have touched upon in Section 4.1. A system in AADL is modeled by specifying components and connections among components within a system component, which is not the case in EAST-ADL. In EAST-ADL a system is being viewed as completely specified according to a specific abstraction level with specific concerns. Note here that each abstraction level does not only provide a level of detail, but also specific concerns, and thus a certain perspective. However, systems are specified hierarchically in EAST-ADL since each architectural element in a specific abstraction level is realized by one or several elements in the subsequent (lower) level. Thus, with respect to the explicit abstraction layers, each component (excluding vehicle/top level and implementation/bottom level components) has relations to a "superior" and a "subordinate" component element(s). Consequently, the fundamental hierarchical differences between the languages are the relations between the members (components) of the hierarchy. In AADL, the hierarchy is generated by the notion of subcomponents, i.e., components are subsumed within another component and thus generates a kind of "subsumptive containment hierarchy". EAST-ADL, on the other hand, generates the hierarchy through the notion of realization. The realization is done through decomposition of components to more concrete elements provided at a subsequent abstraction level. Thus, the hierarchy is a kind of "compositional containment hierarchy" where vehicle level entities are composed of analysis level entities, which are composed of design level entities, which are composed of AUTOSAR entities.

Refinement and traceability. The languages' compositionality nature preserves traceability among properties and relationships throughout the refinement process. EAST-ADL explicitly relate requirement properties to each other, where requirements in the higher abstraction levels are refined to more detailed requirements in the lower levels.

Configurations	AADL	EAST-ADL
Understandability	In-line textual specification with related graphical view	Graphical and partly textual specification
Compositionality	Supported through subcomponents and their connections	Supported through realization relations between abstraction levels
Refinement and traceability	Implicit support (explicitly supported by subtyping, through extends and refines annotations)	Explicit support through realization relations for components and refine relations for requirements
Heterogeneity	Annexes and possible to associate source text	Extension packages
Scalability	Problems due to in-line configurations	Problems due to in-line configurations
Evolution	Supported	Supported
Requirements	Similar as with requirements of components (configuration created inside a component)	Through a model of requirements associated to the configuration (the abstraction level)
N-F properties	Through associated property annotations	Through requirements and constraint models

Fig. 2. Modeling of Configurations

Heterogeneity. AADL and EAST-ADL provide explicit support for specification by multiple specification languages, such as approved annexes (e.g. Behavioral annex, Error Model annex, etc.) for AADL and extension packages (e.g. ErrorBehavior, Requirements, Constraints, etc.) for EAST-ADL. AADL provide additional support for implementation details through predeclared properties where components can be associated with source text written in software languages such as C and Ada, modeling languages such as Simulink, and hardware languages such as VHDL. Implicitly, they support specification by multiple languages through model transformation into formal specification languages.

Scalability. Both languages have scalability issues since both are "in-line configuration ADLs", meaning that components and connectors are not modeled separately from the configurations. Adding new components to a configuration may require modifications to existing connections, since connections within in-line configurations are solely dependent upon the components they connect.

Evolution. Partial architecture specifications are supported by both languages. For example, the AADL language allows architectures of components without component implementation descriptions and with untyped data port interfaces. EAST-ADL allows architectures lacking of entire abstraction levels.

Requirements. Modeling of requirements on configurations is similar as modeling of requirements on components in AADL, since configurations are modeled inside components. EAST-ADL provide possibilities to associate requirements to a complete abstraction level.

Non-functional properties. Both languages support modeling of non-functional properties, such as timing and dependability, for architecture configurations.

4.4 Dependability

EAST-ADL consist of an explicit *dependability package* which provides means, such as hazard analysis, structuring of safety requirements according to their purpose in the safety life-cycle, formalizing requirements through safety constraints, analysis of fault propagation through error models and structuring evidence of safety, to specify and classify dependability. The dependability package is constructed to support the automotive safety standard ISO/DIS 26262. The AADL language does also support dependability modeling through the *Error model annex*, which defines a sub-language for modeling of error models that can be associated with AADL components. Through the error modeling features, the annex enables modeling and assessment of redundancy management, risk mitigation and dependability in architectures.

4.5   Timing

Specification of timing is provided by the AADL language through timing properties (such as deadlines, worst-case execution time, arrival rate, period etc.) as well as predefined concurrency, interaction and execution semantics. AADL has tool support for timing analysis through the Cheddar tool [14] and the Ocarina tool-suite [15]. Cheddar is a free real-time scheduling tool for analysis of temporal constraints. The tool supports both cyclic and aperiodic tasks, as well as a wide range of scheduling policies such as Rate Monotonic (RM), Earliest Deadline First (EDF), Deadline Monotonic, etc. Ocarina provides schedulability analysis of AADL models. EAST-ADL on the other hand has an explicit *timing package*, as with dependability, which provides means for modeling structures of timing constraints and timing descriptions. A timing structure is based on *events* and *event chains* that can be modeled across all abstraction levels. An *event* describes a distinct point in time where a change of state in the system takes place or it may also be an report of the current state. An *event chain* describes the temporal behavior of steps in a system, where the behavior is expressed by two related groups of events: stimulus and response. The chains is also used to specify built-in timing requirements on the different steps in the system. Timing analysis of EAST-ADL models is supported by the MARTE UML profile through the Papyrus add-in [16].

5   Conclusion

In this paper, we addressed the importance of an ADL for dependable software-intensive systems to support activities such as analysis, V&V, code generation/synthesis, etc., and at the same time support understandability and mutual communication. The classification and comparison framework for software Architecture Description Languages [6] developed by Medvidovic and Taylor was extended and used to compare the levels of support AADL and EAST-ADL provide these two aspects. The framework highlighted several areas when the languages were compared. One area was frequently highlighted during the comparison, which is that the metamodel of EAST-ADL has possibilities to describe systems at higher abstraction levels compared to the AADL standard. EAST-ADL provides means to model component types such as features, devices and functions of automotive systems, where a more detailed software architecture of concrete software components can be modeled by AUTOSAR, a complementary language to EAST-ADL. AADL on the other hand, models a system using abstractions of concrete system elements (e.g. processes and threads), which provide less freedom of the structure and how the functionality is obtained in the implementation. As EAST-ADL's point of view is on a higher abstraction level, hiding implementation solutions behind abstract features, devices and functionalities, it concentrates on system aspects of importance between the main parties within the automotive industry (e.g. between suppliers and OEMs) such as modeling of requirements, dependability, variability and timing of the system. This can be concluded in that the gap between an architecture description artifact and its implementation is larger when developing systems using EAST-ADL compared to using AADL, whereas the gap between the understandability of a system (as well as the controllability and the communicability) and its complexity is smaller. Therefore, EAST-ADL tend to primarily focus on understandability and communication of systems whereas AADL tend to be more appropriate for analysis tools, model checkers and compilers.

References

1. Wirsing, M.: Report of the beyond the horizon thematic group 6 on software intensive systems. Technical report, Thematic Group 6: Software-Intensive Systems (2006)
2. As-2 Embedded Computing Systems Committee SAE. Architecture Analysis & Design Language (AADL). SAE Standards no. AS5506 (2004)
3. The ATESST Consortium. East-adl 2.0 specification (November 2010), http://www.atesst.org
4. ATESST2. Advancing traffic efficiency and safety through software technology (November 2010), http://www.atesst.org
5. Medvidovic, N., Rosenblum, D.S.: Domains of concern in software architectures and architecture description languages. In: Proceedings of the Conference on Domain-Specific Languages (DSL 1997), p. 16. USENIX Association, Berkeley (1997)
6. Medvidovic, N., Taylor, R.N.: A classification and comparison framework for software architecture description languages. IEEE Trans. Softw. Eng. 26(1), 70–93 (2000)
7. Feiler, P.H., Gluch, D.P., Hudak, J.J.: The architecture analysis and design language (aadl): An introduction. Technical report (2006)
8. Hudak, J., Feiler, P.: Developing aadl models for control systems: A practitioner's guide. Technical report, CMU Software Engineering Institute (SEI) (2007)
9. As-2 Embedded Computing Systems Committee SAE. Architecture Analysis & Design Language (AADL). SAE Standards no. AS5506A (2009)
10. Cuenot, P., Frey, P., Johansson, R., Lönn, H., Reiser, M.-O., Servat, D., Tavakoli Kolagari, R., Chen, D.J.: Developing automotive products using the east-adl2, an autosar compliant architecture description language. In: European Congress on Embedded Real-Time Software (ERTS), Toulouse, France (2008)
11. AUTOSAR. Automotive open system architecture (November 2010), http://www.autosar.org

12. Franca, R.B., Bodeveix, J.-P., Filali, M., Rolland, J.-F., Chemouil, D., Thomas, D.: The aadl behaviour annex – experiments and roadmap. In: ICECCS 2007: Proceedings of the 12th IEEE International Conference on Engineering Complex Computer Systems, pp. 377–382. IEEE Computer Society, Washington, DC, USA (2007)
13. SysML. Systems modeling language (November 2010), http://www.sysml.org
14. The cheddar project: a free real time scheduling analyzer (November 2010), http://beru.univ-brest.fr/~singhoff/cheddar/
15. Ocarina: An aadl model processing suite (November 2010), http://www.ocarina.enst.fr
16. Papyrus for east-adl (November 2010), http://www.papyrusuml.org

A Formal Approach to Design and Verification of Two-Level Hierarchical Scheduling Systems

Laura Carnevali[1], Giuseppe Lipari[2], Alessandro Pinzuti[1], and Enrico Vicario[1]

Dipartimento di Sistemi e Informatica - Università di Firenze
{laura.carnevali,alessandro.pinzuti,enrico.vicario}@unifi.it
Real-Time Systems Laboratory - Scuola Superiore Sant'Anna
giuseppe.lipari@sssup.it

Abstract. Hierarchical Scheduling (HS) systems manage a set of real-time applications through a scheduling hierarchy, enabling partitioning and reduction of complexity, confinement of failure modes, and temporal isolation among system applications. This plays a crucial role in all industrial areas where high-performance microprocessors allow growing integration of multiple applications on a single platform.

We propose a formal approach to the development of real-time applications with non-deterministic Execution Times and local resource sharing managed by a Time Division Multiplexing (TDM) global scheduler and preemptive Fixed Priority (FP) local schedulers, according to the scheduling hierarchy prescribed by the ARINC-653 standard. The methodology leverages the theory of preemptive Time Petri Nets (pTPNs) to support exact schedulability analysis, to guide the implementation on a Real-Time Operating System (RTOS), and to drive functional conformance testing of the real-time code. Computational experience is reported to show the feasibility of the approach.

Keywords: Real-time systems, Hierarchical Scheduling, ARINC-653, Time Division Multiplexing, preemptive Fixed Priority, verification, preemptive Time Petri Nets, real-time code, real-time testing.

1 Introduction

Hierarchical scheduling (HS) systems consist of real-time applications arranged in a scheduling hierarchy. They can be generally represented as a tree, or a hierarchy, of nodes where each node represents an application with its own scheduler of internal workloads. The tree may have an arbitrary number of levels and each node may have an arbitrary number of children [29]. Hierarchical scheduling is receiving an increasing attention due to its effect of partitioning and reduction of complexity, confinement of failure modes, and temporal isolation among system applications. Among the disparate architectures that may serve the design of HS systems, one way of composing existing applications with different timing characteristics is to use a two-level scheduling paradigm: at the global level, a scheduler selects which application will be executed next and for how long; at

A. Romanovsky and T. Vardanega (Eds.): Ada-Europe 2011, LNCS 6652, pp. 118–131, 2011.

the local level, a scheduler is used for each application in order to determine which tasks of the selected application should actually execute.

Various analytical approaches have been proposed to support schedulability analysis and verification of HS systems under the assumption of local resource sharing [13],[19],[23],[29],[24],[22],[11],[15].In [13], a two-level HS scheme is introduced to manage the execution of both real-time and non real-time applications on a single processor, assuming an Earliest Deadline First (EDF) global scheduler and a Total Bandwidth Server (TBS) [30] for each application. The approach is extended in [19] to encompass Rate Monotonic (RM) scheduling policy at the global level, although the treatment is restricted to the case of periodic tasks with harmonic periods. In [23], an exact schedulability condition is provided for a two-level HS architecture with EDF global scheduling policy and EDF/RM local scheduling policy. In [22], [24], HS systems are described through the periodic server abstraction, providing the class of server parameters that guarantees schedulability for Fixed Priority (FP) local schedulers. Following the approach based on server abstraction, in [11], response time analysis is employed to obtain exact schedulability conditions for HS systems that are handled by FP preemptive scheduling at both the local and the global level, comparing Periodic, Sporadic, and Deferrable Servers. The schedulability analysis techniques of [15], [29] address a hierarchical scheduling framework that employs the bounded-delay resource partition model of [26], providing a compositional method according to which the timing requirements of a parent scheduler are directly derived from the timing requirements of its child schedulers and they are satisfied if and only if the timing requirements of the child schedulers are satisfied. The approach supports the integration of applications developed by independent suppliers, but yields more pessimistic schedulability results.

Recent works address global resource sharing in HS systems. In [12], the response time analysis of [11] is extended with a global resource access policy called Hierarchical Stack Resource Policy (HSRP), which bounds priority inversion and limits the interference due to overruns during resource accesses. In [2], the Subsystem Integration and Resource Allocation Policy (SIRAP) provides temporal isolation between subsystems that share logical resources and thus facilitates the integration of applications developed independently of each other. In [16], compositional techniques support automatic scheduling and correctness verification of ARINC-653 [1] partitions with global resource sharing.

As a major limit, analytical techniques provide pessimistic results for models including sporadic tasks, inter-task dependencies in the time of release, inter-task dependencies due to mutual exclusion on shared resources, and internal sequencing of tasks. Moreover, analytical approaches do not encompass computations associated with a non-deterministic Execution Time, providing schedulability results for assigned values usually coincident with the Worst Case Execution Time (WCET). For complex task-sets that expose any of these factors, the verification of both sequencing and timing correctness may become sufficiently critical to motivate the use of state space analysis of models based on formalisms such as StopWatch Automata [9], preemptive Time Petri Nets (pTPNs) [4], Petri

Nets with hyper-arcs [27], and Scheduling-TPNs [21]. As a common trait, these formalisms encompass temporal parameters varying within an assigned interval and support the representation of suspension in the advancement of clocks. In particular, their semantics can be defined in terms of a state transition rule driving the evolution of a logical location and of a set of densely-valued clocks, which requires that the state space be covered through equivalence classes. In particular, in [4], an efficient approach is proposed which enumerates an approximation of the state space that preserves Difference Bounds Matrix (DBM) encoding [31], [3], [10], supporting the derivation of the tight timing profile of clocks enabled along a path through an algorithm that cleans up false behaviors introduced by the approximation. In [8], the theory of pTPNs is cast in a tailoring of the V-Model SW life cycle that supports design, implementation, and verification of real-time applications within a Model Driven Development (MDD) approach.

In this paper, we extend the methodology of [8] to support the development of two-level HS systems with local resource sharing managed by a Time Division Multiplexing (TDM) global scheduler and preemptive Fixed Priority (FP) local schedulers, according to the scheduling hierarchy prescribed by the ARINC-653 standard [1]. The approach leverages the theory of pTPNs [4] to enable exact schedulability analysis of multiple real-time applications made by periodic, sporadic, and jittering tasks with nondeterministic Execution Times and semaphore/mailbox synchronizations. To this end, the approach of [8] is extended to encompass the representation of a TDM global scheduler, exploiting the induced temporal isolation among system applications to manage the complexity of the model and to keep the analysis viable (Section 2). The pTPN specification model steers the implementation on a Real-Time Operating System (RTOS), yielding code that exposes a readable structure, reflects the organization of the pTPN model, and, especially, preserves pTPN semantic properties. In particular, the coding process of [8] is extended to support the emulation of a TDM global scheduler on RTAI [14] (Section 3). This enables agile verification of the conformance of the implementation to sequencing and timing requirements of its pTPN specification, according to the testing approach of [8] (Section 4). Conclusions are finally drawn in Section 5.

2   Design and Verification through pTPNs

We address *real-time applications* with local resource sharing managed by a TDM global scheduler and FP local schedulers, according to the scheduling hierarchy prescribed by the ARINC 653 standard [1]. Each application is a *task-set* encompassing usual patterns of real-time concurrency [7]: *i)* a task-set is made by *recurrent tasks* which release jobs with *periodic, sporadic,* or *jittering* policy, depending on whether the release time is deterministic, bounded by a minimum but not a maximum value, or bounded by a minimum and a maximum value, respectively; *ii)* a job is a sequence of *chunks*, each associated with an *entry-point* function that implements its functional behavior, with an expected Execution Time interval, and with a priority level (low priority numbers run first); *iii)* a task is subject to a *deadline* which is usually coincident with its minimum inter-release time; *iv)* tasks belonging to the same application (i.e., running in the same time-slots) may have dependencies (e.g., binary semaphore synchronizations), while those belonging to different applications (i.e., running in different time-slots) do not share critical sections.

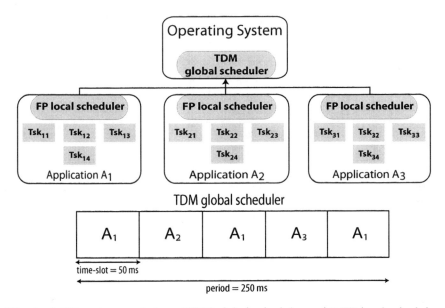

Fig. 1. A HS system made by a TDM global scheduler and 3 FP local schedulers

Fig. 1 illustrates the scheme with reference to the case of 3 applications A_1, A_2, and A_3. The global scheduler partitions a period of 250 *ms* in 5 time-slots of equal length of 50 *ms* and assigns each of them to a single application, i.e., T_1, T_3, and T_5 are assigned to A_1, T_2 is assigned to A_2, and T_4 is assigned to A_3. While the fixed partitioning is a requirement of the approach, equal slots are assumed here without loss of generality to simplify the description of the case. Each application is made by 3 periodic tasks and 1 sporadic task synchronized on 2 binary semaphores, as illustrated in the workload of Table 1.

2.1   PTPN Model of the HS System

PTPNs [5] extend Time Petri Nets (TPNs) [25], [3] with a concept of resource assignment that makes the progress of timed transitions dependent on the availability of a set of preemptable resources, enabling the representation of suspension in the advancement of clocks and thus providing an expressivity that effectively supports the specification of real-time task-sets. In [8], the theory of pTPNs is cast in a V-Model SW process supporting all the steps of development of real-time task-sets running under preemptive FP scheduling. We extend here the approach of [8] to enable design and verification of HS systems managed by

Table 1. The workload of the HS system of Fig.1 (times expressed in ms)

Application	Task	Release	Deadline	Chunk	Priority	Exec. Time	Sem
A_1	Tsk_{11}	$[150, 150]$	150	C_{111}	1	$[1, 2]$	mux_{11}
				C_{112}	1	$[10, 20]$	-
	Tsk_{12}	$[200, 200]$	200	C_{121}	2	$[2, 4]$	mux_{12}
				C_{122}	2	$[1, 2]$	-
	Tsk_{13}	$[250, 250]$	250	C_{131}	3	$[5, 10]$	-
				C_{132}	3	$[1, 2]$	mux_{12}
	Tsk_{14}	$[150, \infty)$	150	C_{141}	4	$[1, 2]$	-
				C_{142}	4	$[1, 2]$	mux_{11}
A_2	Tsk_{21}	$[250, 250]$	250	C_{211}	1	$[2, 4]$	mux_{21}
				C_{212}	1	$[15, 20]$	-
	Tsk_{22}	$[280, 280]$	280	C_{221}	2	$[2, 4]$	-
				C_{222}	2	$[1, 2]$	mux_{22}
				C_{223}	2	$[1, 2]$	-
	Tsk_{23}	$[300, 300]$	300	C_{231}	3	$[10, 15]$	-
				C_{232}	3	$[1, 2]$	mux_{21}
	Tsk_{24}	$[250, \infty)$	250	C_{241}	4	$[1, 2]$	-
				C_{242}	4	$[1, 2]$	mux_{22}
A_3	Tsk_{31}	$[300, 300]$	300	C_{311}	1	$[1, 2]$	mux_{31}
	Tsk_{32}	$[350, 350]$	350	C_{321}	2	$[1, 2]$	-
				C_{322}	2	$[1, 2]$	mux_{31}
	Tsk_{33}	$[350, 350]$	350	C_{332}	3	$[2, 4]$	mux_{32}
	Tsk_{34}	$[250, \infty)$	250	C_{341}	4	$[1, 2]$	mux_{32}

a TDM global scheduler and FP local schedulers. The temporal isolation among tasks of different applications permits to specify each application with a different pTPN model made by the submodels of the task-set and the global scheduler. This reduces the complexity of the problem and enables exhaustive verification of sequencing and timing constraints of complex systems, which could not be afforded through direct analysis of a unique flat model due to the state space explosion problem. We illustrate the approach with reference to the pTPN model of application A_1 of the HS system of Table 1 (see Fig. 2).

The pTPN submodel of the task-set. Recurrent task releases are modeled by transitions with neither input places nor resource request, which thus fire repeatedly with inter-firing times falling within their respective firing intervals, e.g., t_{110} models recurrent job releases of Tsk_{11}. Chunks are modeled by transitions with static firing intervals equal to the min-max range of Execution Time, associated with resource request and static priorities, e.g., t_{112} models the completion of the first chunk of Tsk_{11}, which requires resource cpu with priority level 1 for an Execution Time within $[1, 2]$ ms. Computations in different jobs compete for resource cpu and run under FP preemptive scheduling, e.g., both transitions t_{112} and t_{122} require resource cpu with priority level 1 and 2, respectively, and, if t_{112} becomes enabled while t_{122} is progressing, then t_{112} preempts t_{122} and t_{112}

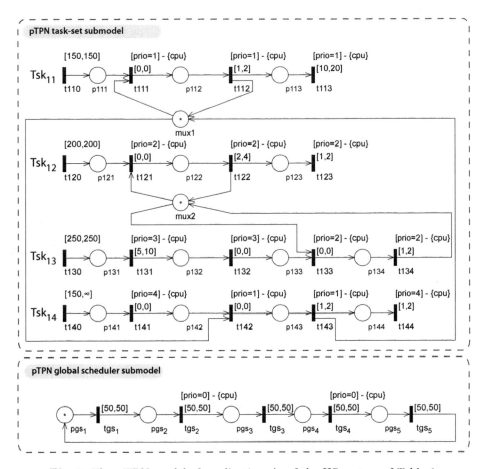

Fig. 2. The pTPN model of application A_1 of the HS system of Table 1

becomes suspended. Binary semaphores are modeled as places initially marked with 1 token; their acquisition operations are represented as immediate transitions, while their release operations are allocated to transitions that also account for chunk completions, e.g., mux_{11} models a binary semaphore synchronizing the first chunk of Tsk_{11} and the first chunk of Tsk_{14}; wait operations are modeled by t_{111} and t_{142}; signal operations are represented by transitions t_{112} and t_{143}, which also model the completion of the two chunks. According to the *priority ceiling emulation protocol* [28], the priority of any chunk synchronized on a semaphore is statically raised to the highest priority of any chunk that ever uses that semaphore, so as to avoid priority inversion. Priority boost operations are explicitly modeled as immediate transitions, while priority lowering operations are allocated to transitions that also account for chunk completions. According to this, the priorities of Tsk_{13} and Tsk_{14} are raised to the priority of Tsk_{12} and Tsk_{11}, respectively, in the sections where they hold a semaphore: priority boost operations are represented by t_{132} and t_{141}, which precede semaphore wait operations; priority lowering operations are represented by t_{134} and t_{143}, which also account for chunk completions.

The pTPN submodel of the global scheduler. The submodel of the global scheduler is made by as many transitions as the number of time-slots in the period, each associated with a static firing interval equal to the duration of the corresponding time-slot and chained to the transition accounting for the previous time-slot through its input place, e.g., transitions tgs_1, tgs_2, tgs_3, tgs_4, and tgs_5 model time-slots T_1, T_2, T_3, T_4, and T_5, respectively. Transitions modeling time-slots assigned to the application are not associated with a resource request, while the other transitions require resource *cpu* with a higher level of priority than any task of the application. In so doing, transitions modeling jobs of the task-set submodel may be progressing and advance their clocks only during the time-slots in which the application is scheduled to execute and they are suspended during the other time-slots. According to this, since tasks of A_1 require *cpu* with a priority level between 2 and 5 and A_1 is scheduled to execute in time-slots T_1, T_3, and T_5, transitions tgs_1, tgs_3, and tgs_5 are not associated with a resource request, while transitions tgs_2 and tgs_4 require *cpu* with priority level 0.

Generalization to multi-level scheduling hierarchies. The proposed approach applies to any tree of schedulers where leaf nodes are FP schedulers and non-leaf nodes are TDM schedulers. The root scheduler partitions its period into a number of time-slots and exclusively assigns each of them to one of its children schedulers. The process is repeatedly applied until each sub-slot is assigned to a leaf FP scheduler. In so doing, each application is exclusively assigned a number of sub-slots and can thus be analyzed in isolation.

2.2 Architectural Verification

The pTPN model of each application is analyzed in isolation, since the embedding environment of the application is completely accounted by the pTPN submodel of the global scheduler. This supports exact schedulability analysis based on correctness verification of the model with respect to logical sequencing and quantitative timing constraints. The analysis is performed through the Oris Tool [18], which supports enumeration of the space of state classes, selection of paths attaining specific sequencing and timing conditions, and tight evaluation of their range of timings. In particular, the identification of all paths that start with a task release and end with its completion enables the derivation of the Best Case Completion Time (BCCT) and the Worst Case Completion Time (WCCT) of each task, thus verifying whether task deadlines are met.

As shown in Table 2, state space analysis enumerates 32084, 183981, and 26147 state classes for A_1, A_2, and A_3, respectively, taking less than 2 minutes and using approximately 300 MB RAM. Note that architectural verification could not be afforded through an unique flat model, which exhausts 4 GB RAM after the enumeration of nearly 10^6 classes in approximately 13 minutes. In fact, as usual in techniques based on state space enumeration [4],[9],[27],[21], the complexity

Table 2. Space and time complexity of state space enumeration on the HS system of Fig.1: structured model vs flat model

Model	# Classes	RAM	Time
model of A_1	32084	$\sim$ 300 MB	$\sim$ 20 sec
model of A_2	183981	$\sim$ 300 MB	$\sim$ 83 sec
model of A_3	26147	$\sim$ 300 MB	$\sim$ 15 sec
flat model	$> 10^6$	> 4 GB (out of memory)	> 13 min

of the analysis notably increases with the number of concurrent tasks and with the number of sporadic tasks.

Table 3 shows the number of paths, the BCCT, the WCCT, the deadline, and the laxity of each task of each application, proving that all deadlines are met. For instance, tasks Tsk_{11}, Tsk_{12}, Tsk_{13}, and Tsk_{14} of A_1 have 11979, 15023, 11069, and 15213 paths, respectively, a BCCT of 61 ms, 14 ms, 6 ms, and 66 ms, and a WCCT of 74 ms, 80 ms, 42 ms, and 82 ms, respectively. This guarantees that all task deadlines are met, with minimum laxity of 76 ms, 120 ms, 208 ms, and 68 ms for Tsk_{11}, Tsk_{12}, Tsk_{13}, and Tsk_{14}, respectively.

Table 3. Results of the architectural verification on the structured model of the HS system of Fig.1, showing the number of paths, the BCCT, the WCCT, the deadline, and the laxity of the tasks of each application (times expressed in ms)

Application	Task	# Paths	BCCT	WCCT	Deadline	Laxity
	Tsk_{11}	11979	61	74	150	76
A_1	Tsk_{12}	15023	14	80	200	120
	Tsk_{13}	11069	6	42	250	208
	Tsk_{14}	15213	66	82	150	68
	Tsk_{21}	31480	67	74	250	176
A_2	Tsk_{22}	66069	39	230	280	50
	Tsk_{23}	139417	30	247	300	53
	Tsk_{24}	57286	82	249	250	1
	Tsk_{31}	13826	101	204	300	96
A_3	Tsk_{32}	20742	53	210	350	140
	Tsk_{33}	28932	55	212	350	138
	Tsk_{34}	13617	156	212	250	38

3   Implementation on RTAI

The specification provided by the pTPN model can be implemented on different RTOSs which natively support HS schemes or not. We illustrate here how a TDM global scheduler can be emulated on RTAI 3.6 [14] by extending the coding process of [8]. The implementation is guided by the structure of the pTPN model and produces code that is responsible for: *i)* task suspension/resumption according to the allocation of time-slots to system applications, *ii)* task releases, *iii)* invocation of semaphore and priority handling operations, and, *iv)* invocation of entry-points. As a characterizing trait, the code has a manageable architecture and preserves the pTPN semantic properties, and it could be equivalently derived in automated manner through an MDD approach. The architecture of the implementation is organized in a kernel module.

Implementation of the entry-point and the exit-point. The kernel module is loaded into the kernel space through the entry-point `init_module`, which creates data structures employed by tasks of the applications (e.g., binary semaphores), creates real-time tasks that implement tasks of the specification, and starts the timer. The kernel module is unloaded at the end of the execution through the exit-point `cleanup_module`, which stops the timer and destroys data structures and real-time tasks.

Implementation of jobs. In order to observe the timely release of jobs, the responsibility of job releases and job executions is given to different real-time tasks, synchronized on a semaphore which is supposed to receive a signal at each release. According to this, each task of the specification is implemented through: *i)* a recurrent real-time task that performs job releases by signaling a semaphore at each activation, and *ii)* a further real-time task that performs job operations by executing a loop that acquires the semaphore at the beginning of each repetition. Real-time tasks performing job releases have a higher priority level than real-time tasks performing job executions.

A code skeleton with two real-time tasks for each task of the specification is adopted also in [8], where an experimental assessment is carried on to evaluate the overhead of the code architecture and the confidence of measurements. Experimental results show that the error due to finite accuracy keeps lower than nearly $1.2\ \mu s$ with recurrent peaks in the order of 3-4 μs, which can be ascribed to timing uncertainties due to processor and bus effects on a general purpose CPU running a hard RTOS [20], [17]. This highlights that the overhead is negligible with respect to the precision of temporal parameters in the model.

Implementation of the global scheduler. The TDM global scheduling policy is emulated through a periodic real-time task with period equal to the duration of a time-slot and with higher priority level than real-time tasks implementing job releases and job executions. At each period, the task suspends the real-time tasks of the applications that are not scheduled to execute during the next time-slot and resumes the real-time tasks of the application that is assigned the next time-slot. Listing 1.1 shows a fragment of the entry-point of the task. For instance, at the beginning of time-slot T_2 (i.e., `case 2` of the `switch` control structure), real-time tasks that implement jobs of A_1 (i.e., `tsk11job`, `tsk12job`, `tsk13job`, and `tsk14job`) are suspended and those that implement task jobs of A_2 (i.e., `tsk21job`, `tsk22job`, `tsk23job`, and `tsk24job`) are resumed. Real-time tasks that implement jobs of A_3 do not need to be suspended since they are suspended also during time-slot T_1, which is in fact assigned to A_1. If time-slots have different duration, the global scheduler could anyhow be implemented as a periodic task by letting it change its period at each activation and set it equal to the duration of the subsequent time-slot.

```
static void tskgs_job(int t)
{
  static int slot = 1;
  while(1) {
    switch(slot) {
      case 1:
        ...
        slot = 2;
        break;
      case 2:
        rt_task_suspend(&tsk11job);
        rt_task_suspend(&tsk12job);
        rt_task_suspend(&tsk13job);
        rt_task_suspend(&tsk14job);
        rt_task_resume(&tsk21job);
        rt_task_resume(&tsk22job);
        rt_task_resume(&tsk23job);
        rt_task_resume(&tsk24job);
        slot = 3;
        break;
      case 3:
        ...
        slot = 4;
        break;
      case 4:
        ...
        slot = 5;
        break;
      case 5:
        ...
        slot = 1;
        break;
    }
    rt_task_wait_period();
  }
}
```

Listing 1.1. Emulation of a TDM global scheduler on RTAI (**t** is a formal parameter of the task function, which is actually not used in the context of our experiment)

4   Testing Conformance with Respect to pTPN Semantics

The close adherence of the code architecture to the pTPN semantic properties enables functional conformance testing of the implementation with respect to sequencing and timing requirements accounted by the pTPN specification [8], as illustrated in the schema of Fig. 3. In particular, the abstraction of pTPNs enables the observation of the following kinds of failures:

- *un-sequenced execution*: an execution run breaking sequencing requirements (e.g., a priority inversion);
- *time-frame violation*: a temporal parameter assuming a value out of its expected interval (e.g., a computation breaking its Execution Time interval);
- *deadline miss*: a job breaking its end-to-end timing requirement.

Each action of the implementation is mapped on a transition in the pTPN model of one of the applications. By construction, these actions are: the completion of suspensions/resumptions of real-time tasks performed by the global scheduler at the beginning of a time-slot, the release of a task job, the completion of a chunk, the completion of a wait operation on a semaphore, the boost of a priority before a semaphore access. The implementation is then instrumented so as to produce a time-stamped log that stores: *i)* each action of the implementation that has a counterpart in the pTPN model of an application and *ii)* the time at which the action occurred. According to this, each run executed by the implementation provides a finite sequence of timed actions $\{\langle a_i, \tau_i \rangle\}_{i=0}^{N}$, where:

- a_i is an action of the implementation, univocally mapped on a transition t_i of the global scheduler submodel or the task-set submodel of an application;
- τ_i is the time at which a_i occurred.

The log produced by the execution of the real-time applications is off-line parsed in order to obtain a separate sub-log for each application, made by the timed actions that correspond to the firings of transitions belonging to the pTPN model of the application. In particular, the sub-log of each application comprises a firing sequence for the pTPN model of the application and it can be compared in isolation against the model itself, in order to determine whether it represents a feasible behavior. More specifically, the decision algorithm starts from the initial state s_0, which accounts for conditions at which the system is started, checks the feasibility of the first timed action $\langle a_0, \tau_0 \rangle$, and computes the subsequent state s_1; at the i-th step, the algorithm checks whether t_i can be fired at time $\tau_i - \tau_{i-1}$ from state s_{i-1} and computes the resulting state s_i. A *failure verdict* is emitted as soon as any timed action $\langle a_i, \tau_i \rangle$ is not accepted by the algorithm, while a *pass verdict* is emitted when the run terminates. In so doing, any un-sequenced execution and any time-frame violation are detected, whereas any stealing of resources are recognized iff the quantity of stolen time exceeds the laxity between the actual Execution Time and its expected upper bound.

The code of the implementation is instrumented by letting real-time tasks write time-stamped actions on an RTAI FIFO queue, since file operations are not available in the kernel space and would in any case take time beyond acceptable limits. The log is subsequently processed and written on a file by a low priority task running in the user space. On the Intel Core 2 Quad Q6600 desktop processor employed in the experiment, the run-time overhead introduced by time-stamped logging is 150 ns on average and it can thus assumed to be negligible with respect to the time scale of the specification [8].

To provide a comprehensive experimental set-up, a busy-sleep function was implemented to emulate computations lasting for a controlled duration and replace entry-point functions [8]. The implementation was run for several times for 2 hours, which corresponds to more than 28000 releases of the shortest period task of application A_1. Logs produced by the execution runs were evaluated and no failure was detected, thus highlighting the conformance of the implementation to its pTPN specification and the feasibility of the proposed approach.

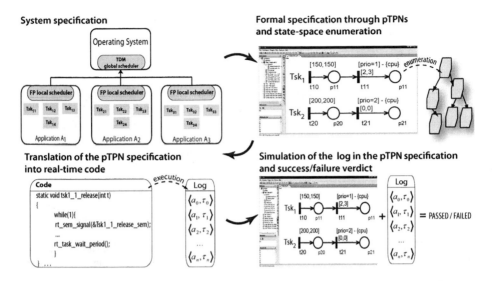

Fig. 3. A schema illustrating the use of pTPNs in the development of HS systems

5   Conclusions

In this paper, we extended the methodology of [8] to support formal specification, architectural verification, implementation, and conformance testing of HS systems managed by a TDM global scheduler and preemptive FP local schedulers, according to the scheduling hierarchy prescribed by the ARINC-653 standard [1]. The approach employs the theory of pTPNs [4] to engineer all the steps of development, addressing complex HS systems made by real-time applications including periodic, sporadic, and jittering tasks, with nondeterministic Execution Times and local resource sharing.

In the design stage, the temporal isolation among different applications is conveniently exploited by leveraging the expressive power of pTPNs in the representation of suspension in the advancement of clocks, which allows the specification of a HS system through a structured model made by a different pTPN for each application. In particular, the pTPN model of each application is made by the submodels of the task-set and the global scheduler, and it can be analyzed in isolation independently of the models of the other applications. This largely reduces the complexity of the problem, facilitates the scalability of the approach, and enables exhaustive architectural verification through state space enumeration, which could not be carried out through direct analysis of an unique flat model due to the state space explosion problem. Moreover, the partitioning of a high number of tasks into subsets and the specification of each of them through a different model eases the assignment of task priorities made by the programmer in the design stage.

In the implementation stage, the coding process of [8] is extended to support the emulation of a TDM global scheduler on RTAI [14]. As a characterizing trait, the resulting code has a readable structure and preserves the semantic properties of the pTPN model. This enables a conformance testing approach where time-stamped logs produced by execution runs are compared against the set of feasible behaviors of the pTPN specification in order to verify whether sequencing and timing requirements are satisfied [8].

The pTPN submodel of the global scheduler of each application comprises a kind of Required Interface [6] accounting for the environment where the local application is embedded. Generalization of the structure of this interface seems a promising way to extend the analysis to more complex schemes of hierarchy that encompass inter-application communication mechanisms as prescribed by the ARINC-653 standard [1].

References

1. ARINC Specification 653-2: Avionics Application Software Standard Interface: Part 1 - Required Services. Technical report, Avionics Electronic Engineering Committee (ARINC) (March 2006)
2. Behnam, M., Shin, I., Nolte, T., Nolin, M.: SIRAP: A Synchronization Protocol for Hierarchical Resource Sharing in Real-Time Operating Systems. In: Proc. of the ACM & IEEE Int. Conf. on Embedded SW, pp. 279–288. ACM, New York (2007)
3. Berthomieu, B., Diaz, M.: Modeling and Verification of Time Dependent Systems Using Time Petri Nets. IEEE Trans. on SW Eng. 17(3) (March 1991)
4. Bucci, G., Fedeli, A., Sassoli, L., Vicario, E.: Timed State Space Analysis of Real Time Preemptive Systems. IEEE Trans. on SW Eng. 30(2), 97–111 (2004)
5. Bucci, G., Sassoli, L., Vicario, E.: Correctness verification and performance analysis of real time systems using stochastic preemptive Time Petri Nets. IEEE Trans. on SW Eng. 31(11), 913–927 (2005)
6. Bucci, G., Vicario, E.: Compositional Validation of Time-Critical Systems Using Communicating Time Petri Nets. IEEE Trans. on SW Eng. 21(12), 969–992 (1995)
7. Buttazzo, G.: Hard Real-Time Computing Systems. Springer, Heidelberg (2005)
8. Carnevali, L., Ridi, L., Vicario, E.: Putting preemptive Time Petri Nets to work in a V-Model SW life cycle. IEEE Trans. on SW Eng. (accepted for publication)
9. Cassez, F., Larsen, K.G.: The Impressive Power of Stopwatches. In: Palamidessi, C. (ed.) CONCUR 2000. LNCS, vol. 1877, p. 138. Springer, Heidelberg (2000)
10. Dill, D.: Timing Assumptions and Verification of Finite-State Concurrent Systems. In: Proc. Workshop on Computer Aided Verification Methods for Finite State Systems (1989)
11. Davis, R.I., Burns, A.: Hierarchical Fixed Priority Pre-Emptive Scheduling. In: Proc. of the IEEE Int. Real-Time Systems Symp., pp. 389–398 (2005)
12. Davis, R.I., Burns, A.: Resource Sharing in Hierarchical Fixed Priority Pre-Emptive Systems. In: Proc. IEEE Int. Real-Time Sys. Symp., pp. 257–270 (2006)
13. Deng, Z., Liu, J.W.-S.: Scheduling real-time applications in an open environment. In: Proc. of the IEEE Real-Time Systems Symp., pp. 308–319 (1997)
14. Dept. of Aerospace Engineering - Polytechnic of Milan. RTAI: Real Time Application Interface for Linux, https://www.rtai.org
15. Easwaran, A., Lee, I., Shin, I., Sokolsky, O.: Compositional Schedulability Analysis of Hierarchical Real-Time Systems. In: Proc. of the IEEE Int. Symp. on Object and Component-Oriented Real-Time Distributed Comp., pp. 274–281 (2007)

16. Easwaran, A., Lee, I., Sokolsky, O., Vestal, S.: A Compositional Scheduling Framework for Digital Avionics Systems. In: Proc. of the Int. Workshop on Real-Time Computing Systems and Applications, vol. 0, pp. 371–380 (2009)
17. Proctor, F.M., Shackleford, W.P.: Real-time operating system timing jitter and its impact on motor control. In: Proc. of SPIE, Sensors and Controls for Intelligent Manufacturing II, December 10-16, vol. 4563 (2001)
18. Bucci, G., Carnevali, L., Ridi, L., Vicario, E.: Oris: a Tool for Modeling, Verification and Evaluation of Real-Time Systems. International Journal of Software Tools for Technology Transfer 12(5), 391–403 (2010)
19. Kuo, T.-W., Li, C.-H.: A Fixed-Priority-Driven Open Environment for Real-Time Applications. In: Proc. IEEE Real-Time Sys. Symp., pp. 256–267 (1999)
20. Dozio, L., Mantegazza, P.: General-purpose processors for active vibro-acoustic control: Discussion and experiences. Control Engineering Practice 15(2), 163–176 (2007)
21. Lime, D., Roux, O.H.: Formal verification of real-time systems with preemptive scheduling. Real-Time Syst. 41(2), 118–151 (2009)
22. Lipari, B.-E., Giuseppe: A methodology for designing hierarchical scheduling systems. Journal of Embedded Computing 1(2), 257–269 (2005)
23. Lipari, G., Baruah, S.K.: Efficient Scheduling of Real-Time Multi-Task Applications in Dynamic Systems. In: IEEE Real Time Tech. and Appl. Symp., p. 166 (2000)
24. Lipari, G., Bini, E.: Resource Partitioning among Real-Time Applications. In: Proc. of the Euromicro Conf. on Real-Time Sys., pp. 151–158 (2003)
25. Merlin, P., Farber, D.: Recoverability of Communication Protocols. IEEE Trans. on Communications 24(9) (1976)
26. Mok, A.K., Feng, A.X., Chen, D.: Resource Partition for Real-Time Systems. In: IEEE Real Time Technology and Applications Symposium, pp. 75–84 (2001)
27. Roux, O.H., Lime, D.: Time petri nets with inhibitor hyperarcs. Formal semantics and state space computation. In: Cortadella, J., Reisig, W. (eds.) ICATPN 2004. LNCS, vol. 3099, pp. 371–390. Springer, Heidelberg (2004)
28. Sha, L., Rajkumar, R., Lehoczky, J.P.: Priority Inheritance Protocols: An Approach to Real-Time Synchronization. IEEE Trans. Comput. 39(9), 1175–1185 (1990)
29. Shin, I., Lee, I.: Periodic Resource Model for Compositional Real-Time Guarantees. In: Proc. of the IEEE Int. Real-Time Systems Symp., pp. 2–13 (2003)
30. Spuri, M., Buttazzo, G.: Scheduling Aperiodic Tasks in Dynamic Priority Systems. Real-Time Systems 10, 179–210 (1996)
31. Vicario, E.: Static Analysis and Dynamic Steering of Time Dependent Systems Using Time Petri Nets. IEEE Trans. on SW Eng. (August 2001)

Architecting a Common Bridge Abstraction over Different Middleware Paradigms[*]

Iago Rodríguez-López and Marisol García-Valls

Distributed Real-Time Systems Lab
Department of Telematics Engineering
Universidad Carlos III de Madrid
Av. de la universidad 30, 28911 Leganés (Madrid), Spain
{irlopez,mvalls}@it.uc3m.es

Abstract. Currently, there are a number of communication middleware technologies that are successful solutions to provide an abstraction for distributed computing in different domains. Although most current middlewares offer different interfaces for a number of programming languages, they are usually bound to use one specific communication paradigm. The usage of middleware decreases programming complexity, but it is not cost-free and fully transparent. Every distributed application using a communication middleware has some degree of dependence over the specific middleware it uses mainly related to the interaction paradigm of the communication. Therefore, there is no fully transparent way to use middleware at present. This paper contributes to increase the transparency between applications and middlewares by presenting a *common bridge* that has been architected in an environment that requires using different middleware technologies interchangeably. This bridge is a software component to abstract the complexity of the middleware solutions requiring minimum porting efforts. Some results are presented to validate the transparency.

Keywords: middleware; interoperability; component-based design, real-time.

1 Introduction

The general idea behind the concept of middleware is to provide a software layer between the operating system and the distributed applications abstracting them from the details of their communication. This definition was fully detailed in [1], that defined a structure of four layers and their specific functionality taking a network-centric point of view.

Over the years, different middleware technologies have appeared solving the problem of distributed communication. In the same way, the different application models and software paradigms have appeared, and new middleware paradigms have provided extended functionality over the common communication facilities. This is the

[*] This work has been partly funded by the iLAND project (ARTEMIS-JU 100026) funded by the ARTEMIS JTU Call 1 and the Spanish Ministry of Industry, Commerce, and Tourism. Also, this work has been partly funded by the ARTISTDesign NoE (IST-2007-214373) of the EU 7th Framework Programme.

A. Romanovsky and T. Vardanega (Eds.): Ada-Europe 2011, LNCS 6652, pp. 132–146, 2011.

case of the middleware developed in [2] where support for service-oriented paradigms, real-time communication, service-based composition, and time-deterministic reconfiguration is provided. This extended functionality is an added-value on top of the communication infrastructure services of the middleware. This added-value functionality can be ported to different underlying infrastructure middleware if the complete architecture is appropriately designed for this goal. Failing in the design of the complete middleware architecture and the appropriate hooks will surely decrease the flexibility and applicability of the full middleware solution. As a matter of fact, the ease of porting the added-value functionality to different communication infrastructure middleware is directly related to how the architecture is conceived.

This paper presents a contribution to develop part of the highly-flexible iLAND middleware. This middleware is flexible enough to use different infrastructure communication levels; its architecture is developed explicitly to be independent of the distribution middleware technologies and upper added-value functionality (see figure 1). To reach this objective, the encapsulation of any middleware-specific details is performed hiding the details of the technologies and even their interaction paradigms, by means of using *common bridge*.

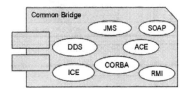

Fig. 1. Shows the *common bridge* component; it hides the complexity of the underlying distribution middleware technologies, increasing its transparency

The interface given by the common bridge to the added-value functionality must be extremely simple; it is necessary to hide the complexity of the communication middleware technologies in use. In fact, abstracting the complexity of the communications to create distributed systems is a clear objective of the communication middleware, and it is kept at all times by the common bridge. However, current solutions still manage a high complexity degree. This is because the creation of an abstraction enabling a distributed system to perform as standalone requires managing complex communication interactions which is not an easy task. This task becomes even harder when the different middleware solutions introduce the quality of service (QoS) parameters used to model, in a more accurate manner, the communications between different hosts. However, managing QoS parameters is key for the middleware in distributed real-time embedded systems (DRE).

An essential part of this work is the creation of mechanisms to provide a generic way to interact from the developed *common bridge* with the QoS parameters of the abstracted distribution middleware technologies.

The creation of standards mitigates in part the complexity problem and enables the use of independent middleware components. Nevertheless, even some standard middleware as DDS [3] or CORBA [4] present have highly complex interfaces to be used straightforward. Therefore, this is another problem that adds to the traditional (and understandable) resistance of some networked real-time domains and software developers to integrate middleware technologies. The use of an external software that will be an essential part of the developed applications implies a risk in terms of software obsolescence, licensing and in sum, control over the final software product. For example, some DDS standard compliant implementations are mainly used as a technology for aerospace, military and transportation projects but not in other domains like domotics or e-health where it would be as useful but more costly.

To present the developed *common bridge*, this paper is structured as follows. Section 2 defines in detail the concept of middleware in its traditional communication-oriented view and similar approaches for maximum flexibility, independence, and portability. Section 3 presents the main abstractions of the common bridge and its structure. Section 4 details the proposed API. Finally, in section 5, the validation of the component is performed. Section 6 presents the conclusions and future work.

2 Background and Related Work

This section presents interesting background work on the definition of the middleware concept and a brief explanation of the architectural model taken as reference in its *classical meaning*. Also, the different approaches for architecting middleware transparency are presented, as well as the issues involved in the attempt to decrease its complexity and other derived issues like maximizing interoperability.

There are multiple uses of the concept of *middleware*, but not all of them are appropriate nor even informed. As mentioned before, this work is based on the classical definition of middleware provided by Schantz and Schmidt [1] related to the origin of this term: *communication middleware*. To be more precise, they divide the middleware in four layers and explain the functionalities of each one. The focus of this work is on the *distribution middleware layer*, which enables to program the distributed systems like stand-alone applications. The objective is to increase the transparency of the enabling technologies (see figure 2). The distribution middleware technologies are diverse: DDS, RMI[5], JMS[6], CORBA, RT_CORBA[7], ICE[8], etc., and they communicate using paradigms as message oriented middleware (MOM), remote procedure call (RPC), object remote broker (ORB), peer-to-peer (P2P), or more innovative ones like publish/subscribe (P/S), and any other not yet classified. Depending of the communication paradigm the enabling solutions will require a different degree of sophistication and complexity. The classifying of all these middleware depends of multiple variables and points of view, and there are researches focused just in this task as it is done in [9, 10].

The use of different middleware as communication backbone has already been done in [11]. PolyORB is presented as a *schizophrenic* middleware that can support distribution with different personalities: CORBA, RT-CORBA, or DSA [12]. With the *common bridge* component the target is similar, but it has been created in a different way. The iLAND common bridge focuses at not only giving different personalities to the middleware, but also at providing a transparent component to use the different middleware technologies. The component transparency is one of the principles in the architecture of the software ecosystems [13]. This kind of systems, manage the complexity using transparency and modular design with translucence interfaces. In this work, some of the ideas of the software ecosystems are going to be used to provide the maximum transparency to the developed *common bridge* component. Moreover, interface uncertainty is used to manage the QoS parameters of the different middleware technologies.

Another similar approach is the presented in the work of [14] where an abstraction over the peer-to-peer overlays is given to "facilitate independent innovation in overlay services and applications" based on an API proposal. Although there is some distance between our proposal and [14], the theoretical problems faced are similar; therefore, proposing an API is an essential part our work too.

Up to now, in this section, we have explained how transparency has been tackled in other approaches where complexity and interoperability problems appear as lateral issues overcome by the fact of increasing the transparency.

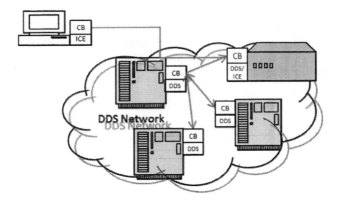

Fig. 2. Illustrates the interoperability of different communication middleware technologies using the common bridge

There are, however, other approaches that focus directly on the interoperability and complexity problems. Frameworks like [15] or the protocol-bridging are presented in [16] for achieving interoperability through introducing more complexity to the system. Other solutions, as DDS, deal with complexity by creating a standard API that enables the use of independent middleware components. However, even with the standard, the complexity degree is high, and simpler APIs are merging. The best example is SimD [17], an API based on DDS (but outside of the standard) to simplify the creation of DDS applications.

3   The *Common Bridge* Abstraction

This section explains the main ideas that lead to the creation of an abstraction level developed as a piece of software in the middleware architecture (the iLAND middleware *common bridge*) and how it has been defined.

Every system must provide higher level abstractions in order to be used with a reasonable effort. In this case the created abstraction increases the transparency of the different upper levels with the distribution middleware. The upper levels are the applications and the middleware layers: *common middleware functionality* and *domain-specific middleware functionality*.

Another important issue to be explained are the QoS parameters; most distribution middleware technologies for real-time environments have some level of QoS parameters to model the communication and even the execution characteristics of local and distributed threads. The type of QoS parameters used is mostly specific of the technology and target domain so having some kind of mechanism that enables their usage becomes a key issue.

3.1 Communication Abstraction

The architecting of the *common bridge* component requires to keep in mind a clear separation among the existing distribution middleware technologies; two are the main identified: event communication and client/server communication technologies. This division allows to benefit from the performance characteristics of both worlds that mainly provide synchronous and asynchronous communication models, respectively.

This work names both approaches as the synchronous and asynchronous modes. To be more specific, following the defined communication schemes defined for WS*, the most widespread services architecture defined in [18], the synchronous communication implements *request/response* scheme and the asynchronous communication implements the *fire&forget* scheme.

In the request/response scheme, a source service sends a message to a destination, and it waits until it receives the response (either full-content message or a message indicating no response). In the other hand, the destination entity receives the request message, processes it, and transmits back the response. In the fire&forget scheme, the sending source sends a message with a destination address without any kind of synchronism with the destination entity. The decision taken of having two models for two communication schemes will affect to the full *common bridge* component, especially in the interaction with higher levels. The API proposal will need to manage functions enabling the two different ways to communicate. This introduces some more logic inside the common bridge at the cost of architecting a powerful communication model supporting the two major communication paradigms.

The next step is defining the architecture of the *common bridge* component. Taking as main reference how the middleware definition in layers was performed, this component is structured following a three layered hierarchy, as it can be seen in figure 3.

The top layer of the component is the *common bridge layer*. The name coincides with the naming of the whole component since it is its interface to both sides: (1) the applications and (2) the backbone communication infrastructure of the underlying middleware. The main goals of the *common bridge layer* are:

- To maximize the degree of independence enabling transparency,
- To achieve a high degree of simplicity in the design,

One of the key elements for achieving these objectives is the API definition. It is defined as generic as possible as it will be explained in the next paragraphs; the specific data types and functions are detailed in section 4.

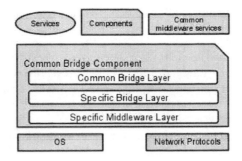

Fig. 3. Presents the general architecture of the *common bridge*

As it is stated in software ecosystems, to provide transparency, the information in the component interfaces must be minimized. So, the different parameters, structures, or entities involved in a middleware communication have been divided by their functionality in *common* ones (the minimal and essential information), and *modeling* ones. In the first group includes principal characteristics as source, destination, and data to be exchanged. This does not mean every middleware uses them in a direct way; for example, MoM aggregated these characteristics to define a queue. However, with these principal characteristics, the basic communication in middleware technologies can always be created. Moreover, modeling structures, parameters and entities allow to shape the communication. Following again the MoM example, modeling parameters define the number of elements in the message queue or the queuing disciple, among others.

To create the communication in a transparent way, the interactions between the higher levels and the *common bridge* must be defined in a generic way in order to satisfy all the middleware technologies. Furthermore, in these interactions, only the common parameters will be directly involved; modeling parameters will be encapsulated and managed through a QoS structure as explained in section 3.2.

The strategic location of the *common bridge* makes it receive and send data to the applications. Reception is performed through the specific receptacle parameters of its API. Data is sent by using callback functions, that is either data exchanged in the communications or data related to the communications (communication states essentially).

A different way to perform this task is through the return parameters of the functions. This option was discarded because this can only be used on synchronous models. Also, the wait/notify mechanism between middleware and the applications has been tested. It can be implemented with the provided API, but for simplicity (one of our objectives), the callbacks are preferred.

The second layer is the *specific bridge* (see figure 4) and its main objectives are:

- The transformation of the provided data and the datatypes of the *common bridge*,
- The creation of the different structures involved in the communication.

In this layer, programmers with expertise in the specific middleware technology that is chosen can hide the complexity of the distribution middleware using the *common bridge* interface. For this purpose, the communication entities must be created and modeling parameters for the communication must be initialized. This is done by using the API of the specific middleware technology and implementing additional logic to cover unsolved issues. Finally, it also has to deal with the different data types proposed in the *common bridge* API and with the data types that the distribution middleware handles.

Finally, in the low level layer there is the *specific middleware layer* consisting of the specific implementation of a distribution middleware paradigm. This distribution middleware manages the common communication issues (serializing, de-serializing, addressing, discovering); if any of these is not provided, it must be created in the *specific bridge* logic.

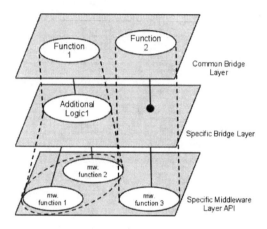

Fig. 4. Shows the *specific bridge* functionality in the context of the three layers of the *common bridge* component

As a final remark, with the proposed architecture, it is possible to have different middleware technologies to be used for the modeling of the synchronous and the asynchronous communication modes. The cost of this improvement is an increase of the complexity of the *specific middleware* layer because of the need of some mechanisms to share data in the different technologies. When supporting both communication modes, it is the usual case that the system performs better for one of them. As an example, DDS middleware has better performance for the fire&forget scheme, but it loses performance implementing request/response.

3.2 QoS Abstraction

Different middleware approaches model the communication performance in a non homogeneous way. Mostly, it is done by specifying QoS parameters but other entities may be involved as well.

In our approach, we focus on the analysis of the QoS parameters of the different middleware technologies to determine the communication behavior. In the *common bridge*, the management of the QoS properties uses two concurrent mechanisms:

- Additional logic in the *specific bridge* to manage the static QoS,
- A QoS component that uses information of the *common bridge* component interface and interacts with the *specific bridge* to handle the dynamic QoS.

In the additional logic of the *specific bridge*, the QoS parameters common for all the communications of the system are set. It means that we configure the middleware technology to manage the communication with this QoS.

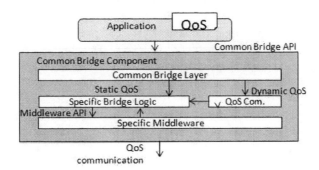

Fig. 5. Shows that the QoS component interactions handle the dynamic QoS and the specific bridge logic handles the static QoS

The QoS component models one specific communication. This component in its simpler version consists in a mapping of the high level QoS parameters specified by the applications into structures, entities, or QoS parameters of the specific middleware technology.

This component must be located over the *common bridge*; although, it is not a requirement of the proposed architecture, it adds dynamism to the system communications. Figure 5 shows the interaction among components.

4   Common Bridge API

The *common bridge* API (summarized in table 1) is described in a language closer to C; however, it can be easily defined and implemented for Ada and even Java. This section first defines the types used in the API; later, the functions are defined and explained.

4.1   Data Types

- Domain is a 20 Bytes String to identify a service domain in the system. *Source* and *destination* are domains of services.
- The cb_data is a structure containing two elements:
  - Length, a 32 bits integer representing the size of the sent data.
  - Data, a sequence of bytes containing the information.

- The QoS is a structure which contains a sequence of QoS parameters.
- The rec_ptr is the pointer to a callback function in the service to receive the data. It also can be used as pointer to implement the reception of wait/notify signals.

4.2 Asynchronous Functions

- int create_listener (domain, rec_ptr). This operation initializes all the needed structures to create a listening connection attached to a specific domain. When a message is received, the data is stored in a local variable through the rec_ptr. This is very similar to the way the hardware interruptions work. The function returns an int type to notify if the operation has been completed or to send to the upper levels an error code.
- int close_listener (domain). This function closes the specific listening connection associated to a domain. The int type that the operation returns works in the same way as explained in the creation of the listener.
- void send_async (domain, cb_data, qos). This operation sends a specific number of bytes to a destination domain where a listener is supposed to be waiting to receive the data. This sending operation is non-blocking and no response is expected as it was explained for the fire&forget scheme.

4.3 Synchronous Functions

- int create_server (domain, rec_ptr). It starts all the needed structures to create a receiving connection attached to a specific domain for the service, and it uses the callback function to manage the data and answer to each request.
- int close_server (domain). This function closes the specific listening connection associated to a domain.
- cb_data send_sync (source, destination, cb_data, qos). It sends a specific number of bytes to a destination domain where a server is supposed to be waiting to receive the data. The source entity domain is specified because the replying entity needs to know who is going to get the response. This sending operation blocks the sender until the reception of the response message.

Table 1. Shows the *common bridge* API

Model	Function	Parameters	Return
Fire&Forget	create_listener	domain, rec_ptr	int
	close_listener	domain	int
	send_async	destination, cb_data, qos	void
Request/ Response	create_server	domain, rec_ptr	int
	close_server	domain	int
	send_sync	destination, source, cb_data, qos	cb_data

5 Validation

In this section, the architecture and the API presented are going to be applied DDS and to the complete iLAND architecture. This scenario has been chosen for various reasons. First, DDS middleware is a standard, implementing one of the newest communication paradigms for the distribution middleware based on *publish/subscribe* and decoupled communication between entities. The modeling of the communication is performed through a comprehensive set of QoS parameters also related to time that provide soft real-time capacities. Second, the composition of services over a SOA (service-oriented architectures) for networked embedded systems is a new and interesting field of research on the real-time technologies that are progressively integrating it. To provide the distribution capabilities to the SOA paradigm, the *common bridge* layer must support different kinds of interactions between the services and the infrastructure.

The validation work is described in two sections. Section 5.1 explains the use of the *common bridge* API with the service architecture defined in [2], and then, in section 5.2, the implementation of the *common bridge* is explained over the DDS standard.

5.1 Use of the *Common Bridge* in the iLAND Middleware

The iLAND project creates an architecture defined and explained in [2]. iLAND targets at supporting real-time distributed service oriented systems. In such a context, application services perform several interactions types among themselves and also with the iLAND middleware. Further details are provided in [19], but in essence, the middleware supports registering of application services in the system, composition of services, and it controls their execution. Every application service is mapped to a single task execution, and it has associated QoS parameters. A set of tasks (services) can be composed in a sequence to offer an enhanced functionality; such a set is called an application.

Following, we present a validation by providing a simplified model that uses two kinds of interactions: application and infrastructure. The infrastructure interactions take place in two forms (see figure 6): (1) between services and the middleware components, or (2) among the middleware components. On the other side, the application interactions happen only between application services.

Any application will have a set of services and a set of infrastructure components to carry out diverse functionalities that work as a distributed system over the *common bridge*. This means that the *common bridge* API supports that the architecture may execute in a standalone mode.

The infrastructure interactions take place as commands; therefore, a request/ response interaction is appropriate for this scheme. Infrastructure components communicate via the synchronous API. In the case of the interactions between applications, the asynchronous API is the natural option.

The next step is the definition of domains and QoS properties related to the infrastructure and application interactions. In the case of the infrastructure, they are set in a specific range reserved for the system. In the case of the services, they are uniquely identified in the architecture; this ID defines the domain of their communications and enables dynamic creation. The definition of QoS properties is, therefore, application/service dependent; therefore, it will be established by the service/application programmer.

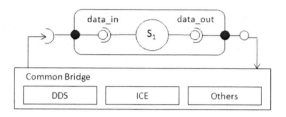

Fig. 6. Shows iLAND service interaction model over the common bridge

Several validation demonstrators have been created, ranging from the typical (and simple) `HelloWorld` to a data-streaming real-time video surveillance. In the first example, each service adds a word to the string "`Hello iLAND world`" every second. This requires to send small amounts of data periodically. Observing the actual behavior of this example indicates that the kind of data managed by the applications is better supported by a specific middleware approach. In the same way, RTP transport protocol is used for isochronous communication or TCP for information that requires higher reliability, since it uses its connection oriented approach and retransmission windows to avoid packet loss. This is the key point to creating a transparent middleware component.

5.2 *Common Bridge* Implementation

This section shows how an existing distribution middleware technology (DDS) can be integrated in the proposed *common bridge* API without losing language specific expression capabilities. The validation takes a functional point of view since the objective of the *common bridge* is providing transparency of the middleware. This way, the main advantages and performance issues of the architecture will be given by the different middleware technologies to be used; the selection must be carefully studied to maximize performance. The main challenge has been to check if the *common bridge* could maximize the use of the complex DDS standard with an Ada front-end.

In the next paragraphs, it will be detailed the essentials of the implementation of the *common bridge* for the synchronous and asynchronous models in the DDS standard followed by a description of the QoS parameters management.

The asynchronous scheme is modeled through the creation of a DDS *topic*: asynchronous topic. This topic is then divided in subtopics through the specific DDS *partition* QoS parameter. The partitions are created only when a new domain requests it through the `create_listener` or `send_async` functions of the *common bridge* API. So, the management of the DDS entities is related essentially to the domain parameter of the *common bridge* API. Finally, the pointer parameter specified in the creation of a listener is attached to a specific DDS entity, called *listener*, which manages the reception of data.

The definition of the asynchronous topic contains the fields: id (to implement different queues for instances) and length&data (to implement the cb_data structure defined by the API).

Regarding the QoS parameters of DDS, some of them are directly set in this *specific bridge* layer and others are set at a higher level (service level). The low level specified parameters will be the same for every asynchronous communication, static. The service level parameters will model the services communication dynamically. The DDS QoS parameters specified as static are the *data availability* which is specified as transient, the *data delivery* which is not reliable, the *resource consumption* which is set to use the minimum data possible; finally, the *timeliness QoS parameters* are the dynamic ones.

The synchronous scheme requires more complexity than the asynchronous one. The reason for this is that DDS provides decoupled event communication. To create the request/response scheme, two main approaches were studied:

- Creating two different topics for the request and the response,
- Adding a new parameter in the topic to define if a message is a request or a response.

This last solution is the implemented approach because it was prioritized having the minimum topics possible and also, this solution boosts the performance with other mechanisms of the DDS standard as the content_filtered_topic. Figures 7 and 8 show the asynchronous and the synchronous topic definitions in IDL and adapted for Ada.

The management of the DDS entities and the different queues are developed in a similar way. In the asynchronous communication, it is done by using the domain parameter of the function create_server and send_sync of the *common bridge* API.

```
module Common_Bridge {
    struct async_topic {
        long domain_id;
        struct cb_data {
            long length;
            sequence <octet, 2000> data;
        }
    }; #key async_topic domain_id
    struct sync_topic {
        long domain_id;
        octet type;
        struct cb_data {
            long length;
            sequence <octet, 200> data;
        }
    }; #key sync_topic domain_id
};
```

Fig. 7. Shows the DDS topics definition for the *common bridge* in IDL

```
package Common_Bridge is
async_topic_TypeName:DDS.String := DDS.To_DDS_String ("async_topic");
   type async_topic is record
       domain_id : DDS.Long;
       length : DDS.Long;
       data : DDS_OctetSeq;
   end record;
pragma Convention (C,async_topic);

sync_topic_TypeName:DDS.String := DDS.To_DDS_String("sync_topic");
   type sync_topic is record
       domain_id : DDS.Long;
       type : DDS.Octet;
       length : DDS.Long;
       data : DDS_OctetSeq;
   end record;
pragma Convention (C, sync_topic);
```

Fig. 8. Shows the DDS topics definition for the *common bridge* in Ada

Regarding the management of the QoS parameters, the functionality is the same exposed in the asynchronous model. Also, the value specified for the data availability is transient. Similarly, the value specified for the data delivery is reliable, for the minimal resource consumption to improve reliability. Finally, the timeliness QoS parameters are left to be established at higher level in the QoS component.

Table 2. Using distribution middleware technologies with the *common bridge*

	DDS	ICE	RTSJ	JMS
Complexity of the implementation	Simple (implemented)	Simple	Hard	Hard
Managing QoS	Static: good Dynamic: fine (worst performance)	Good	Good	Good
Interoperability over CB	Good	Good	Good	Good
Remarkable issues	Depending of the implementation needs launching external processes.	ICE needs to run a server process and addressing it.	Interaction with the Virtual Machine.	The use of JMS is difficult due to the interacting with J2EE server.

Although the current implementation is over DDS, other technologies have been analyzed for obtaining conclusions about the ease of usage of the common bridge with other relevant approaches with different programming languages. DDS has already been integrated since it most naturally fits the service oriented paradigm and decoupled interaction. However, other technologies such as Ada Glade also offer interesting properties that are currently being considered for adapting the *common bridge*. Table 2 shows how different middleware technologies perform with the *common bridge* as a result of the current analysis.

6 Conclusions

The presented work has presented the architecture of a software component, the *common bridge*, to use distribution middleware technologies in a more transparent way, especially considering the management of QoS parameters. Also, it has been presented the common bridge API, that enables the interaction of the higher levels with the developed component abstracting the complexity of the distribution middleware layer.

The component has been validated by (1) implementing it over a specific middleware standard, DDS, and (2) creating the infrastructure of a service oriented application containing different services that used the component to interact as a standalone system. The implementation of this component using DDS middleware technology demonstrates that the proposed architecture provides sufficient expression capabilities to support not only the middleware communication under a publish/subscribe paradigm, but also the management of a full set of QoS parameters.

Current and future work is developing new full implementations over other middleware technologies, measuring the complexity of the provided *common bridge* API by software design methods compared to the standard middleware APIs.

References

1. Schantz, R.E., Schmidt, D.C.: Middleware for distributed systems. In: Evolving the Common Structure for Network-Centric Applications. Encyclopedia of Software Engineering (2001)
2. García-Valls, M., Rodríguez-López, I., Fernández-Villar, L., Estévez-Ayres, I., Basanta-Val, P.: Towards a middleware architecture for deterministic reconfiguration of service-based networked applications. In: Proc. of the 15th IEEE Int'l Conference on Emerging Technologies and Factory Automation - ETFA 2010, Bilbao, Spain, September 13-16 (2010)
3. OMG.: A Data Distribution Service for Real-time Systems Version 1.2. Real-Time Systems (2007)
4. OMG.: Common Object Request Broker Architecture (CORBA) Specification, Version 3.1. Interfaces (2008)
5. Wollrath, A., Riggs, R., Waldo, J.: A Distributed Object Model for the Java System. USENIX Computing Systems 9(4) (1996)
6. Hapner, J.M., et al.: Java Message Service (JMS) Specification v1.1. (April 2002)
7. OMG.: Real-time CORBA Specification (2005)
8. ZeroC Inc.: The Internet Communications Engine (2003), http://www.zeroc.com/ice.html
9. Ibrahim, N.: Orthogonal Classification of Middleware Technologies. In: 3rd International Conference on Mobile Ubiquitous Computing, Systems, Services and Technologies UBICOMM 2009, pp. 46–51 (11-16, 2009)

10. Pérez, H., Gutiérrez, J., Sangorrin, D., Harbour, M.: Real-time distribution middleware from the ada perspective. In: Kordon, F., Vardanega, T. (eds.) Ada-Europe 2008. LNCS, vol. 5026, pp. 268–281. Springer, Heidelberg (2008)
11. PolyORB, http://polyorb.objectweb.org/
12. Tucker Taft, S., Duff, R.A., Brukardt, R.L., Plödereder, E., Leroy, P.: Ada 2005 Reference Manual. LNCS, vol. 4348. Springer, Heidelberg (2006)
13. Cataldo, M., Herbsleb, J.D.: Architecting in software ecosystems: interface translucence as an enabler for scalable collaboration. In: Proceedings of the Fourth European Conference on Software Architecture: Companion Volume, pp. 65–72. ACM, New York (2010)
14. Dabek, F., Zhao, B., Druschel, P., Kubiatowicz, J., Stoica, I.: Towards a common API for structured peer-to-peer overlays. Peer-to-Peer Systems II, 33–44 (2003)
15. Berler, A., Pavlopoulos, S., Koutsouris, D.: Design of an interoperability framework in a regional healthcare system. In: Conference Proceedings: Annual International Conference of the IEEE Engineering in Medicine and Biology Society, vol. 4, pp. 3093–3096 (2004)
16. Moon, K.-d., Lee, Y.-h., Lee, C.-e., Son, Y.-s.: Design of a universal middleware bridge for device interoperability in heterogeneous home network middleware. IEEE Transactions on Consumer Electronics 51, 314–318 (2005)
17. Data Distribution Portal, Simple DDS (2010),
    http://www.omgwiki.org/dds/content/document/
18. W3C: Web Services Architecture Usage Scenarios
19. http://www.w3.org/TR/2002/WD-ws-arch-scenarios-20020730 (2002)
20. Garcia-Valls, M., Basanta-Val, P., Estevez-Ayres, I.: A component model for homogeneous implementation of reconfigurable service-based distributed real-time applications. In: Proc. of the 10th Annual Int'l Conference on New Technologies of Distributed Systems (NOTERE - DANCE Workshop), pp. 267–272 (2010)

Using Robotics as a Motivational Tool: An Ada Interface to a Pioneer Robot*

Rigoberto Chil, Diego Alonso, Francisco Ortiz, Juan Pastor

Division of Systems and Electronic Engineering (DSIE)
Technical University of Cartagena, Campus Muralla del Mar, E-30202, Spain
diego.alonso@upct.es

Abstract. The new European Higher Education Area encourages student centred learning, which puts the focus on the learner and his needs, rather than being
centred around the teacher's input. This paper presents an initiative that revolves
around the use of a real robot and a robot simulator with two main objectives: make
learning programming languages more appealing to undergraduate students, and
to have a platform that can be still used in postgraduate and master courses. The
interface with the simulator and the real robot has been programmed in Ada, and
it is also being used in our current Research and Development projects.

1 Introduction and Motivation

Motivating students when teaching programming languages is an arduous and difficult
task. One of the main reasons for this, in our opinion, is that the simplicity and limitations of the used examples and proposed problems do not motivate students enough
to go into knowing programming languages in depth. Also, they give students the false
impression that what they are learning is of little use, since all they do is solving simple calculations, like quadratic equations, calculating Fibonacci numbers, a number's
factorial, bubble sort ten numbers, etc.

The purpose of the Bologna Process [1] is to create the *European Higher Education
Area* (EHEA) by making academic degree standards and quality assurance standards
more comparable and compatible throughout Europe. The Bologna Process currently
has 46 participating countries, whereas there are only 27 Member States of the European Union. The new EHEA encourages the development and adoption of new learning
techniques [2], such as autonomous and problem-based learning [3] for students. In this
new reality, the kind of exercises described above does not meet the requirements of
the EHEA. This situation is even more important when considering higher and master courses, since students must then apply transversal skills, such as teamwork ability,
ability to put knowledge into practice, adaptation to new situations, etc.

Laboratories and practical classes play a crucial role in the curriculum of scientists
and engineers [4], and the acquisition of practical skills is one of the main requirements
of the Bologna process. In this vein, it is worth mentioning related initiatives such as
the one described in [5], where the authors describe a laboratory for teaching Robotics.

* This work has been partially supported by the Spanish CICYT Project EXPLORE
(ref. TIN2009-08572) and the Séneca Proyect MISSION-SICUVA (ref. 15374/PI/10).

A. Romanovsky and T. Vardanega (Eds.): Ada-Europe 2011, LNCS 6652, pp. 147–159, 2011.
© Springer-Verlag Berlin Heidelberg 2011

With this in mind, we think that building simple robotics control programs will allow us to achieve a number of closely related objectives. Firstly, we think that the use of a simulator will increase students motivation as well as show them the usefulness of what they are learning. Secondly, using a simulator enables us to propose problems of different size and levels of complexity, according to the students level, without being limited by the access to a single robot. Lastly, Robotics is a traditional research area for the DSIE Research Group, and in this sense, using a robot or a simulator enables us to transfer part of our research to students, as well as to attract interested students.

On the other hand, the use of simulators is justified by itself, since before these robots are put to work, they need to be tested under different conditions. As mobile robots are used extensively for their ability to navigate and perform tasks in unstructured environments (space exploration, military surveillance, nuclear power industry, security, etc.), simulators play a key role during these early stages of the robot development, as they will give designers an idea of how the robot is going to behave [6]. Their use can avoid the robot suffering damage in the early tests, while it makes it possible to have many people working in parallel, testing their algorithms against their own simulators. This last advantage is crucial for teaching, since students can safely and concurrently crash their virtual robots while testing their programs.

In 2010 we started teaching the subject *"Applied Computing"* in the first year of the *Bachelor in Industrial Electronics and Automation Engineering* [7], and in two years' time we will start teaching *"Real-Time Systems Programming"*. Finally, we also teach *"Software Development for Real-Time Systems"* in *Master in Information and Communication Technologies* [8]. And we plan to use the simulator and the real robot in all of them.

Our research background began in the early 90s., integrating new paradigms in the service robot development process as they emerged [9,10]. During the early years (1993–1998), our efforts were directed at the development of software for various kinds of tele-operated robots to perform maintenance tasks in nuclear power plants; during a second phase (1999–2006),we built applications for ship-hull cleaning robots. All this time, we have been applying all the possibilities offered by Software Engineering, from the use of Structured and Object-Oriented programming paradigms in early developments, to the recent adoption of the Model-Driven Software Development (MDSD) approach.

Nowadays, we are involved in the EXPLORE Research and Development project, whose main objective is to develop and implement a set of methods and tools for real-time systems development incorporating design patterns, a component-oriented approach, and MDSD techniques for the design and validation as well as for the automatic code generation for the target platform. We use three robots as case study: a small robot developed by us, a golf cart also modified by us, and a commercial Pioneer 3–AT robot. And we want to use the same interface with all of them. This reason led us to develop the application described in this paper.

The Pioneer robot has helped us uniting our teaching and researching facets. On the teaching hand, its manufacturer provides a simulator that has the same interface and that accepts the same commands with the same protocol as the real robot. Thus, we have an excellent platform in which students can test their programming skills. On the other hand, the Pioneer is an excellent and robust platform that already provides the

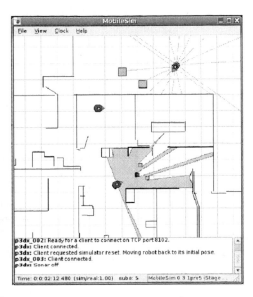

Fig. 1. Pictures of the Pioneer P3–AT robot (left) and screen shot of the MobileSim simulator (right). Simulator screen capture extracted from http://robots.mobilerobots.com/wiki/MobileSim

low-level control facilities, which allows developers to focus on higher-level aspects. Fig. 1 shows a couple of pictures of the robot and a screen-shot of the simulator.

This paper presents the design and implementation details of the already mentioned interface with both the real Pioneer P3–AT robot [11] and the MobileSim simulator [12] in Ada, as a continuation and improvement of a previous work [13]. The following two sections are devoted to present a brief review of the technical background, and to describe the developed interface with the Pioneer robot and its simulator. Section 4 presents some examples of the kind of applications that students must develop, depending on the course level. And finally section 5 concludes and presents some future work.

2   Technical Background: Hardware and Software Involved

Since the target robot of the software described in this paper is a *Pioneer 3-AT* mobile robot (P3–AT), it is worth describing first its main characteristics, the software installed in the robot and the available software for controlling it.

The Pioneer family of robots is sold as a research tool, used in many universities and companies around the world as the main physical research platform. These kind of robots are programmable intelligent platforms equipped with the basic devices for navigation and sensing in the real world. They are part of an extensive family of robots released in 1995 by the company Mobile Robots [14]. Specifically, the P3–AT is provided with high resolution motion encoders with inertial correction to compensate for skid steering (that is, when the wheels skid encoders are still counting revolutions even though the robot is not really moving as the encoders indicate), reversible DC motors and motor controllers, as well as the four-wheel skid steer which carries out the balanced drive system of the robot. The P3–AT robot can carry a payload of up to 40 kg, reaches speeds up to 0.7 m/s, it can climb steep up to 45% grades and sills of 9 cm. The P3–AT is equipped with eight front and eight rear sonars, and a SICK laser scanner that senses obstacles from 15 cm to 7 m. In order to handle the low-level control details of the mobile robot (e.g. maintaining the platform's drive speed and heading, acquiring sensor readings, etc.), the P3–AT uses a high-performance 32-bits micro-controller with the embedded robot control software developed by its manufacturer, ARCOS (*Advanced Robot Control and Operations Software*).

The Pioneer 3–AT requires a PC to run client software for intelligent robotics command and control operations. As shown in Fig. 2, the robot follows a client-server architecture: ARCOS operates as a server that manages all the low-level details of the mobile robot, while the client role is played by the software running on a computer connected with the robot micro-controller via the host serial link. The high-level functionality and behaviour of the robot, such as obstacle avoidance, path planning, features recognition, localization, navigation, and so on, must be provided by the client software.

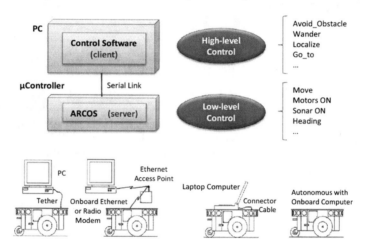

Fig. 2. Some possibilities to connect a client PC to the robot server

As said in the introduction, the manufacturer also offers *MobileSim*, a 2D simulator for their robots, together with its C++ source code distributed under the terms of the GNU General Public License. Communication with the simulator is done through TCP/IP using the same protocol as with the real robot (ARCOS commands), although not each and every feature and command are currently supported by the simulator. The simulator is also capable of simulating several robots, which are controlled through different network sockets. This feature provides additional possibilities to the use of the simulator, since it is now possible to develop applications where the simulated robots must collaborate.

While using ARCOS for the low-level control of the robot is mandatory, there are two main options for selecting the client software, namely: (i) use any of the available robotic frameworks, including the one provided by the manufacturer, or (ii) write your own robotics control software in order to have greater control of its behaviour. After describing briefly in the following paragraphs the advantages and disadvantages of both options, we will justify why we have adopted the second option.

Specific middleware and framework technologies for developing software for autonomous mobile robots have matured, evolved and improved during the last years. They all facilitate design reuse and provide the typical functionality that is common in the domain. The fact that robots from different manufacturers have completely different hardware platforms and their own development environments, has forced developers to pay special attention to the abstraction of the lowest levels, trying thereby to design a common API for programming them all. Thus, many manufacturers provide development platforms for their robots, like ARIA (for the robots built by MobileRobots), Mobility (for the robots developed by iRobot), Open-R (for the Sony Aibo), etc. There are also other initiatives that are not promoted by any manufacturer, such as Player/Stage, which provides a common abstraction for many robotic platforms that facilitates the development of control applications. It is possible to find a very detailed comparison of their characteristics in [6].

These frameworks standardize and simplify the low-level control aspects of the chosen robot. They usually provide access to abstract sensors and actuators, which exhibit a simpler interface and greater functionality than directly accessing the hardware through the operating system. Further raising the level of complexity, other frameworks such as OROCOS, CARMEN, ORCA, and MARIE, to mention a few, include features commonly used in robotics, such as control algorithms, localization and mapping, safe navigation, etc. A summary of the main features of these kind of high-level frameworks together with a comparison chart of their characteristics can be found in [15,16]. Finally, the manufacturer of the P3–AT offers ARIA (*Advanced Robotics Interface for Applications*), which provides a client-side interface to a variety of intelligent behaviours already programmed. ARIA is released under the GNU Public License, fully documented C++, Java and Python libraries and source code, but there is no Ada version available.

Though robotics frameworks provide much tested and working code, which enables developers to start programming the robot easily and quickly, there are some cases in which you want to have strict control of what the robot is executing, or in which using a framework is not suitable. For instance, frameworks such as ARIA offer typical algorithms for localization and mapping, but they offer no temporal guarantees and suffer the "inversion of control" (or the "Hollywood principle") problem [17], in which the flow of control of a system is inverted in comparison to procedural programming. That is, the framework code deals with the program execution order, but the business code is encapsulated by the called subroutines (developed by framework users). Thus, developers have no control over tasking characteristics, e.g. number of tasks, type, priority, etc., since they are determined by the framework design.

At the educational level, ARIA is written in C++, and though we could have used the facilities for interfacing with other languages that Ada offers, as described in [18], we decided not to do that. In that work, a Player-Ada binding is built using import C facilities. We did not do something similar because it would still present the inversion of control problem, and because using the ARIA framework would still be complex, making the student feel overwhelmed by the overall structure of the framework.

Besides, the objective we pursue in our courses is not teaching students to manage any of these frameworks (which might be of interest to other subjects more related to robotics), but using the robot as a platform for setting out different types of problems. Thus, we simply need to have direct access to the basic functionality offered by the robot, as discussed in the next section. In such cases, it is necessary to control the P3–AT robot simply via the ARCOS client-server interface.

As an added value for our research and for the robotics community, we offer a very simple Ada interface, which is as transparent as possible, so that developers know at all times what data is being used and also have complete control over tasking issues, e.g. their number, periods, priorities, etc.

3   Architecture of the Application

As explained in the previous section, in order to have strict control of the execution of tasks in the robot, we decided to develop an abstraction layer to access directly to ARCOS. Fig. 3 shows a deployment diagram of the two considered scenarios: direct access to the real robot through a serial port, and communication with the simulator through network sockets.

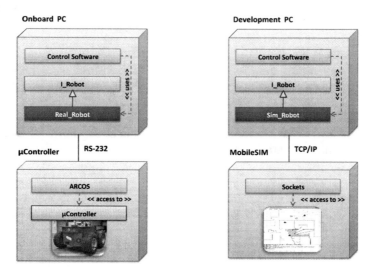

Fig. 3. Deployment diagram depicting the two considered scenarios: communication with the real robot and the simulator

As said before, one of the key requirements in the development was that the same program should drive the real and the simulated robots with minimum changes to the code. This is possible because the MobileSim simulator shares the same commands with the real Pioneer robot. Thus, we decided to create an interface (I_Robot, see Figures 3 and 4) that provides the functionality that is shared by both the simulator (Sim_Robot) and the real robot (Real_Robot), which are implemented as types derived from the already mentioned interface (see Fig. 5). These two types were implemented as protected objects, since they ensure mutual exclusion in the reading and writing access to

```
 1  package Pioneer_P3at is
 2     type T_Robot_Comm is (Serial , Socket);
 3     type Rt_Robot_Comm_Config (Comm : T_Robot_Comm) is record
 4        case Comm is
 5           when Serial =>
 6              Port_Number  : Positive := 1;
 7              Rate         : Gnat.Serial_Communications.Data_Rate :=
 8                             Gnat.Serial_Communications.B9600;
 9           when Socket =>
10              Address_Rec : GNAT.Sockets.Sock_Addr_Type := (Addr => Inet_Addr
11              ("127.0.0.1"), Port => 8101, Family => Family_Inet);
12        end case;
13     end record;
14
15     type I_Robot is synchronized interface;
16     procedure Read_Data (This : in out I_Robot) is abstract;
17     procedure Begin_Comm (This : in out I_Robot; Comm_Parm :
                 Rt_Robot_Comm_Config) is abstract;
18     procedure Write_Data (This : in  out I_Robot; Buffer : in Ada.Streams.
                 Stream_Element_Array) is abstract;
19     function Get_Posx (This : in  I_Robot) return Integer is abstract;
20     function Get_Posy (This : in  I_Robot) return Integer is abstract;
21        ...
22  end Pioneer_P3at;
```

Fig. 4. Definition of the synchronized interface and its (abstract) subprograms. Only 4 subprograms are shown, but a total of 14 have been defined.

```
 1
 2  package Pioneer_P3at.Real_Robot is
 3     type Pioneer_P3at is synchronized new I_Robot with private;
 4  private
 5     protected type Pioneer_P3at is new I_Robot with
 6        overriding procedure Read_Data;
 7        overriding procedure Begin_Comm (Comm_Parm : Rt_Robot_Comm_Config);
 8        overriding procedure Write_Data (Buffer : in Ada.Streams.
                 Stream_Element_Array);
 9        overriding function Get_Posx return Integer;
10        overriding function Get_Posy return Integer;
11        ...
12     end Pioneer_P3at;
13  end Pioneer_P3at.Real_Robot;
```

Fig. 5. Definition of the synchronized type implementing the communication with the real P3AT robot through a serial port. The Ada package for interfacing with the simulator is similar to this one.

the serial port and the network socket, through which the communication with the real robot and the simulator takes place. In this case, we decided to use the synchronized interface facility provided by Ada 2005 in order to implement the common interface and both protected objects. We created a totally passive structure comprising two protected types, since we decided that concurrency issues should be considered in higher layers by the code using the provided protected types. In this vein, we have a very versatile code, since it can be used in both single and multi-tasking applications.

ARCOS SIP packet structure

2 bytes	1 byte	1 byte	n bytes	2 bytes
Header	Byte Count	Type	Robot Data	CRC

ARCOS client command packet structure

2 bytes	1 byte	1 byte	1 byte	n bytes	2 bytes
Header	Byte Count	Command Number	Argument Type	Argument	CRC

Fig. 6. Structure of ARCOS commands: SIP command sent by the robot (top) and command sent by the client (bottom)

Once the communication is started, ARCOS sends periodically every 100 ms a special packet containing the robot status, the *Server Information Packet* (SIP). This packet is sent without waiting for the client to request it. The client program can read data sent from the robot, and send commands back to it asynchronously. The robot can send different types of information, each one of them has a specific data structure, but the packet structure remains always the same for the Header, Byte Count and Type bytes. Fig. 6 depicts the typical structure of ARCOS commands.

On the other hand, client commands have a different structure, but as can be seen in Fig. 6, it is almost always the same, changing only the arguments that depend on the chosen command. ARCOS commands can contain four different types of argument, namely none (the argument is empty), integer (16 bits signed integer), unsigned (16 bits unsigned integer), or string (array of characters with variable length). A brief description of some of the most frequently used ARCOS commands is shown in Table 1.

Table 1. Some of the most frequently used ARCOS=commands

Command	Number	Data	Description
PULSE/SYNC0	0	—	Keep the watchdog alive/ First synchrony packet
OPEN/SYNC1	1	—	Begin communication with the robot/Second synchrony packet
CLOSE/SYNC2	2	—	Finish communication with the robot/Third synchrony packet
ENABLE	4	Int	Enable or disable the motors
SONAR	28	Int	Enable or disable all the sonars, or some specific array of sonars
CONFIG	18	—	Request a configuration SIP
MOVE	8	Int	Translate X mm forward(+) or backward(-)
ROTATE	9	Int	Rotate X degrees counter-clockwise(+) or clockwise(-)
VEL	11	Int	Translate at a velocity X (mm/sec) forward(+) or backwards(-)

The client receives the SIP commands from ARCOS and stores the data in a structured way, allowing other parts of the program to access it. The client also takes care of sending to the robot the commands received from the higher layers, as well as keeping communications alive, by sending the ARCOS watchdog PULSE command every 100 ms.

3.1   Implementation of the Protected Objects

Figure 7 shows the package structure in which the code for communicating with the real and the simulated robot has been organized into. As can be seen, there is a parent package that contains the definition of the common synchronized interface (I_Robot), the common data types to be used, and the functions that generate the byte arrays corresponding to the ARCOS command to be sent (*Output_Gen* set of functions). Both protected types are implemented in separate child packages. They store the last update of the robot status and the communication configuration parameters. Finally, we have defined two private child packages that contain the data types that are used internally, and the supporting subprograms shared by both protected types, such as CRC calculation. It is worth describing some key details:

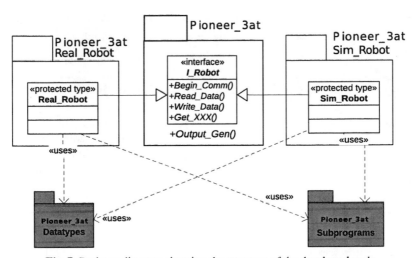

Fig. 7. Package diagram showing the structure of the developed code

- The *Begin_Comm* procedure must be called with the adequate configuration parameter, depending on whether the real robot or the simulator is going to be used. As said before, it is important to remember that the simulator can simulate one or more robots, which are available through different network ports. Thus, the configuration parameter (*Rt_Robot_Comm_Config*) must be set accordingly.
- The *Read_Data* procedure reads the last SIP command sent by the robot and updates the inner variables stored in the protected object. Then, it sends the watchdog command back to the robot in order to keep it alive, every 100 ms (the time that takes for ARCOS to send a new SIP). These variables can then be read by a set of *Get_XXX* functions, for instance *Get_Pos, Get_Vel, Get_Sonars*, etc.
- The *Output_Gen* functions receive a command number and optionally a set of arguments, and generate the adequate ARCOS commands. These functions only return the desired ARCOS command. It must then be sent to the robot by using the *Write_Data* procedure.

Lastly, this structure allows for a smooth transition between the code developed for the simulator and for the real robot, since it is only necessary to change the type of the protected object being used, as shown in Fig. 8. Thanks to the dispatching facilities obtained by the use of Ada interfaces, subprograms calls need not be modified.

```ada
1    — Using the simulator
2    Robot : Pioneer_3at.I_Robot'Class := new Pioneer_3at.Sim_Robot;
3    Robot_Config : Pioneer_3at.Rt_Robot_Comm_Config (Socket);
4
5    — Using the real robot
6    Robot : Pioneer_3at.I_Robot'Class := new Pioneer_3at.Real_Robot;
7    Robot_Config : Pioneer_3at.Rt_Robot_Comm_Config (Serial);
8
9    — Subprograms calls need not to be modified:
10   Robot.Begin_Comm (Robot_Config);
11   Robot.Write_Data (Pioneer_3at.Cmd'(Watchdog));
```

Fig. 8. Changing between the simulated and the real robot

4   Using the Developed Software: Templates for Students

The structure of the code presented before lends itself to different experiments with various levels of complexity for undergraduate, graduate or master students. Grade students can avoid the complexity added by concurrency and develop a simple single-tasking application that implements a *Sense-Plan-Act* control loop. At this level, students only

```ada
1    with Pioneer_3at; use Pioneer_3at; with Pioneer_3at.Sim_Robot;
2    use Pioneer_3at.Sim_Robot; with Ada.Real_Time; use Ada.Real_Time;
3
4    procedure Test_Simulator is
5       Next_Time : Time := Clock;
6       Period : constant Time_Span := Milliseconds (100);
7       Robot : Pioneer_3at.I_Robot'Class := new Pioneer_3at.Sim_Robot;
8       Robot_Config : Pioneer_3at.Rt_Robot_Comm_Config (Socket);
9                — we are going to use the simulator
10   begin
11      — Configuration
12      Robot.Begin_Comm (Robot_Config);
13      Robot.Write_Data (Pioneer_3at.Cmd'(Config));
14      Robot.Write_Data (Pioneer_3at.Cmd'(Motors_On));
15      Robot.Write_Data (Pioneer_3at.Cmd'(Sonars_On));
16      — Sense—Plan—Act loop
17      for I in 1 .. 1000 loop
18         Robot.Read_Data; — 'Sense'
19         — 'Plan' and 'Act' code here!
20         — Pos_X := Robot.Get_Pos_X;
21         — Sonars := Robot.Get_Sonars;
22         — Robot.Write_Data (Pioneer_3at.Output_Gen(Cmd'(Motors), 20, 20));
23         — etc.
24         Robot.Write_Data (Pioneer_3at.Cmd'(Watchdog));
25         Next_Time := Next_Time + Period;
26         delay until Next_Time;
27      end loop;
28   end Test_Simulator;
```

Fig. 9. Excerpt of the code template given to undergraduate students

have to fill the "Plan" part of the control loop with the code that solves the proposed problem. We provide a sample template code (see Fig. 9) that students must reuse and complete.

We propose simple problems, since students do not have enough programming experience, like:

- Make the robot accelerate as time passes.
- Make the robot draw circles.
- Make the robot follow a path generated from its initial position.
- Make the robot wander in a big map without colliding with any object.

Regarding postgraduate and master students, they are presented two different kind of problems, depending on their profile. On the one hand, they have to implement a concurrent solution for the problem of controlling the simulated robot, since writing and reading commands can be sent to the robot, at most, every 100 ms. Thus, they have to design an application with two or more tasks, and one or more protected objects to store the robot's status data in order to avoid polling the simulator. Besides, the MobileSim simulator is capable of simulating more than just one robot. This makes it possible to develop harder problems, where students must design an application where two or more robots must be controlled and must cooperate in order to fulfil a given mission. The usual structure of such programs is shown in Fig. 10.

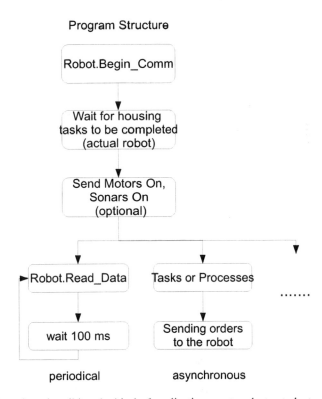

Fig. 10. Flow chart describing the kind of applications postgraduate students must develop

On the other hand, master students must also solve harder problems regarding robot navigation, path planning, mapping, etc. These are mainly algorithmic problems and we are not going to describe them in this paper, but the interested reader can find more information in [19].

5   Conclusions and Future Research

This paper has described ongoing work that aims at developing a common Ada infrastructure that can be used in both our teaching and research duties. This infrastructure revolves around the development of an Ada interface to a real Pioneer P3–AT robot and its simulator. We hope the use of such platform will make learning programming languages more appealing to undergraduate students, while at the same time it allows us to prepare more difficult problems to postgraduate and master students, involving concurrency control and robot cooperation in complex missions.

The Ada interface has been programmed by using the synchronized interface facility provided by Ada and then implementing to protected objects: one for interfacing with the real robot and another for the simulator. We found variant records very useful for the configuration procedure, since the protected type representing the real robot and the one representing the simulator have different configuration parameters (serial port number and serial port parameters versus IP and port number), and we were able to define a single procedure to perform the configuration using a variant record instead of adding two configuration subprograms. However, we experienced some troubles using the library distributed with GNAT for the control of the serial port in Linux.

Regarding future research, we plan to develop a thin network layer in order to make it possible to use any programming language to interact with the Ada interface with the MobileSim. We will then be able then to extend this to other courses where we teach different programming languages.

References

1. The Bologna Process web page,
   http://ec.europa.eu/education/higher-education/doc1290_en.htm
   (checked February 2011)
2. Benlloch-Dualde, J.V., Blanc-Clavero, S.: Adapting Teaching and Assessment Strategies to Enhance Competence-Based Learning in the Framework of The European Convergence Process. In: Proceedings of the 37th ASEE/IEEE Frontiers in Education Conference, Milwaukee, USA (October 2007)
3. Markham, T., Larmer, J., Ravitz, J.: Project Based Learning. A Guide to Standards-Focused Project Based Learning for Middle and High School Teachers, Buck Institute (2003)
4. Boud, D., Dunn, J., Hegarty-Hazel, E.: Teaching in Laboratories. Society for Research into Higher Education, Guildford (1986)
5. Hassan, H., Domnguez, C., Martnez, J.M., Perles, A., Albaladejo, J.: Remote Laboratory Architecture for the Validation of Industrial Control Applications. IEEE Transactions on Industrial Electronics 54(6), 3094–3102 (2007)
6. Kramer, J., Scheutz, M.: Development environments for autonomous mobile robots: A survey. Autonomous Robots 22(2), 101–132 (2007)

7. Web page of the School of Industrial Engineering of the Universidad Politcnica de Cartagena, Bachelor in Industrial Electronics and Automation Engineering, `http://www.etsii.upct.es/giti_en.htm` (checked November 2011)
8. Web page of the Master in Information and Communication Technologies of the Universidad Politcnica de Cartagena (in Spanish), `http://www.dte.upct.es/doctorado` (checked November 2010)
9. Iborra, A., Alonso, D., Ortiz, F.J., Franco, J.A., Snchez, P., Álvarez, B.: Design of service robots. IEEE Robotics and Automation Magazine, Special Issue on Software Engineering for Robotics 16(1), 24–33 (2009)
10. Ortiz, F.J., Alonso, D., Álvarez, B., Pastor, J.A.: A reference control architecture for service robots implemented on a climbing vehicle. In: Vardanega, T., Wellings, A.J. (eds.) Ada-Europe 2005. LNCS, vol. 3555, pp. 13–24. Springer, Heidelberg (2005)
11. Pioneer 3 operations manual web page, `http://robots.mobilerobots.com/docs/alldocs/P3OpMan6.pdf` (checked November 2010)
12. Web page of the MobileRobots/ActivMedia MobileSim simulator, `http://robots.mobilerobots.com/wiki/MobileSim` (checked November 2010)
13. Chil, R.: Desarrollo de un protocolo de comunicacin en tiempo real, usando el lenguaje Ada, para comunicarse con el robot Pioner P3–AT, Master Thesis (in Spanish), Universidad Politcnica de Cartagena (2010)
14. Web page of the MobileRobots company, `http://www.mobilerobots.com` (checked November 2010)
15. Mohamed, N., Al-Jaroodi, J., Jawhar, I.: Middleware for Robotics: A Survey. In: Proceedings of the 2008 IEEE Conference on Robotics, Automation and Mechatronics, Chengdu, China, pp. 736–742 (September 2008)
16. Web page of the Robot Standards and Reference Architectures (RoSTa), Coordination Action funded under EU's FP6, `http://wiki.robot-standards.org/index.php/Current_Middleware_Approaches_and_Paradigms`
17. Fayad, M., Schmidt, D.: Object-Oriented Application Frameworks. Special Issue on Object-Oriented Application Frameworks, Comm. of the ACM 40(10), 32–38 (1997)
18. Mosteo, A., Montano, L.: SANCTA: an Ada 2005 general-purpose architecture for mobile robotics research. In: Abdennahder, N., Kordon, F. (eds.) Ada-Europe 2007. LNCS, vol. 4498, pp. 221–234. Springer, Heidelberg (2007)
19. Murphy, R.: Introduction to AI robotics. The MIT press, Cambridge (2000) ISBN 0-262-13383-0

ORK+/XtratuM: An Open Partitioning Platform for Ada[⋆]

Ángel Esquinas[1], Juan Zamorano[1], Juan A. de la Puente[1],
Miguel Masmano[2], Ismael Ripoll[2], and Alfons Crespo[2]

[1] Universidad Politécnica de Madrid (UPM), E-28040 Madrid, Spain
aesquina@datsi.fi.upm.es,jzamora@fi.upm.es,jpuente@dit.upm.es
[2] Universidad Politécnica de Valencia (UPV), E-46022 Valencia, Spain
mmasmano@ai2.upv.es, {iripoll,alfons}@disca.upv.es

Abstract. The ARINC 653 standard defines an Integrated Modular Avionics (IMA) architecture for building complex systems consisting of several real-time applications with different levels of criticality running in the same hardware platform. Applications execute in *partitions* that are isolated from each other in the temporal and spatial (i.e. storage) domains. The standard defines an architecture and an applications program interface (API) for an operating system or *application executive* (APEX) supporting these concepts.

This paper describes an implementation of a partitioning platform for Ada based on a similar approach. The platform is built with two components: the XtratuM hypervisor, which supports multiple virtual machines on a single computer, and the Open Ravenscar Kernel (ORK+), a small, reliable real-time kernel supporting the Ada Ravenscar tasking profile. This combination provides an open-source platform that enables high-integrity Ada applications to share the same computer board with other, possibly less critical, applications.

Keywords: Ada 2005, real-time systems, high-integrity systems, integrated modular avionics, partitioned systems, ORK, Ravenscar profile.

1 Introduction

Current avionic systems are often composed of several applications that may have different levels of criticality. In such kind of systems, applications must be isolated from each other, so that their integrity is not compromised by failures occurring in other applications. A common approach to isolation has been based on using a *federated* architecture, i.e. on allocating different applications to different computers. However, the growth in the number of applications and the increasing processing power of embedded computers have opened the way to *integrated* architectures, in which several applications are executed on a single computer platform. In this case, alternate mechanisms must be put in place in order to isolate applications

---

[⋆] This work has been partly funded by the Spanish Ministry of Science, project TIN2008-06766-C03 (RT-MODEL).

A. Romanovsky and T. Vardanega (Eds.): Ada-Europe 2011, LNCS 6652, pp. 160–173, 2011.

from each other. A common approach is to provide a number of *logical partitions* on each computer platform, in such a way that each partition is allocated a share of processor time, memory space, and other resources. Partitions are thus isolated from each other both in the temporal and spatial domains. Temporal isolation implies that a partition does not use more processor time than allocated, and spatial isolation means that software running in a partition does not read or write into memory space allocated to other partitions.

Partitioning has been successfully implemented in the aeronautics domain by the so-called Integrated Modular Avionics (IMA) concept [15]. The IMA architecture requires a specialized operating system layer that provides temporal and spatial isolation between partitions. The ARINC 653 standard [3] defines an architecture and an applications program interface (API) for such an operating system or *application executive* (APEX), in ARINC terms.

Temporal isolation is achieved by using a two-level scheduling scheme. A global *partition scheduler* allocates processor time to partitions according to a static cyclic schedule, where partitions run in turn for the duration of a fixed slice of time (see figure 1). The global scheduler is a variant of a static cyclic executive, while the local schedulers are priority-based. Spatial isolation between partitions is provided by implementing a separate address space for each partition, in a similar way as process address spaces are protected from each other in conventional operating systems.

It should be noted that the Ada 2005 advanced real-time mechanisms allow other approaches to time and space partitioning, which may be simpler to implement and provide more flexibility in scheduling real-time tasks [14,18]. However, there is a strong demand for IMA systems in industry, and support for such

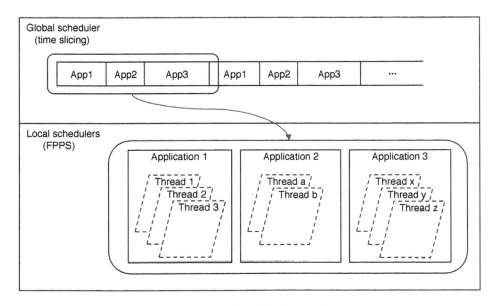

Fig. 1. Hierarchical scheduling architecture

architectures must be made available to Ada software developers as well. Indeed, there are multiple industrial ARINC 653 implementations available from a variety of vendors, and the standard has been successfully used in a number of commercial and military avionics systems. However, there is currently no open source platform available which can be used to build partitioned systems. This paper shows how an open-source platform following the IMA approach can be built by combining the XtratuM hypervisor [12] with the Ada 2005 version of the Open Ravenscar Kernel (ORK+) [19]. The hardware platform is LEON2 [8], a radiation-hardened implementation of the SPARC V8 architecture [16] that is commonly used in European space systems.

The rest of the paper is organized as follows: Section 2 introduces the architecture and the main features of the XtratuM hypervisor. The architecture of ORK+ is described in Section 3. Section 4 describes the approach and some issues that arose during the porting of ORK+ to run on top of XtratuM. A preliminary evaluation of the performance of the platform compared to ORK+ running directly on a bare board is included in Section 5. Related work is summarized in Section 6. Finally, some conclusions about the resulting partitioning platform are drawn and plans for the near future are exposed in Section 7.

2   Overview of XtratuM

XtratuM [12] is an open-source hypervisor that has been designed to meet safety critical real-time requirements in embedded systems. Its most relevant features are:

- Bare machine (type 1) hypervisor.
- Para-virtualization. The virtual machine interface is similar, but not identical, to the underlaying hardware.
- Dedicated devices: some devices can be directly and exclusively managed by a designated partition.
- Strong temporal isolation by enforcing a static cyclic plan to execute partition in a major temporal frame.
- Strong spatial isolation by allocation partitions at specified memory regions that cannot be accessed by other partitions.
- Safe partition execution: partitions are executed in processor user mode, whereas the hypervisor is executed in privileged processor mode.
- Fine-grained resource allocation via a configuration file that specifies the resources available on the board and the way they are allocated to partitions.
- Robust inter-partition communication mechanisms based on sampling and queuing ports.
- Some restricted services can only be used by *system* partitions, not by *normal* partitions (the default).
- Fault management model. Faults are detected and handled by the hypervisor, as a consequence of a system trap or a hypervisor-generated event.

XtratuM provides a virtual machine interface that is close to the native hardware. The virtual machine interface gives access to the system resources: CPU registers, clock, timer, memory, interrupts, etc., through a set of system calls (*hypercalls*). Each virtual machine defines a partition that can contain either a bare machine application or an operating system on top which applications can run. An operating system that runs in a partition has to be *para-virtualized*, which implies that some parts of the operating system hardware abstraction layer (HAL) have to be replaced with the corresponding hypercalls.

The Xtratum architecture is shown in figure 2. The figure shows several partitions based on ORK+/XtratuM, and an additional partition based on a bare machine C code running directly on top of XtratuM. Other configurations are also possible. In the figure, only one partition is defined as a *system* partition, while the other ones are *normal* or user partitions. In general, several partitions can be configured as system partitions.

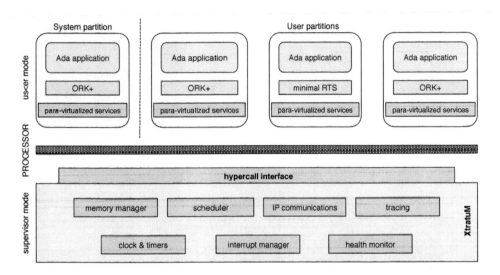

Fig. 2. XtratuM architecture

The services provided by XtratuM are summarized in table 1. As shown in the table, some services are constrained or partially constrained to be used only in system partitions. As an example, partition management is restricted in such a way that any partition can halt, stop, resume, reset, or shutdown itself, but only system partitions can execute these actions on other partitions. Likewise, only system partitions have access to the health monitor events in order to analyse errors detected at run time.

XtratuM provides some additional services for managing specific hardware resources that depend heavily on the processor architecture. Table 2 shows the specific services for the SPARC V8 architecture.

XtratuM version 2.2 is currently being used by CNES (Centre National d'Études Spatiales, France) as a time and space partitioning (TSP) based solution for building highly generic and reusable on-board payload software for space applications [1,2].

Table 1. XtratuM general hypercalls

Group of services	Hypercalls	Partition
Clock management	get clock; define timers	normal
IRQ Management	enable/disable IRQs, mask/unmask IRQs	normal
IP Communication	create ports read/receive/write/send messages	normal
IO management	read/write IO	normal
Partition management	mode change halt/reset/resume/ suspend/shutdown partitions	system
Health monitoring management	read/seek/status HM events	system
Audit facilities	read/status	system

Table 2. XtratuM SPARC V8 specific hypercalls

SPARC V8 hypercalls
XM_sparcv8_atomic_add
XM_sparcv8_atomic_and
XM_sparcv8_atomic_or
XM_sparcv8_flush_regwin
XM_sparcv8_get_flags
XM_sparcv8_inport
XM_sparcv8_iret
XM_sparcv8_outport
XM_sparcv8_set_flags

3 Overview of ORK+

ORK [19] is an open-source real-time kernel which provides full compliance with the Ada Ravenscar profile [4, D.15] on embedded computers. The kernel has a reduced size and complexity, and has been carefully designed to allow developers to build reliable software systems for embedded applications on LEON-based computers. It is integrated with a cross-compilation system based on GNAT[1]. The current version, ORK+, includes support for the new Ada 2005 timing features, such as execution-time clocks and timers, group budgets and timing events. Restricted support for execution-time timers and group budgets is provided, despite not being part of the Ravenscar profile, as these mechanisms have been found useful to ensure some temporal properties at run time [13].

The kernel functions can be grouped as follows:

- Task management, including task creation, synchronization, and scheduling.
- Time services, including absolute delays, real-time clock, execution time clocks and timers and timing events.

---
[1] http://www.dit.upm.es/ork

– Interrupt handling, including attaching a protected parameter procedure to a hardware interrupt vector, dealing with interrupt priorities and initializing vectors in the interrupt table.

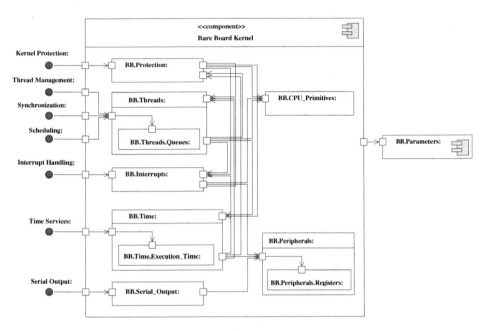

Fig. 3. ORK+ architecture

The kernel components implementing the above functions are depicted in figure 3. Most of the components are fully independent from the underlying platform. The lower-level components, which are hardware-dependent —namely BB.CPU_Primitives, BB.Time, BB.Peripherals, and BB.Interrupts— have platform-independent specifications. Consequently, only the implementations of these components have to be rewritten in order to port the kernel to the XtratuM virtual machine interface. Overall, 1398 out of 7316 lines of code have been modified. This figure accounts for the XtratuM interface as well as low-level assembly routines that are part of the implementation of the above packages.

4   Porting ORK+ to XtratuM

4.1   Adapting the XtratuM Interface

As a general rule, the kernel components that closely depend on the processor characteristics have to be re-implemented in order to port ORK+ to different hardware platforms. In the case of XtratuM, the porting strategy is slightly different, as the question is not to port the kernel to a different processor, but to the virtual processor interface provided by the hypervisor for a partition. As previously stated, the virtual processor is similar, but not identical, to the original processor architecture. Therefore, the processor-dependent components of ORK+ have to be para-virtualized, i.e. some of the processor resources have to be accessed by means of the Xtratum hypercalls.

ORK+ is written mostly in Ada, except for a few low-level routines that are written in SPARC assembly language. On its side, the XtratuM native interface is coded in C, which is its main implementation language. Therefore, an Ada interface to XtratuM has to be built as a first step so that the ORK+ code can use the XtratuM hypercalls. To this purpose, the standard Interfaces.C package and pragma Import [4, Ap. B] have been used to write a new kernel package, named System.BB.XtratuM, which provides the hypercall interface. The parts of this package that are related to interrupt support are shown in listing 1 as an example.

4.2   CPU Management

The context switch operation is one of the first things to be re-implemented when porting a kernel to a different architecture, as it is highly dependent on the processor. In this case, the SPARC architecture includes a set of register windows that are especially complex to handle [16]. At the lowest level, XtratuM provides some basic support for this feature, including register window underflow and overflow trap handlers. However, the basic context switch operations have still to be provided by ORK+ in order to support Ada tasking at the application level.

An important difference when running ORK+ on top of XtratuM with respect to the original, bare machine implementation, is that now the kernel runs in user processor mode, as all XtratuM partitions do. As a result, the ORK+ context switch routine cannot access privileged processor registers, which are only available to the hypervisor, running in supervisor mode. Consequently, the ORK+ context switch routine has been rewritten so that all the assembly language code referencing privileged processor registers uses specific SPARC V8 hypercalls (see table 2). These hypercalls have a lightweight implementation in order to keep context switches and other low-level operations efficient.

4.3   Interrupt Support

XtratuM virtualizes the 16 interrupt sources of the SPARC architecture, and defines 32 additional virtual interrupt sources that are intended to be used for Xtratum services. For instance, XM_VT_HW_TIMER is a virtual interrupt source for a software elapsed-time timer defined by the hypervisor. Therefore, the number of interrupt sources in XtratuM is greater than in the original SPARC architecture. This has been reflected in the kernel System.BB.Interrupts package, as well as the standard Ada.Interrupts and Ada.Interrupt.Names packages, so that application code can attach protected parameterless procedures to all interrupt sources, including the XtratuM virtual interrupts.

XtratuM does not support priorities for interrupt sources. Therefore, all the interrupt sources have the same priority, as it is customary for hypervisor and

Listing 1. Interrupt support in the Xtratum Ada API

```ada
pragma Restrictions (No_Elaboration_Code);
with Interfaces .C;

package System.BB.Xtratum is
   pragma Preelaborate;

   use type Interfaces .C.unsigned;

   ------------------
   -- INTERRUPTS --
   ------------------
   XM_VT_EXT_FIRST : constant Interfaces.C.unsigned := 32;

   XM_VT_EXT_HW_TIMER : constant Interfaces.C.unsigned := 0 + XM_VT_EXT_FIRST;

   XM_VT_EXT_EXEC_TIMER : constant Interfaces.C.unsigned := 1 +
                           XM_VT_EXT_FIRST;
   procedure Disable_Interrupts ;
   pragma Import (C, Disable_Interrupts , "XM_disable_irqs" );
   -- All external interrupts (asynchronous traps) are disabled

   procedure Enable_Interrupts ;
   pragma Import (C, Enable_Interrupts , "XM_enable_irqs" );
   -- Interrupts are enabled

   function Mask_IRQ (Irq :  Interfaces .C.unsigned) return Integer ;
   pragma Import (C, Mask_IRQ, "XM_mask_irq" );
   -- Mask an interrupt
   -- [1 .. 15] Hardware Interrupts . Traps from 0x11 to 0x1F
   -- [31 .. 63] Extended Interrupts . Interrupts trigger the traps from
   --            0x100 to 0x11F.

   function Unmask_IRQ (Irq : Interfaces .C.unsigned) return Integer ;
   pragma Import (C, Unmask_IRQ, "XM_unmask_irq" );

   ...

end System.BB.Xtratum;
```

operating systems. Consequently, ORK+ has been modified so that the System.
Interrupt_Priority range has only one value.

4.4   Time Services

ORK+ provides direct support for the Ravenscar profile time services, i.e. Ada.
Real_Time.Clock, absolute delays, global timing events, and execution-time clocks.

It also supports execution-time timers and group budgets, as an extension to the Ravenscar profile. The original implementation of these time services is based on two hardware timers: a periodic timer and a single-shot timer [19].

It must be noted that hardware timers are indeed elapsed-time timers. However, the XtratuM hypervisor, as it is common in partitioned systems, has a dual concept of time: in addition to the common notion of elapsed real-time, there is the notion of *partition-time*, which only advances when a partition is scheduled. Accordingly, Xtratum provides two kinds of software timers, as well as two kinds of clocks: elapsed-time clocks and timers, and partition-time clocks and timers.

The real-time mechanisms, i.e. Ada.Real_Time.Clock, absolute delays, and global timing events, are implemented in ORK+/XtratuM in a similar way to the bare machine version, i.e. by using the elapsed-time clock and timer. However, execution-time clocks cannot be implemented in the same way. Since the hypervisor switches the running partition without giving any notice to the software running in the partitions, implementing execution-time clocks on elapsed-time timers would also account for the time the partition is not running. In order to avoid this inconvenience, all execution-time mechanisms, i.e. execution-time clocks and timers, as well as group budgets, are implemented using partition time timers.

5   Performance Evaluation

5.1   General Approach

Possible losses in performance are a key issue when running critical real-time software on a partitioned system. We have carried out some experiments in order to quantify the loss of performance incurred by an application running on an ORK+/XtratuM partition with respect to using ORK+ on a bare LEON2 computer. To this purpose, we have developed a set of scenarios in order to evaluate which is the performance loss incurred by the hypervisor layer when different partition sets are defined.

There are two possible approaches to performance evaluation in this context:

- Direct measurements: the hypervisor is instrumented with breakpoints at the hypercall entry/exit points so that clock registers can be dumped in order to compute the execution time of every service.
- Indirect measurements: the application code executes some workload. The difference in the amount of work that is performed when running in a partition compared to what is done on the bare board provides a measurement of the effect of the hypervisor on the application.

We have opted for the indirect measurements approach as it is simpler to implement and does not require any special equipment nor instrumenting the hypervisor code. In order to get a good accuracy in the estimation of the overhead introduced by the hypervisor, an extremely simple workload, consisting on incrementing a counter whose value is sampled at periodic time intervals, has been used. The total increment in an interval provides a good estimation of the number of instructions executed in it. It should be noted that the duration of the slot assigned to the partition must be long enough to guarantee that XtratuM will not perform a partition switch during the interval, in order to avoid additional overheads on the measurement.

The platform used for the evaluation is the TSIM/LEON SPARC simulator, version 2.0.6 (professional version) running at 80 MHz with 4 MB of RAM and separate instruction and data caches of 4 KB. During the evaluation the LEON2 processor was running at 2.25 CPIs (clock cycles per instruction), which means a performance of 35 MIPS. This is a typical value for current space systems.

5.2 Scenario Description

The evaluation scenario consists of three tasks:

- *Counter* task: a background, low priority task that continously increases a counter. The counter value is global and can be read by other tasks.
- *Timer* task: a periodic task with an intermediate priority level. The period of the task is calculated so as to generate a specified number of preemptions of the counter task in a reader task period.
- *Reader* task: a high priority service that periodically reads the counter value and stores the increment in the period. In the experiments the task period has been set to 1 second.

Figure 4 shows an execution diagram for the above tasks. This scenario has been executed several times for different values of the number of preemptions incurred by the counter task in a period of the reader task. The values used for the evaluation go from 1 to 1000 preemptions per second, which correspond to timer task periods between 1000 and 1 milliseconds. This scenario has been executed in a slot in the XtratuM schedule which is longer than the total duration of the experiment, so that no additional interference due to partition context switch is incurred.

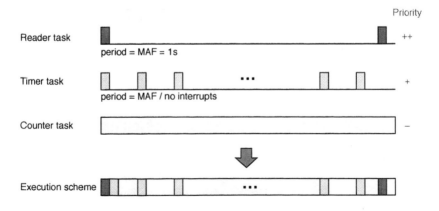

Fig. 4. Evaluation scenario

Table 3 shows the results of the evaluation for ORK+ running on a native LEON2 platform, and ORK+ running in a XtratuM partition. The numbers are the average, maximum, and minimum count values in a reader task period over a 50-second interval, which is the total duration of the experiment. The results are shown for different values of the timer task period (TTP).

Table 3. Evaluation results

ORK+ on native LEON2						
TTP	1000	500	100	50	10	5	1
AVG	9999113	9998618	9994117	9988498	9943509	9887269	9444166
MAX	9999131	9998642	9994141	9988522	9943520	9887280	9445368
MIN	9999046	9998558	9994056	9988436	9943462	9887222	9437370
DIF	0	495	4996	10615	55604	111844	554947
PL1	0,000%	0,004%	0,049%	0,106%	0,556%	1,118%	5,549%
ORK+ on XtratuM						
TTP	1000	500	100	50	10	5	1
AVG	9997222	9994785	9975228	9950780	9755212	9510748	7555050
MAX	9997235	9994791	9975236	9950790	9755216	9510760	7555056
MIN	9997185	9994750	9975195	9950749	9755176	9510719	7555019
DIF	0	2437	21994	46442	242010	486474	2442172
PL2	0,000%	0,024%	0,219%	0,464%	2,42%	4,866%	24,428%
PL3	0,02%	0,03%	0,19%	0,38%	1,89%	3,80%	20,00%

The first column, for a TTP of 1000 ms, provides a basic value for the performance, as there are no preemptions of the counter task in a reader task period. For the rest of the TTP values, the difference (DIF) between the average values and the reference value provides an indication of the performance losses (PL) of the counter task due to the task switching overhead of the timer task. The following performance loss indicators are shown:

- *PL1*: performance loss for ORK+ with respect to its best case (TTP = 1000).
- *PL2*: performance loss for ORK+/XtratuM with respect to its best case (TTP = 1000).
- *PL3*: performance loss for ORK+/XtratuM with respect to ORK+.

Figure 5 shows the performance loss values for different values of the timer task period.

The above results show that for ORK+ on native LEON2, the performance loss due to task switching (PL1) is negligible when the timer period is longer than 10 ms, and only reaches a significant value for a timer period of 1 ms, which is seldom found in the kind of space applications we have in mind. The performance loss for ORK+ on XtratuM (PL2) follows a similar pattern. The PL3 figures give an indication of the cost of virtualization, i.e. the difference in performance between the ORK+/XtratuM and the native ORK+ configurations. Again, it can be seen that it is only significant for very short periods, far below the values

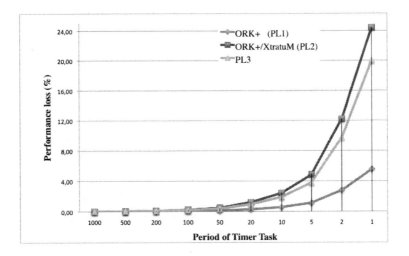

Fig. 5. Evaluation scenario

that are commonly found in on-board software applications. These results can be considered very satisfactory, taking into account the advantages of having several applications running in an isolated (temporal and spatial) partitioning framework.

Finally, it must be noted that PL2 values are about 5 times the corresponding PL1 values. This result roughly means that the periodic task switching overhead in ORK+/XtratuM is about 5 times the native ORK+ overhead. This increment is mainly due to clock management, as XtratuM general hypercalls have to be made not only to set the elapsed timer for the absolute delay, but also to keep the values of the execution-time clocks using the partition time clock. It can thus be concluded that the implementation of Ada timing services on top of a virtualization layer deserves further research.

6   Related Work

Although hypervisors were first developed by IBM in the 1960s, there has been a recent revival of interest in this technology, due to projects such as Xen [7], VMWare [20] and L4 [11]. These projects were aimed at building virtualizers for general purpose systems, including desktop PCs and servers.

More recently, hypervisors have been used in embedded and real-time systems. For example, PikeOS [10] is a microkernel based on L4 which is targeted to embedded systems and uses virtualization techniques. Although microkernels were first developed as an architectural approach for building large and complex operating systems, they can also be used as bare-metal supervisors. The PikeOS architecture has two main components, namely the *separation kernel* and the *system software*. The former runs in supervisor mode and provides a set of basic services: scheduling, memory management and interrupt handling. The latter runs in user mode and is shared by all partitions. It provides services for inter-partition communication and device drivers. The services provided by the microkernel can be used to build several different operating systems, resulting in a virtualized system.

Other related projects are NOVA [17], which is aimed at constructing a secure virtualization environment, and OKL4 Microvisor [9], which is designed as a highly-efficient hypervisor for use in embedded systems.

Generally speaking, it can be said that para-virtualization is the virtualization method that better fits the requirements of embedded systems with real-time constraints. Other methods which can provide full virtualization introduce a siginficant overhead in the system execution, with a direct impact on the predictability of the the applications running in the different partitions. For example, binary translation works by catching the execution of conflicting instructions and replacing them on the fly, which has a clear cost in terms of execution time.

7   Conclusions and Future Work

Combining ORK+ and Xtratum builds up an efficient partitioning platform that enables real-time Ada applications with different criticality levels to run on a LEON2 platform. Time and space isolation between partitions is implemented by the XtratruM hypervisor, and ORK+ provides timing predictability within each partition. The temporal behaviour of applications running on a hierarchical scheduling environment like that provided by ORK+/XtratuM can be statically analysed using an extension of response-time analysis methods [6,5]. It should be noted that ORK+ provides an additional level of enforcement of the required temporal behaviour by means of execution time clocks and timers [13].

XtratuM and ORK+ are currently targeted to LEON2-based computers. The LEON2 support for spatial isolation is rather primitive, consisting only of a set of fence registers, which do not provide any protection against incorrect read operations. This kind of limited memory protection mechanism also imposes a rigid memory sharing scheme between different partitions. This limitation is expected to be overcome with the next-generation of LEON3 processors, which have a full-featured MMU.[2] Future plans include porting the platform to LEON3 and other common embedded processor architectures.

References

1. Arberet, P., Metge, J.J., Gras, O., Crespo, A.: TSP-based generic payload on-board software. In: DASIA 2009, Data Systems in Aerospace, Istanbul (May 2009)
2. Arberet, P., Miro, J.: IMA for space: status and considerations. In: ERTS 2008, Embedded Real-Time Software, Toulouse France (Jannuary 2008)
3. ARINC: Avionics Application Software Standard Interface — ARINC Specification 653-1 (October 2003)

---

[2] Memory Management Unit.

4. Tucker Taft, S., Duff, R.A., Brukardt, R.L., Plödereder, E., Leroy, P.: Ada 2005 Reference Manual. LNCS, vol. 4348. Springer, Heidelberg (2006) ISBN 978-3-540-69335-2
5. Balbastre, P., Ripoll, I., Crespo, A.: Exact response time analysis of hierarchical fixed-priority scheduling. In: Proceedings of 15th IEEE International Conference on Embedded and Real-Time Computing Systems and Applications (August 2009)
6. Davis, R., Burns, A.: Hierarchical fixed priority pre-emptive scheduling. In: Proceedingsof the 26th IEEE International Real-Time Systems Symposium — RTSS 2005 (2005)
7. Dragovic, B., Fraser, K., Hand, S., Harris, T., Ho, A., Pratt, I., Warfield, A., Barham, P., Neugebauer, R.: Xen and the art of virtualization. In: Proceedings of the ACM Symposium on Operating Systems Principles (October 2003), http://www.citeseer.ist.psu.edu/dragovic03xen.html
8. Gaisler Research: LEON2 Processor User's Manual (2005)
9. Heiser, G., Leslie, B.: The OKL4 Microvisor: Convergence point of microkernels and hypervisors. In: Proceedings of the 1st Asia-PacificWorkshop on Systems, New Delhi, India, pp. 19–24 (August 2010)
10. Kaiser, R., Wagner, S.: Evolution of the PikeOS microkernel. In: MIKES 2007: First International Workshop on MicroKernels for Embedded Systems, Sydney, Australia (2007)
11. Liedtke, J.: On microkernel construction. In: Proceedings of the 15th ACM Symposium on Operating System Principles (SOSP-15). Copper Mountain Resort, CO (December 1995), http://www.l4ka.org/publications/
12. Masmano, M., Ripoll, I., Crespo, A., Metge, J., Arberet, P.: Xtratum: An open source hypervisor for TSP embedded systems in aerospace. In: DASIA 2009, Data System in Aerospace, Istanbul (May 2009)
13. Mezzetti, E., Panunzio, M., Vardanega, T.: Preservation of timing properties with the ada ravenscar profile. In: Real, J., Vardanega, T. (eds.) Ada-Europe 2010. LNCS, vol. 6106, pp. 153–166. Springer, Heidelberg (2010)
14. Pulido, J.A., Urueña, S., Zamorano, J., Vardanega, T., de la Puente, J.A.: Hierarchical scheduling with ada 2005. In: Pinho, L.M., González Harbour, M. (eds.) Ada-Europe 2006. LNCS, vol. 4006, pp. 1–12. Springer, Heidelberg (2006)
15. Rushby, J.: Partitioning for safety and security: Requirements, mechanisms, and assurance. NASA Contractor Report CR-1999-209347, NASA Langley Research Center (June 1999), also to be issued by the FAA
16. SPARC International, Upper Saddle River, NJ, USA: The SPARC architecture manual: Version 8 (1992), http://www.sparc.com/standards/V8.pdf
17. Steinberg, U., Kauer, B.: Nova: a microhypervisor-based secure virtualization architecture. In: EuroSys, pp. 209–222 (2010)
18. Urueña, S., Pulido, J.A., López, J., Zamorano, J., de la Puente, J.A.: A new approach to memory partitioning in on-board spacecraft software. In: Kordon, F., Vardanega, T. (eds.) Ada-Europe 2008. LNCS, vol. 5026, pp. 1–14. Springer, Heidelberg (2008)
19. Urueña, S., Pulido, J.A., Redondo, J., Zamorano, J.: Implementing the new Ada 2005 real-time features on a bare board kernel. Ada Letters XXVII(2), 61–66 (2007); Proceedings of the 13th International Real-Time Ada Workshop (IRTAW 2007)
20. White paper: Virtualization overview (2006), http://www.vmware.com/pdf/virtualization.pdf

Implementing Mixed Criticality Systems in Ada

Sanjoy Baruah[1] and Alan Burns[2]

[1] Department of Computer Science, The University of North Carolina, USA
[2] Department of Computer Science, University of York, UK

Abstract. Many safety-critical embedded systems are subject to certification requirements. However, only a subset of the functionality of the system may be safety-critical and hence subject to certification; the rest of the functionality is non safety-critical and does not need to be certified, or is certified to a lower level. The resulting mixed criticality system offers challenges both for static schedulability analysis and run-time monitoring. This paper considers both of these issues and indicates how mixed criticality applications can be implemented in Ada. In particular, code is produced to illustrate how the necessary run-time mode changes can be supported. This support makes use of a number of the new features introduced into Ada 2005.

1 Introduction

One of the ways that standard real-time systems has been extended in recent years is the removal of the assumption that all tasks in the system have the same level of criticality. Models have been produced that allow mixed criticality levels to co-exist on the same execution platform. For systems that contain components that have been given different criticality designations there are two, mainly distinct, issues: run-time robustness [7] and static verification [12,3].

Run-time robustness is a form of fault tolerance that allows graceful degradation to occur in a manner that is mindful of criticality levels: informally speaking, in the event that all components cannot be serviced satisfactorily the goal is to ensure that lower-criticality components are denied their requested levels of service before higher-criticality components are.

Static verification of mixed-criticality systems is closely related to the problem of *certification* of safety-critical systems. The current trend towards integrating multiple functionalities on a common platform (for example in Integrated Modula Avionics, IMA, systems) means that even in highly safety-critical systems, typically only a relatively small fraction of the overall system is actually of critical functionality and needs to be certified. In order to certify a system as being correct, the certification authority (CA) must make certain assumptions about the worst-case behavior of the system during run-time. CA's tend to be very conservative, and hence it is often the case that the assumptions required by the CA are far more pessimistic than those the system designer would typically use during the system design process if certification was not required. However, while the CA is only concerned with the correctness of the safety-critical part of the system the system designer wishes to ensure that the entire system is correct, including the non-critical parts.

A. Romanovsky and T. Vardanega (Eds.): Ada-Europe 2011, LNCS 6652, pp. 174–188, 2011.

In this paper, we consider some of the scheduling issues involved in static verification. But we consider in more detail the run-time robustness requirements and show how they can be supported in Ada.

2   System Model

A system is defined as a finite set of components $\mathcal{K}$. Each component has a defined level of criticality, L. Each component contains a finite set of tasks. Each task, τ_i, is defined by period, deadline, computation time and criticality level: (T_i, D_i, C_i, L_i). These parameters are however not independent, in particular the following relations are assumed to hold (for the same task) between L and the other parameters in any valid mixed criticality system:

- The worst-case computation time, C_i, will be derived by a process dictated by the criticality level. The higher the criticality level, the more conservative the verification process and hence the greater will be the value of C_i.
- The deadline of the task may also be a function of the criticality level. The higher the criticality level, the greater the need for the task to complete well before any safety-critical timing constraint and hence the smaller the value of D_i.
- Finally, though less likely, the period of a task could depend on criticality. The higher the criticality level, the tighter the level of control that may be needed and hence the smaller the value of T_i.

These relations are formalised with the following axioms: if a component is reclassified so that task, τ_i is moved to criticality level L_i^1 from criticality level L_i^2 then

$$L_i^1 > L_i^2 \Rightarrow C_i^1 \geq C_i^2$$
$$L_i^1 > L_i^2 \Rightarrow D_i^1 \leq D_i^2$$
$$L_i^1 > L_i^2 \Rightarrow T_i^1 \leq T_i^2$$

At run-time a task will have fixed values of T, D and L. Its actual computation time is however unknown; it is *not* directly a function of L. The code of the task will execute on the available hardware, and apart from catching and/or dealing with overruns the task's actual criticality level will not influence the behaviour of the hardware. Rather the probability of failure (executing beyond deadline) will reduce for higher levels of L (due to C monotonically increasing with L).

In a mixed criticality system further information is needed in order to undertake schedulability analysis. Tasks can depend on other tasks with higher or lower levels of criticality. In general a task is now defined by: (T, D, C, L), where C is a vector of values – one per criticality level, with the constraint:

$$L1 > L2 \Rightarrow C^{L1} \geq C^{L2}$$

for any two criticality levels $L1$ and $L2$.

The general task τ_i with criticality level L_i will have one value from its C_i vector that defines its *representative* computation time. This is the value corresponding to L_i, ie. $C_i^{L_i}$. This will be given the normal symbol C_i.

Definition 1 (Behaviors). During different runs, any given task system will, in general, exhibit different *behaviors*: different jobs may be released at different instants, and may have different actual execution times. Let us define the *criticality level of a behavior* to be the smallest criticality level such that no job executed for more than its C value at this criticality level.

As previously stated, two distinct issues have been addressed concerning the scheduling of mixed-criticality systems: *static verification*, and *run-time robustness*.

Static verification. From the perspective of static verification, the correctness criterion expected of an algorithm for scheduling mixed-criticality task systems is as follows: for each criticality level ℓ, *all jobs of all tasks with criticality $\geq \ell$ will complete by their deadlines in any criticality-ℓ behavior.*

Run-time robustness. Static verification is concerned with *certification* – it requires that all deadlines of all tasks τ_i with $L_i \geq \ell$ are guaranteed to be met, provided that *no* job executes for more than its level-ℓ worst-case execution time (WCET). Run-time robustness, in addition, seeks to deal satisfactorily with *transient overloads* due either to errors in the control system or to the environment behaving outside of the assumptions used in the analysis of the system. Even in behaviors that have a high criticality level by Definition 1 above, it may be the case that all jobs executing beyond their WCET's at some lower criticality level did so only for a short duration of time (i.e., a transient overload can be thought to have occurred from the perspective of the lower criticality level). A robust scheduling algorithm would, informally speaking, be able to "recover" from the overload once it was over, and go back to meeting the deadlines of the lower-criticality jobs as well. This is illustrated in the latter half of the paper.

3   Scheduling Analysis for Fixed Priority Scheduling

The distinctive feature of *mixed criticality* as opposed to *partitioned criticality* is that schedulability is obtained from optimising the temporal characteristics of the tasks rather than their important parameters.

Consider the common fixed priority deadline-monotonic scheduling scheme. Here the key operational parameter priority (P) is derived solely from the deadlines of the tasks. For any two tasks τ_i and τ_j: $D_i < D_j \Rightarrow P_i > P_j$. As noted earlier there will be a natural tendency for high criticality tasks to have shorter deadlines, but this is not a strong enough rule to result in a partitioning of deadlines (and hence priorities) via criticality levels.

In general therefore we must consider mixed criticality systems in which a task may suffer interference from another task with a higher priority but a lower criticality level. A phenomenon that could be referred to as *criticality inversion*.

To test for schedulability, the standard Response Time Analysis (RTA) [9,1] approach first computes the worst-case completion time for each task (its response time, R) and then compares this value with the task's deadline D (ie. tests for $R_i \leq D_i$ for all tasks τ_i). The response time value is obtained from the following (where $\mathbf{hp}(i)$ denotes the set of tasks with priority higher that than of task τ_i):

$$R_i = C_i + \sum_{\tau_j \in \mathbf{hp}(i)} \left\lceil \frac{R_i}{T_j} \right\rceil C_j \tag{1}$$

This is solved using a recurrence relation.

Three cases need to be considered depending on whether the arbitrary higher priority task τ_j has an equal, higher or lower criticality. For each case the correct value of C_j must be ascertained:

1. If $L_i = L_j$ then the tasks are at the same level of criticality and the normal representative value C_j is used.
2. If $L_i < L_j$ then it is not necessary to use the large value of computation time represented by C_j, rather the smaller amount corresponding to the criticality level of C_i should be used (as this is the level of assurance needed for this task). Hence eqn (1) should use $C_j^{L_i}$.
3. If $L_i > L_j$ then we have criticality inversion. One approach here would be to again use $C_j^{L_i}$, but this is allowing τ_j to execute for far longer than the task is assumed to do at its own criticality level. Moreover, it would require all low criticality tasks to be verified to the highest levels of importance, which would be prohibitively expensive (and in many ways undermine one of the reasons for having different criticality levels in the first place). Rather we should employ C_j, **but the run-time system must ensure that τ_j does indeed not execute for more than this value.**

The latter point is crucially important. Obviously all the shared run-time software must be verified to the highest critically level of the application tasks. One aspect of this is the functionality that polices the execution time of tasks and makes sure they do not ask for more resource that was catered for during the analysis phase of the system's verification. We note that Ada 2005 provides this functionality as illustrated in Section 5.

The response time equation (eqn 1) can be rewritten as:

$$R_i = C_i + \sum_{\tau_j \in \mathbf{hp}(i)} \left\lceil \frac{R_i}{T_j} \right\rceil C_j^{min(L_i, L_j)} \tag{2}$$

Note that this use of minimum implies that values of C are only required for the task's criticality level and all lower criticality levels (ie. not for higher).

3.1 Shared Objects

With a more realistic system model, tasks will not be independent but will exchange data via shared objects protected by some mutual exclusion primitive or access control protocol (as in Ada's protected objects).

If an object is only used by tasks from the same component then it itself can be assigned the criticality level of the component. More generally if a shared object is used to exchange data between tasks from different components with different criticality level then the object must be produced and analysed at the ceiling criticality level of the components that use it.

As a consequence of the use of shared objects, a blocking term must be introduced into the scheduling equation:

$$R_i = C_i + B_i + \sum_{\tau_j \in \mathbf{hp}(i)} \left\lceil \frac{R_i}{T_j} \right\rceil C_j^{min(L_i, L_j)} \qquad (3)$$

where B_i is the blocking term; its value is the maximum execution time of any operation on a shared object that has a ceiling priority equal or higher than the priority of task τ_i, and which is also used by a task of lower priority.

3.2 Optimal Priority Ordering for Fixed Priority Scheduling

Using the analysis outlined above it is possible to allocate priorities to tasks in a way that optimises schedulability whilst being aware of criticality levels. Vestal [12] was the first to address this issue by assigning priorities to the tasks using Audsley algorithm [2]. That is, it first identifies some task which may be assigned the lowest priority; having done so, this task is removed from the task system and a priority assignment is recursively obtained for the remaining tasks. If the tasks are 'tested' in lowest criticality first order then, if the system is indeed schedulable, a priority ordering is found that delivers a schedulable task set and is as close as possible to being in criticality order (ie. lower criticality tasks are given lower priorities as often as possible). Vestal's claim of optimality for the algorithm was recently proved by Dorin et al [8].

Once a priority ordering is found then an implementation in Ada is straightforward. Tasks are assigned static priorities and a standard, even Ravenscar compliant, program can be developed. However, the run-time behaviour of a mixed-criticality system is not as straightforward. This issue is considered in the rest of this paper.

4   Managing Overruns and Increasing Robustness

As indicated in the introduction one of the important uses of criticality levels is to increase the robustness of the run-time behaviour of a system. This dynamic use of criticality levels can control overloads, either those that are derived from component failure or from excessive work load. The latter could involve a 'best effort' system that must deal with some level of work, but the environment cannot be constrained to never exceed this level. Whatever the level, the system should try and cope. Its main weapon for doing so is to drop less critical work and assign this capacity to the more critical tasks.

The golden rule here is that an overrun by a task at criticality M should not impact on tasks of higher criticality, but can steal resource from tasks with lower criticality. The problem with this rule of course is that for schedulability the priority of a high criticality task may be below that of the M crit task.

To make run-time trade-offs between tasks of different criticality, it is important to define more precisely the measurement scale of the 'criticality' metric [10]. In the literature on mixed criticality systems there is no evidence to use anything other than an ordinal scale. Hence one task of criticality H is worth more than any number of tasks at criticality M (with $H > M$). It follows that a task, τ_i can execute for no longer than C_i (which is the value corresponding to its criticality level) unless it exploits slack in the system or steals execution time from strictly lower criticality tasks.

There could be a number of implementation schemes that could ensure this 'sharing' of computation time - ie. allow a task to use capacity statically allocated to lower criticality tasks. For example the use of execution time servers [5,6,4]. However all of these schemes have considerable run-time complexity and are not currently supportable on high integrity systems. Therefore here we exploit a simple scheme that only involves changes to task priorities. As a change to a task priority will impact on all aspects of the system's schedulability we identify this behaviour as a *mode change*.

The mode change to a more criticality aware priority ordering is triggered by the identification of an overrun of a task's execution time. For a long running system it is likely that the overload situation will eventually pass, and hence it is necessary to return to the original priority ordering. A mode change back to the original ordering must, however, be taken with care as it could cause a high criticality task to miss its deadline if undertaken prematurely. The simplest, and safest, protocol to undertake for this priority change is to wait until there is an idle tick and only switch priority at this time [11]. At this point all effects of the old mode are concluded and the new mode can proceed. The 'idle' tick can actually be of zero duration, but it must be a genuine point at which there is no existing load.

5 Implementation of the Run-Time Protocol in Ada

To illustrate the run-time behaviour described above, and to demonstrate that the proposal is implementable, a simple example is programmed in Ada. The example uses just four tasks and two criticality levels (H and L). The details of the task set are given in Table 1.

Table 1. Example Task Set

Task	L_i	T_i	D_i	C_i	$C_i(overload)$
τ_1	H	100	25	12	
τ_2	L	100	50	10	50
τ_3	L	100	70	15	
τ_4	H	100	100	25	

The C values for each task relate to their criticality levels. On the assumption that the two lower critical tasks do not execute for more than their C values, the system is schedulable with the static priorities in the order (highest first) τ_1, τ_2, τ_3 and then τ_4. In this example task τ_2 is allowed to enter an overloaded state in which its execution time is not 10 but rises to 50. This breaks the schedulability constraint, and hence a mode change is required in which the priority ordering changes to one that is more criticality based, ie τ_1, τ_4, τ_3 and then τ_2.

5.1   Implementation Details

This section describes a prototype implementation of the priority changing protocol. The compiled code executed on a bare machine implementation. All priorities are changed from within a protected object (`Pri_Changer`). This object is called by a handler for a `Timer` object, and by the background task. It makes use of the dynamic priorities package. It therefore needs to record the task IDs of the system's tasks, and the specific priorities to be used in the two modes. These values are embedded in the code but in a real implementation would by taken from an external source. The priority changer is specified in the following package:

```ada
with System;
with Ada.Task_Identification; use Ada.Task_Identification;
with Ada.Execution_Time; use Ada.Execution_Time;
with Ada.Execution_Time.Timers; use Ada.Execution_Time.Timers;
with Ada.Text_IO; use Ada.Text_IO;
with Ada.Integer_Text_IO; use Ada.Integer_Text_IO;
with Ada.Real_Time; use Ada.Real_Time;
with Ada.Dynamic_Priorities; use Ada.Dynamic_Priorities;
package Overload_Control is
   Max_Tasks : constant natural := 4;
   type Mode is (Normal, Overload);
   type Task_Ids is array(1..Max_Tasks) of Task_ID;

   protected Pri_Changer is
      pragma Priority(Min_Handler_Ceiling);
      procedure Change(M : Mode);
       -- called by background task
      procedure Changer(TM : in out Timer);
       -- called by a Timer
      procedure Register(N : Natural);
       -- called once by each of the four system tasks
   private
      Current_Mode : Mode := Normal;
      IDs : Task_Ids;
   end Pri_Changer;
end Overload_Control;
```

The body of this package is as follows:

```ada
package body Overload_Control is
   Task_Pris : array(1..Max_Tasks, Mode) of positive;
   protected body Pri_Changer is
      procedure Change(M : Mode) is
      begin
         if not (M = Current_Mode) then
            put("Mode_Change_to_"); put("Normal"); new_line;
            Current_Mode := M;
            for I in 1..Max_Tasks loop
              Set_Priority(Task_Pris(I,Normal),IDs(I));
            end loop;
         end if;
      end Change;
      procedure Changer(TM : in out Timer) is
      begin
```

```
         if Current_Mode = Normal then
           put("Mode_Change_to_"); put("Overload"); new_line;
           Current_Mode := Overload;
           for I in 1..Max_Tasks loop
               Set_Priority(Task_Pris(I,Overload),IDs(I));
           end loop;
         end if;
     end Changer;
     procedure Register(N : Natural) is
     begin
        IDs(N) := Current_Task;
     end Register;
   end Pri_Changer;

begin
   -- the following static values represent the required
   -- priorities in the two modes
   Task_Pris(1, Normal) := 10;   Task_Pris(1, Overload) := 10;
   Task_Pris(2, Normal) := 9;    Task_Pris(2, Overload) := 4;
   Task_Pris(3, Normal) := 8;    Task_Pris(3, Overload) := 8;
   Task_Pris(4, Normal) := 7;    Task_Pris(4, Overload) := 9;
end Overload_Control;
```

The main part of the program contains a task type for the four application tasks and a single background task. The task type uses discriminates to set its temporal characteristics:

```
task type Periodic(Id, Pri, Period, Deadline, WCET, LifeSpan : Natural);
```

LifeSpan is used to give a finite duration to the execution of the program.

The 'work' of each task is simulated by a busy loop that executes for the required time, using an execution time clock:

```
procedure Work(Initial : CPU_Time; C : natural) is
   X : integer := 0;
begin
   loop
     X := X + 1;
     exit when Clock - Initial > Milliseconds(C);
   end loop;
end Work;
```

The start of each of the tasks is coordinated by a 'starter' protected object:

```
protected Starter is
   pragma Priority(12);
   procedure Get_Start_Time(T : out Time);
private
   First : boolean := true;
   St : Time;
end Starter;

protected body Starter is
   procedure Get_Start_Time(T : out Time) is
   begin
     if First then
```

```
         St := Clock;
         First := false;
      end if;
      T := St;
   end Get_Start_Time;
end Starter;
```

The background task has a low priority and whenever its get to run it calls Change in protected object Pri_Changer and attempts to return the system to the normal mode. For most executions of the task this will be a 'null op' as the system will be in this mode. However execution time is not wasted as this task only runs when the system is otherwise idle. Note an entry cannot be used for this interaction; if the task called an entry (and was blocked) then as soon as the mode is changed to Overload and the barrier made True then the blocked task would execute and set the mode back to Normal!

If a more efficient version of the protocol is needed, so that other non-real-time tasks can execute at the lowest priority level in the normal mode, then this background task would need to be prevented from executing when the mode is Normal. A further action to take when the overload occurs would be the release (from suspension) of the 'background' task.

```
task Background is
   pragma Priority(1);
end Background;

task body Background is
   Epoc : constant Duration := 4.5;
   End_Time : Time := Clock + Seconds(30);
begin
   delay Epoc;
   -- needs to delay until tasks have registered
   loop
      Pri_Changer.Change(Normal);
      exit when Clock > End_Time;
   end loop;
end Background;
```

The code for each periodic task has the usual form. It gets a (common) start time, waits 5 seconds to allow all initialisation to occur. It then sets up its temporal parameters. For all but the second task (which is involved with the overload) the repeating code is essentially:

```
loop
   Work(CPU,WCET);
   if Clock > Next_Release + Relative_Deadline then
      put("Task "); put(Id); put(" missed a deadline"); new_line;
   else
      put("Task "); put(Id); put(" met a deadline"); new_line;
   end if;
   Next_Release := Next_Release + Release_Interval;
   exit when Next_Release > End_Time;
   CPU := Clock;
   delay until Next_Release;
end loop;
```

For the second task a `Timer` is set (and canceled if it does not fire). Also the duration of the work is extended for 3 iterations of the loop:

```
loop
    Count := Count + 1;
    Set_Handler(Overrun, Milliseconds(WCET), Pri_Changer.Changer'Access);
    if Id=2 and (Count > 4 and Count < 8) then
      Put("Overload in Task "); put(Id); new_line;
      Work(CPU,WCET*5);
    else
      Work(CPU,WCET);
    end if;
    Cancel_Handler(Overrun, TempB);
    ... -- as other tasks
end loop;
```

Note for completeness, all tasks have Timers set, but they are not called on to execute in the example executions (as execution time is less than WCET by construction).

The full code for the main program is continued in the Appendix.

5.2   Example Execution

The task set runs for a number of iterations and meets all its deadlines. The overload then occurs in task τ_2 for three consecutive jobs. After that the task returns to its 'normal' behaviour. If no changes are made to the system then deadlines are missed in tasks τ_2, τ_3 and τ_4; τ_1, still has the highest priority and therefore is not impacted by the overload. A sample run of the code, on a bare board single processor platform, for this situation is as follows:

```
Main Started
Task              1 met a deadline
Task              2 met a deadline
Task              3 met a deadline
Task              4 met a deadline
Task              1 met a deadline
Task              2 met a deadline
Task              3 met a deadline
Task              4 met a deadline
Task              1 met a deadline
Task              2 met a deadline
Task              3 met a deadline
Task              4 met a deadline
Task              1 met a deadline
Task              2 met a deadline
Task              3 met a deadline
Task              4 met a deadline
Task              1 met a deadline
Overload in Task          2
Task              2 missed a deadline
Task              3 missed a deadline
Task              1 met a deadline
Overload in Task          2
Task              2 missed a deadline
Task              3 missed a deadline
Task              4 missed a deadline
Task              1 met a deadline
Overload in Task          2
Task              2 missed a deadline
Task              3 missed a deadline
```

```
Task            4 missed a deadline
Task            1 met a deadline
Task            2 met a deadline
Task            3 met a deadline
Task            4 missed a deadline
Task            4 met a deadline
Task            1 met a deadline
Task            2 met a deadline
Task            3 met a deadline
Task            4 met a deadline
Task            1 met a deadline
Task            2 met a deadline
Task            3 met a deadline
Task            4 met a deadline
Task            1 met a deadline
...
```

After the overload and nine missed deadlines the system does eventually return to a stable situation in which all deadlines are met.

To implement the mode change protocol, a `Timer` is defined for task τ_2 that is executed only when the task executes for more than its WCET (10). The handler calls a protected object that changes the priorities of all tasks to the 'overload' setting. A background, low priority, task is used to change the system back to the 'normal' priority settings. This task will only execute if there is slack in the system, in which case it is appropriate to reinstate the original priorities. An example run of the system when the protocol is engaged is as follows:

```
Main Started
Task            1 met a deadline
Task            2 met a deadline
Task            3 met a deadline
Task            4 met a deadline
Task            1 met a deadline
Task            2 met a deadline
Task            3 met a deadline
Task            4 met a deadline
Task            1 met a deadline
Task            2 met a deadline
Task            3 met a deadline
Task            4 met a deadline
Task            1 met a deadline
Task            2 met a deadline
Task            3 met a deadline
Task            4 met a deadline
Task            1 met a deadline
Overload in Task        2
Mode Change to Overload
Task            4 met a deadline
Task            3 met a deadline
Task            1 met a deadline
Task            4 met a deadline
Task            3 met a deadline
Task            2 missed a deadline
Overload in Task        2
Task            1 met a deadline
Task            4 met a deadline
Task            3 met a deadline
Task            2 missed a deadline
Overload in Task        2
Task            1 met a deadline
Task            4 met a deadline
Task            3 met a deadline
Task            2 missed a deadline
Task            2 missed a deadline
```

```
Mode Change to Normal
Task          1 met a deadline
Task          2 met a deadline
Task          3 met a deadline
Task          4 met a deadline
Task          1 met a deadline
Task          2 met a deadline
Task          3 met a deadline
Task          4 met a deadline
Task          1 met a deadline
```

As evident in this print out, all tasks apart from τ_2 meet their deadlines even when there is an overload. Of course τ_2 misses a series of four deadlines but once it has 'caught up' and the priorities changed by the background task then all tasks behave correctly.

6   Conclusion

In this paper we have considered some of the issues involved in supporting the production of mixed criticality systems. A type of system that is increasingly being considered in a wide range of applications. To verify such systems an extended form of scheduling analysis is needed and a somewhat more complex method of assigning priorities is required. Both of which are now available; and neither of which presents any significant problems for implementation languages such as Ada.

The required run-time characteristics are however beyond what is available in, say, a Ravenscar compliant real-time kernel. As tasks with low criticality may be executing with priorities higher than tasks with higher criticality it is imperative that tasks are not allowed to execute for more than their allotted execution time. Fortunately Ada 2005 allows task execution times to be monitored and code executed when bounds are violated. Such code can manipulate priorities so that critical tasks are protected. In this paper we have illustrated how such a protocol can be supported in Ada. An illustrative prototype multi-tasking program has been produced and executed on a bare-board single processor platform. Example executions of this code illustrate the required isolation between the 'failing' low criticality task and all higher criticality tasks. The code patterns provided by this prototype are such that their use in real industrial high-integrity applications should be seriously evaluated.

References

1. Audsley, N.C., Burns, A., Richardson, M., Tindell, K., Wellings, A.J.: Applying new scheduling theory to static priority preemptive scheduling. Software Engineering Journal 8(5), 284–292 (1993)
2. Audsley, N.C.: On Priority Assignment in Fixed Priority Scheduling. Information Processing Letters 79(1), 39–44 (2001)
3. Baruah, S.K., Vestal, S.: Schedulability analysis of sporadic tasks with multiple criticality specifications. In: ECRTS, pp. 147–155 (2008)
4. Bernat, G., Broster, I., Burns, A.: Rewriting history to exploit gain time. In: Proceedings Real-time Systems Symposium, Lisbon, Portugal, pp. 328–335. IEEE Computer Society, Los Alamitos (2004)

5. Bernat, G., Burns, A.: Multiple servers and capacity sharing for implementing flexible scheduling. Real-Time Systems Journal 22, 49–75 (2002)
6. Caccamo, M., Buttazzo, G., Sha, L.: Capacity sharing for overrun control. In: Proceedings 21th IEEE Real-Time Systems Symposium (2000)
7. de Niz, D., Lakshmanan, K., Rajkumar, R.: On the scheduling of mixed-criticality realtime task sets. In: Proceedings of the IEEE Real-Time Systems Symposium, pp. 291–300 (2009)
8. Dorin, F., Richard, P., Richard, M., Goossens, J.: Schedulability and sensitivity analysis of multiple criticality tasks with fixed-priorities. Real-Time Journal (2010)
9. Joseph, M., Pandya, P.: Finding response times in a real-time system. BCS Computer Journal 29(5), 390–395 (1986)
10. Prasad, D., Burns, A., Atkin, M.: The measurement and usage of utility in adaptive realtime systems. Journal of Real-Time Systems 25(2/3), 277–296 (2003)
11. Tindell, K., Alonso, A.: A very simple protocol for mode changes in priority preemptive systems. Technical report, Universidad Politecnica de Madrid (1996)
12. Vestal, S.: Preemptive scheduling of multi-criticality systems with varying degrees of execution time assurance. In: Proceedings of the IEEE Real-Time Systems Symposium, pp. 239–243 (2007)

Appendix -Example Code

The full code of the example used in this paper is as follows (note the package
Overload_ Control is as given earlier).

```ada
pragma Task_Dispatching_Policy(FIFO_Within_Priorities);
pragma Locking_Policy(Ceiling_Locking);
with System;
with Ada.Task_Identification; use Ada.Task_Identification;
with Ada.Execution_Time; use Ada.Execution_Time;
with Ada.Execution_Time.Timers; use Ada.Execution_Time.Timers;
with Ada.Text_IO; use Ada.Text_IO;
with Ada.Integer_Text_IO; use Ada.Integer_Text_IO;
with Ada.Real_Time; use Ada.Real_Time;
with Ada.Dynamic_Priorities; use Ada.Dynamic_Priorities;
with Overload_Control; use Overload_Control;
procedure Mixedcrit is

   task type Periodic(Id, Pri, Period, Deadline, WCET, LifeSpan :
      Natural) is pragma Priority(Pri);
   end Periodic;

   task Background is
      pragma Priority(1);
   end Background;

  protected Starter is
    pragma Priority(12);
    procedure Get_Start_Time(T : out Time);
  private
    First : boolean := true;
    St : Time;
  end Starter;

  procedure Work(Initial : CPU_Time; C : natural) is
    X : integer := 0;
  begin
   loop
     X := X + 1;
     exit when Clock - Initial > Milliseconds(C);
     end loop;
  end Work;

  task body Periodic is
    Epoc : constant Time_Span := Seconds(5);
    Next_Release, Start_Time, End_Time : Time;
    Release_Interval : constant Time_Span := Milliseconds(Period);
    Relative_Deadline : constant Time_Span := Milliseconds(Deadline);
    CPU, CPU_New : CPU_Time;
    T_ID : aliased Task_ID := Current_Task;
    Overrun : Timer(T_ID'Access);
    TempB : Boolean;
    Count : integer := 0;
  begin
    Starter.Get_Start_Time(Start_Time);
```

```
      Pri_Changer.Register(Id);
      Next_Release := Start_Time + Epoc;
      End_Time := Start_Time + Epoc + Seconds(LifeSpan);
      delay until Next_Release;
      CPU := Clock;
      loop
        Count := Count + 1;
      Set_Handler(Overrun, Milliseconds(WCET), Pri_Changer.Changer'Access);
         if Id=2 and (Count > 4 and Count < 8) then
            Put("Overload_in_Task_"); put(Id); new_line;
            Work(CPU,WCET*5);
         else
            Work(CPU,WCET);
         end if;
         Cancel_Handler(Overrun, TempB);
         if Clock > Next_Release + Relative_Deadline then
             put("Task_"); put(Id); put("_missed_a_deadline"); new_line;
         else
             put("Task_"); put(Id); put("_met_a_deadline"); new_line;
         end if;
         Next_Release := Next_Release + Release_Interval;
         exit when Next_Release > End_Time;
         CPU := Clock;
         delay until Next_Release;
       end loop;
    end Periodic;


    task body Background is
      Epoc : constant Duration := 4.5;
      End_Time : Time := Clock + Seconds(30);
    begin
      delay Epoc;
      loop
        Pri_Changer.Change(Normal);
        exit when Clock > End_Time;
      end loop;
    end Background;


    protected body Starter is
      procedure Get_Start_Time(T : out Time) is
      begin
        if First then
          St := Clock;
          First := false;
        end if;
        T := St;
      end Get_Start_Time;
     end Starter;

  A : Periodic(1,10,100,25,12,1);   B : Periodic(2,9,100,50,10,1);
  C : Periodic(3,8,100,70,15,1);    D : Periodic(4,7,100,100,25,1);
begin
  put_line("Main_Started");
end Mixedcrit;
```

Programming Languages Meet Multicore

Erhard Ploedereder

University of Stuttgart, Universitaetsstr. 38, 70569 Stuttgart, Germany
Erhard.Ploedereder@informatik.uni-stuttgart.de

Abstract. This introduction to a panel presents topics that need to be addressed by language designers as they strive to support the move towards multicore applications and much higher degrees of concurrency in the execution of programs.

Keywords: multicore, memory models, programming language design.

1 Introduction to the Panel

Multicore architectures have rekindled the discussion about suitable strategies to exploit the physical parallelism offered by them. While it is easy to keep two or four cores busy, mostly with independent concurrent activities, it is far from clear how one can fill 32, 64, or 1024 cores with useful work while the speed of the single cores declines or, at least, no longer increases. History provides little guidance towards a conclusive answer to this question. Successfully exploiting large-scale parallelism has been the traditional domain of "embarrassingly simple problems", whose computational structure lends itself to a direct mapping onto the hardware structures. Numerical applications on vector machines are early examples, graphics algorithms on GPUs are today's forerunners of such problems. In these restricted domains, amazing performance gains have been realized by parallelization. But not all problems are "embarrassingly simple". Quite the contrary, most of today's software does not exhibit the replicable and regular structures needed to easily distribute the computation over a large number of individual processors. And yet, in order to exploit the performance promises of multicore architectures, such distribution onto the available cores is necessary while minimizing the communication and synchronization across cores.

Crucial to the design of new languages and run-time environments is a concept of what the concurrent code units consist of and how they are to be composed. The spectrum starts at a view that sees concurrency as an implementation issue to be dealt with mostly by the tools used in producing the systems. Here compilers are made responsible for subdividing a given program into code portions that can then be farmed out to the different cores for concurrent execution. Demands on the design of a programming language are then relatively modest at first glance. They deal mostly with better decidability of data and control dependencies and on minimizing or at least strictly controlling the communication among concurrent entities. This approach has been quite successful in the past but only in very restricted problem domains, e.g., in the afore-mentioned numerics area. Implicit parallelization for irregular problems

A. Romanovsky and T. Vardanega (Eds.): Ada-Europe 2011, LNCS 6652, pp. 189–192, 2011.

or software in general has been singularly unsuccessful when targeted to a significant number of parallel hardware units. Alternatively, tools can be used to generate source code and feed it into parallel entities supported by a particular programming language. This approach requires appropriate language features but leaves it negotiable where the constraints needed for data-race-free execution (see below) are enforced. Enforcement by the tools allows the language designer to provide highly efficient, flexible mechanisms, possibly difficult to validate in all possible combinations. Engineering of embedded systems goes this route but requires a business model that ensures the tool-based validation of the absence of dangerous data races. Finally, languages that take on this responsibility or cater directly to the programmers in the more traditional sense of software production will have to solve both problems of offering a sufficiently rich model of concurrent program units and a way to ensure data-race-free execution. As always, many parameters influence the language design: is the distribution to be established statically or opportunistically during execution? How much explicit synchronization is inherent in the provided features? Most importantly, is the concurrency model adequate for the way programmers will think about parallel execution? An interesting and rather fundamental question to ask any language designer is where he or she positions the language in this wide spectrum of options.

For about a decade, designers of hardware, programming languages, compilers, and run-time kernels have struggled to develop a memory model that supports reliable semantics of programs in the presence of concurrency. A good overview of the topic is [1]; several of the following issues are paraphrased from this publication. The issues with memory models are amazingly difficult to formalize, understand and argue about, once sequential consistency is at stake or, worse, particular programmer expectations are violated by the semantics implied by the memory model. Performance concerns at the hard- and software levels, capabilities for analysis and detection of endangering execution characteristics, and the fundamental desire and need for non-deterministic execution orders of independent code portions interact to make simplistic memory models infeasible. One could go as far as to say that the memory models developed for present languages in many years of hard work are a major step towards understanding the issues but have ultimately failed to provide a solid basis for program execution without surprises. Users are still very unsure about what to expect and what to exclude as possible behavior of a concurrent program.

As we face the added dimension of multicore architectures with parallel accesses to shared memory via a hierarchy of separate and joint caches and the ensuing issues for providing a consistent view of "memory" contents and operations on these contents across cores, it can be argued that the model of threads (or anything similar) operating on and communicating via shared variables unrestrictedly is an evolutionary dead end for our model of parallel execution. Yet it is the most common paradigm in today's notions of concurrency and one wonders whether popular familiarity will win over technically better alternatives. At a different point in the spectrum, we have the well-established models of distributed systems without the concept of shared variables. The simplistic answer of mapping the methods of distributed system design and communication by message passing onto multicore architectures runs counter to the design of these architectures and partly forgoes the significant performance advantages of shared memory. A more constrained and more efficient model is highly desirable. Several such models have been proposed and much of the work on memory models has gone into providing sound semantics for these more constrained models. Increasingly, "programmer beware" as the attitude to deal with intentional or unintentional violations of the constraints imposed by such models is becoming unacceptable. Too many applications are being developed where data-race situations in the execution of code with unexpected impacts on functional behavior are simply unacceptable. Medical equipment, automotive control, robots, communication systems, and power grids are examples of domains where unsafe or unsound execution characteristics need to be verifiably avoided. The next generation of programming languages and run-time execution libraries will need to be designed with these concerns in mind. Hence, a primary question to be answered for future technologies is how the communication and synchronization of concurrently executing code portions is to be achieved with a guaranteed absence of unintended data races, presumably by language constructs and enforcement rules constraining communication and synchronization, but also with an efficiency that is commensurate with the frequency of these operations.

Thirty years of research and practice have established a wealth of knowledge and experience with scheduling concurrent units on single-CPU systems. Unfortunately, quite a few properties that were appreciated by users no longer hold true on multicore architectures. For example, priority protection models, a.k.a. ceiling protocols, can no longer protect resources by virtue of priority assignments. Languages or run-time environments will have to take a stand on the question which scheduling paradigms will be the most advantageous ones on multicore architectures. Possible answers still have to reach the user community.

2 Questions to the Panelists

For the following questions, please consider the term "language" as including run-time environments and libraries.

- Does the programmer have to identify concurrent units in the code? If so, what are these units, were they specifically designed for massively parallel execution, and how are they to be used? If not so, what is the underlying concept to arrive at concurrent execution?
- How does your language support communication and synchronization among concurrent units?
- How did you address efficiency concerns that arise from synchronization on multicore architectures?
- Which guarantees do your concepts provide regarding the avoidance of data races and general races?
- Can programmers step outside the safe bounds, i. e., write programs with races after all? How likely is an accidental violation of any such bounds?
- Which mapping of your language constructs to multicore architectures do you have in mind?
- Did transactional memory influence your choice of language constructs, resp. is it a good match to any of your existing constructs?

- Who or what decides about distribution of concurrent units to the available cores? Does your language make assumptions about when that decision is made? Can the user influence the decision?
- Which scheduling paradigms do you see as the winners on manycore architectures? Which ones does your language support?
- If you could radically change some concepts of your existing language to achieve a better match to multicore targets, what would these changes be?

Reference

1. Adve, S.V., Boehm, H.J.: Memory Models: A Case for Rethinking Parallel Languages and Hardware. Comm. of the ACM 53(8), 90–101 (2010)

Programming Languages for Real-Time Applications Executing on Parallel Hardware

Alan Burns

Department of Computer Science, University of York, UK

Panel Position Statement

If there were only one type of parallel hardware then perhaps the problem of designing programming languages for this domain would be tractable. Unfortunately, there are many: multicores, SMPs, MPSoCs, FPGAs, GPGPUs and dataflow machines to name just a few. And even the single architecture of 'multicore' represents a host of alternatives specifically with respect to memory management and scale. The scale issue being a particular source of concern – dual and four cores chips are currently problematic, but we know 1024 cores are not too far away. Even a focus of 1024 cores is sometimes criticized as being redundant and a wasted effort as 10,000 cores per chip is just around the corner.

It is clear that certain forms of parallel hardware are best exploited by tools that extract the necessary concurrency from the application's program which may be sequential or agnostic in this respect. But it is also clear that some forms of hardware and some kinds of application need to let the programmer control the mapping of their code on to the available platform. One of these platforms is SMPs (possibly a multicore chip) and one of the application areas is real-time systems.

Real-time systems have timing constraint, typically deadlines, that must be satisfied. A non real-time system may have considerable non-determinacy; as long as it is making progress, correctness does not depend on the detailed ordering of the large set of possible execution sequences. Real-time system must be more constrained; resources must be managed so that temporal constraints are taken into account. For a relatively small number of cores, the best way of managing this resource usage, at the programming language level, would appear to be the use of the well formed abstraction of a task/process/thread – I'll use the term *task* here.

On single processor system, the execution behaviour of a collection of tasks can be adequately controlled, from a scheduling point of view, by the use of priority and/or explicit task deadlines. What multicore architectures bring, in addition, is the notion of affinity – the relation of a task to the core (or cores) on which it must/may execute. For a real-time system, executing on a multicore platform, control over affinity is as important as the control of priority or deadline.

Most languages used for programming real-time systems provide the abstraction of a task. Sometimes this is well integrated into the language (as with Ada) and sometimes it is more of an add-on only available via a standard library (as with Java). These languages all support the notion of priority and priority based scheduling of tasks, and some even support deadlines and EDF scheduling (Earliest Deadline First). So how should they support affinities?

A. Romanovsky and T. Vardanega (Eds.): Ada-Europe 2011, LNCS 6652, pp. 193–195, 2011.
© Springer-Verlag Berlin Heidelberg 2011

From the scheduling theoretic point of view, there are a number of task management schemes that all have merit [3]:

– Partitioned allocation – each task is assigned to just one core
– Global allocation – all tasks can execute on all cores
– Migration – some tasks can migrate to some cores
– Zoned allocation – cores are grouped into zones, within which any one of the other schemes may be applied.

So, for an example of the latter scheme, an 80 task application running on a 16 core platform may be structured as four 4-core zones. Within each zone most tasks are partitioned, but three tasks can migrate, each between two statically defined cores [1]. Such a structure has the advantage of giving near optimal performance whilst minimizing overheads – as only 9 tasks migrate, and they do so between just two cores.

The natural place to support these aspects of a task (priority, deadline and affinity) is from within the programming language – even if a different kind of programmer deals with these aspects. It is to be commended that Ada is moving to give this level of support [2].

Turning now to issues of inter-task communication and synchronisation. As the Chair's paper discusses[1], this is a difficult area. What works well on single processors does not even generalise to two cores let alone, 10, 100 or 10,000. At the platform level there are various features that allow fast and predictable parallel code to execute. From the programming language designers point of view, what are the abstractions that allow these features to be accessed? Unlike the uniprocessor situation, it is unlikely that a single scheme will satisfy all application requirements.

One issue that must be addressed is control over the order of execution: when can code be reordered and when must the sequential order in the program be maintained – even when there does not seem to be any functional dependency between the statements. The use of unprotected shared variables is usually deemed undesirable in concurrent programming, but there are a number of lock free schemes that deliver good levels of performance on parallel hardware. These schemes, however, require explicit control over the order of execution of key *volatile* variables. Control over ordering can be extended to define blocks of code as being *atomic*. This allows the compiler and run-time to exploit transactional memory which is becoming more common; although perhaps not yet for real-time systems.

In conclusion, for small numbers of cores the current notion of a sequential task would appear to be the correct abstraction for real-time code. But this simple notion of a task must be augmented by allowing affinity to be controlled, and atomic or volatile variables and blocks to be directly supported in the programming language. There are, however, a number of important issues that are not addressed by this approach:

– Worst-case execution time (WCET), a vital parameter in real-time applications, is not easily obtained/measured on many forms of multicore chips.
– Not all platforms will have homogeneous processors, many will contain various heterogeneous components that will need different forms of abstraction to be available at the language level.

---

[1] Contained in these proceedings.

– The notion of a task is perhaps not the right abstraction for highly parallel hardware.

Not all of these issues can be solved at the programming language level, but it is to be hoped that the languages available to application developer are more of a help than a hindrance.

References

1. Burns, A., Davis, R.I., Wang, P., Zhang, F.: Partitioned EDF scheduling for multiprocessors using a C=D scheme. In: Proceedings of 18th International Conference on Real-Time and Network Systems (RTNS), pp. 169–178 (2010)
2. Burns, A., Wellings, A.J.: Dispatching domains for multiprocessor platforms and their representation in ada. In: Real, J., Vardanega, T. (eds.) Ada-Europe 2010. LNCS, vol. 6106, pp. 41–53. Springer, Heidelberg (2010)
3. Davis, R.I., Burns, A.: A survey of hard real-time scheduling algorithms for multiprocessor systems. Accepted for publication in ACM Computing Surveys (2011)

Multicore Programming in ParaSail

Parallel Specification and Implementation Language

S. Tucker Taft

SofCheck, Inc.
`tucker.taft@sofcheck.com`

Abstract. The advent of multicore processors requires a new approach to programming. ParaSail is an example of such a new approach. It is a marriage of implicit parallelism and formal methods integrated into a simplified yet powerful programming language.

Keywords: parallel programming, formal methods, multicore processor, race-free.

1 Introduction

ParaSail [1] is a new language for race-free parallel programming, with a distinct approach to supporting parallelism. ParaSail has two overarching themes: language semantics should be parallel by default, forcing the programmer to work harder if sequential execution is required; and all checking, for race conditions, user-defined assertions, and other potential run-time problems such as null values or array out of bounds, should be performed at compile-time.

ParaSail was created not by bolting parallelism and formal annotations onto an existing language, but rather by going back to basics, and building parallelism and formal annotations into the language from the beginning, while simplifying and unifying concepts wherever possible.

2 Implicitly Parallel

All expression evaluation in ParaSail is parallel by default. Explicitly parallel, explicitly sequential, or (by-default) data-dependence-based execution of statements and loops is provided. Annotations such as preconditions, postconditions, assertions, constraints, invariants, etc., are woven into the syntax, and are enforced at compile-time. Both sequential and concurrent data structures are supported, with both lock-based and lock-free concurrency mechanisms provided.

To enable its full compile-time checking, ParaSail eliminates global variables to operations, requiring all outputs and non-constant inputs of an operation to be explicitly declared. In addition, no aliasing is permitted between a writable parameter that is of a non-concurrent type, and any other parameter to the operation.

A. Romanovsky and T. Vardanega (Eds.): Ada-Europe 2011, LNCS 6652, pp. 196–200, 2011.

3   Simplified and Unified Language Concepts

To make *conceptual room* for including implicit parallelism and formal annotations in ParaSail, a conscious attempt was made to eliminate from the language all extraneous concepts, and to unify those that remain. ParaSail has four basic concepts – modules, types, objects, and operations. All modules are parameterized (like a generic template). Every type is an instance of a module. Every object is an instance of a type. Operations are defined in modules and operate on objects.

There is no special syntax for built-in types. Instead, all aspects of a type are definable by the user, including what literals are appropriate for the type, whether the type is indexable like an array, the comparison operations available on the type, any other operators available on the type, etc. Modules may be sequential or concurrent, with their instances being sequential or concurrent types, respectively. Instances of a concurrent type support concurrent access by multiple threads. Synchronization for concurrent objects may be indicated as locked, conditionally queued, or lock-free.

There is no explicit use of the heap or pointers in ParaSail. All ParaSail objects effectively live on the stack, in a region associated with the scope where they are declared. Objects are extensible and shrinkable as the result of assignment, but never share space with any other object. Storage management is automatic within each region, but there is no need for asychronous garbage collection since all size-changing operations are explicit and there is no sharing.

There are no exceptions in ParaSail, though it is possible for one thread to explicitly "exit" or "return" from a lexically enclosing construct, and as a side-effect terminate all other threads active within the construct. Large objects are generally passed by reference, but since there is no aliasing for non-concurrent objects and no exceptions, passing non-concurrent objects by copy is feasible as well.

4   Parallel Run-Time Model and Pico-Threading

ParaSail's run-time model is most closely related to that of Intel's Cilk language [2], where small computations are spawned off as pico-threads, which are then served by a set of worker processes running on separate processors or cores. Computations spawned by a given worker are served last-in, first-out (LIFO) by that worker. When a worker runs out of threads to serve, it steals from the queue of another worker, but in this case using first-in, first-out (FIFO).

Because of the lack of aliasing and the concurrent looping constructs, ParaSail is also amenable to the stream computing model of CUDA [3] and OpenCL [4], where the body of a concurrent loop becomes a "kernel" which is executed on each element of the container or stream over which the iteration applies. Because of the lack of pointers and exceptions, passing parameters by copy, as might be required when communicating with a Graphics Processing Unit (GPU), is straightforward.

5   Deterministic and Non-deterministic Race-Free Parallel Programming

ParaSail makes it easy for the programmer to achieve determinism when desired, but also does not force overspecification, so that, for example, the iterations of a (non-concurrent) loop over a sequence are by default unordered, but the programmer may specify "forward" or "reverse" explicitly. This enables the compiler to more readily interleave or run in parallel non-data-dependent parts of the loop. Similarly, by default the execution of sequential statements are limited only by data dependencies involving non-concurrent data structures, but it is possible for the programmer to force strictly sequential execution by using ";;" rather than simply ";" to separate statements. Or the programmer can go the other way, and effectively declare there are no non-concurrent data structure dependencies by using "||" rather than ";" to separate statements, essentially "forcing" parallel execution.

6   Object-Oriented Programming in Parasail

As far as object-oriented programming, ParaSail supports inheritance and polymorphism. Each module has an "interface," and if not declared as abstract, a "class" that defines it. Modules may inherit operation interfaces from one or more other modules, and may inherit operation code and data components from at most one other module. Named sets of operations may be effectively appended to a module, without disturbing the original module, largely bypassing the need for "visitor" operations. A polymorphic variant of a type, identified by appending a "+" to the type name, may be used anywhere a type is used, to represent any type that implements the associated interface.

7   Conclusion

Our position is that languages like ParaSail are the way to bring safe and efficient parallel programming to the masses, which will be mandatory as we move into the era of multi-core on the desktop. ParaSail fosters the use of parallel programming by making programs parallel by default, while eliminating programmer concerns like race conditions and run-time failures, thereby easing the debugging burden. This burden is further reduced by eliminating exceptions, the heap, and reassignable pointers, and unifying the typically distinct concepts of generic templates, packages, namespaces, modules, interfaces, classes, objects, and structs, into a single notion of module, with all types being an instance of a module, and all objects being an instance of a type.

References

1. Taft, S.T.: ParaSail Programming Language blog (2011),
   `http://parasail-programming-language.blogspot.com`
2. Blumofe, et al.: Cilk: An Efficient Multithreaded Runtime System (1995),
   `http://publications.csail.mit.edu/lcs/pubs/pdf/MIT-LCS-TM-548.pdf`

3. NVIDIA: What is CUDA (2011),
   http://www.nvidia.com/object/what_is_cuda_new.html
4. Khronos Group: OpenCL - The open standard for parallel programming of heterogeneous systems (2011), http://www.khronos.org/opencl/

Appendix

As an example of the syntax of ParaSail, here is a parallel version of the Quick-
sort algorithm in ParaSail. The expressions in braces are annotations which are
checked for validity at compile-time. Comments start with "//". Reserved words
are in lower case. In this example, user identifiers are in mixed case, though that
is not required. Note that rather than explicit recursion, a parallel "continue
loop" is used to perform the sorting of the two partitions of the original array.

```
interface Sorting<One_Dim_Array<>> is
    // Non-recursive parallel quicksort
    procedure Quicksort(Arr : ref var One_Dim_Array;
      function Before(Left, Right : One_Dim_Array::Element_Type)
        -> Boolean is "<");
          // Sort Arr according to the sorting function "Before"
          // which returns True if Left must appear before Right
          // in the sorted order.
          // Before returns False if Left = Right.
end interface Sorting;

class Sorting is
    // Non-recursive parallel quicksort
  exports
    procedure Quicksort(Arr : ref var One_Dim_Array;
      function Before(Left, Right : One_Dim_Array::Element_Type)
        -> Boolean is "<")
    is
      for A => Arr while Length(A) > 1 loop
        // Handle short arrays directly. Partition longer arrays.
        if Length(A) == 2 then
          if Before(A[A.Last], A[A.First]) then
            // Swap the elements if out of order
            A[A.Last] :=: A[A.First];
          end if;
        else
          // Partition array
          const Mid := A[A.First + Length(A)/2];
          var Left : Index_Type := A.First;
          var Right : Index_Type := A.Last;
          until Left > Right loop
            var New_Left : Index_Type := Right+1;
            var New_Right : Index_Type := Left-1;
            block
              // Find item in left half to swap
              for I in Left .. Right forward loop
                if not Before(A[I], Mid) then
                  // Found an item that can go into right partitition
                  New_Left := I;
                  if Before(Mid, A[I]) then
                    // Found an item that *must* go into right part
                    exit loop;
                  end if;
                end if;
              end loop;
            ||
              // In parallel, find item in right half to swap
              for J in Left .. Right reverse loop
```

```
                    if not Before(Mid, A[J]) then
                      // Found an item that can go into left partitition
                      New_Right := J;
                      if Before(A[J], Mid) then
                        // Found an item that *must* go into left part
                        exit loop;
                      end if;
                    end if;
                  end loop;
                end block;

                if New_Left > New_Right then
                  // Nothing more to swap
                  // Exit loop and recurse on two partitions
                  Left := New_Left;
                  Right := New_Right;
                  exit loop;
                end if;

                // Swap items
                A[New_Left] :=: A[New_Right];

                // continue looking for items to swap
                Left := New_Left + 1;
                Right := New_Right - 1;
              end loop;

              // At this point, "Right" is right end of left partition
              // and "Left" is left end of right partition
              // and the partitions don't overlap
              // and neither is the whole array
              // and everything in the left partition can precede Mid
              // and everything in the right partition can follow Mid
              // and everything between the partitions is equal to Mid.
              {Left > Right;
               Right < A.Last;
               Left > A.First}
              {(for all I in A.First .. Right => not Before(Mid, A[I]));
               (for all J in Left .. A.Last => not Before(A[J], Mid));
               (for all K in Right+1 .. Left-1 =>
                 not Before(Mid, A[K]) and not Before(A[K], Mid))}

              // Iterate on two halves (in parallel)
            then
              continue loop with A => A[A.First .. Right];
              ||
              continue loop with A => A[Left .. A.Last];
            end if;
        end loop;
      end procedure Quicksort;
  end class Sorting;
```

Why Parallel Functional Programming Matters: Panel Statement

Kevin Hammond

School of Computer Science, University of St. Andrews, UK
kh@cs.st-andrews.ac.uk

Abstract. Parallel programming is returning to importance. Functional programming ideas offer a way to break through the barriers that restrict parallel programmers, dramatically simplifying how parallelism can be exploited. This paper explores some ideas of abstraction from functional programming, showing how functional programming offers opportunities to deal with real problems of parallelism.

1   Introduction

In a possibly unguarded moment, Carnegie Mellon professor Bob Harper said[1]:

> "The only thing that works for parallel programming is functional programming"

While this statement might need some qualification, it conveys a kernel of truth that has led to an epiphany moment for many programmers and system designers. Parallel programming is *fundamentally* about avoiding or minimising side-effecting conflicts, and functional programming can clearly help with this: *if a language has no side-effects, or makes all side-effects explicit, it becomes much easier to write programs that run in parallel.*

For a long time, parallel programming was seen as a specialised activity, relevant only to high-performance applications. This situation is currently changing, *and changing extremely rapidly*. Future multi-core/many-core hardware will not be *slightly parallel*, like today's dual-core and quad-core processor architectures, but will be *massively parallel*. It is becoming increasingly obvious that the traditional sequential *von Neumann* programming model has reached, or will soon reach, its limits, even when packaged into a threading model.

> "Ultimately, the advice I'll offer is that developers should start thinking about tens, hundreds, and thousands of cores now in their algorithmic development and deployment pipeline. This starts at a pretty early stage of development; usually, the basic logic of the application should be influenced because it drives the asymptotic parallelism behaviors."
> **Anwar Ghuloum, Principal Engineer, Intel Corporation**

---

[1] Pers. comm., March 2011.

A. Romanovsky and T. Vardanega (Eds.): Ada-Europe 2011, LNCS 6652, pp. 201–205, 2011.

It is not enough simply to program in a language that *permits* parallelism and to hope that adequate performance can be obtained; rather, programmers must think about parallelism as a fundamental part of their program structure, in the same way that they think about loops, conditionals and other constructs. Parallelism cannot be "bolted on" to an existing program (or language) as an afterthought, it must be present in a fundamental way in the original design. Failure to do this will yield a program with unacceptable parallel performance, or one that cannot be scaled to meet future requirements. This paper discusses these issues, building on substantial experience with Parallel Haskell [1,2,3,4].

2   What Are the Key Challenges to Writing Effective Parallel Programs?

Parallel programmers face many challenges that are not present in sequential code, and which may not be obvious from the outset. The key problems include:

Decomposition: the parallel tasks within the program must be identified.

Race conditions: the order in which expressions are evaluated and/or the order of communications may affect the outcome of the parallel program.

Locking: Shared memory locations must be *locked* to avoid conflicts that could give inconsistent results; this locking is often expensive and very error-prone.

Deadlock/Livelock: the programmer must avoid creating dependencies that block program execution.

Granularity: It is necessary to achieve the correct level of granularity - too fine-grained and the system will be swamped with small tasks; too coarse-grained and there will be insufficient granularity. Unfortunately, a fixed choice will generally not *scale*.

Scalability: programs should scale to take advantage of increased numbers of parallel processors.

Load balancing: work may be unevenly distributed among the available processing resources, especially where tasks have *irregular* granularity, and it may be necessary to rebalance the work allocation.

2.1   How does Functional Programming help with These Challenges?

Fortunately, good high-level language and implementation design can help with many of these challenges. Purely functional languages such as Haskell have several advantages when it comes to parallel evaluation. The most fundamental is that because there are no side effects, it is always safe to execute computations in parallel, so **decomposition** is easy. Regardless of the order in which computations are executed, the result of the program will always be the same. In fact, even more strongly, the result will be identical to that obtained when the program is run sequentially. Moreover, provided all the parallel computations are needed as part of the result of the program, if the program terminates when it is run sequentially, it will also terminate when run in parallel. These two points mean that programs can be debugged sequentially, which represents a huge saving in effort. The parallel implementation adds only behavioural effects in terms of e.g. performance and memory usage. In addition, because the order in which any I/O operations are performed is fully defined by the language[2], there can *never* be **race conditions** or unexpected outputs caused by interleaving I/O operations in the wrong order. Much or all of the required **locking** and synchronisation can be handled entirely within the implementation. In addition, **deadlock** can *never* occur: the data and control dependencies in the functional language ensure that there can be no unresolved mutual dependencies between tasks. Finally, **scalability** and **load balancing** are made much simpler if **granularity** can be varied by the runtime system: it is much easier to rebalance fine-grained tasks, and to absorb increased processing capabilities. However, care needs to be taken to avoid both excessive per-thread overheads and excessive numbers of threads. Ultra-lightweight threading can help with this.

2.2 Shared Memory and Locking

Avoiding memory conflicts is very important in shared-memory systems. The usual solution to this problem is to use a memory-locking protocol, often using very slow and bandwidth-hogging atomic operations. If nothing is known about the behaviour of other parallel threads, as in most imperative/object-oriented languages, then it is necessary to lock very conservatively in order to avoid possible conflicts. This can lead to a high level of locking and poor performance, especially when the programmer has (as often happens) been over-cautious with the use of locking. One solution is to avoid shared memory and to provide threads with their own completely private and independent memory spaces. Sharing then occurs only if it is necessary, using either a shared-memory or a message-passing abstraction. Maintaining this discipline manually is extremely difficult, but it is easily handled as part of a well-designed runtime system for a parallel functional language, for example.

3 Parallel Patterns or Skeletons

Recognising and using patterns of parallelism can dramatically simplify the programming task. Pattern-based programming is one of the key weapons in getting programmers to "think parallel". There is a long history of using parallel patterns in functional programming, where they are usually called *skeletons* [5]. Higher-order functions naturally describe high-level programming patterns, the use of higher-order functions allows them to be combined easily and generically, and the advanced type systems allow these patterns to be safely reused in a variety of settings. For example, a simple parallel map where a function f is mapped over a list of elements $[x_1, \ldots, x_n]$ to give $[fx_1, \ldots, fx_n]$ can be given a simple direct parallel implementation as shown in Figure 1, which maps easily

---

[2] e.g. using the IO monad in Haskell

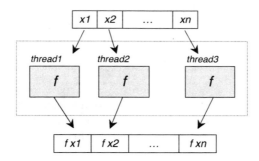

Fig. 1. Simple Implementation of Parallel Map Pattern

onto a data-parallel system. Alternative parallel patterns for the same construct include control-parallel *task farms* or *parallel workpools* or even, if the dependencies are correct, *pipelines*. These high-level patterns can easily be selected and changed by the programmer.

4   Influences on Real-World Languages/Systems

Functional languages such as Haskell [6], Erlang [7] and Micrososft's F# [8] are rapidly growing in popularity. Such languages naturally support parallelism. Functional programming concepts are also finding their way into other, mainstream notations. For example: **Apple's Grand Central Dispatch scheduler** uses *closures* to capture very lightweight threads; C++0x uses *futures* to encode potential threads, and allows anonymous functions to be defined using *lambda functions* and *closures*; dataflow ideas are widely used in parallel computer architectures; CUDA is based around the idea of stateless threads with bulk synchronisation; and Google has very successfully deployed pattern-based programming in the form of its **mapReduce** pattern, which is a classic functional programming construct. These are just a few instances of the idea that "the only thing that works is functional programming".

5   What about Sequential Performance?

This is a mantra that is often raised. Sequential imperative programs are faster than the corresponding functional programs, so we should aim to parallelise them rather than the functional programs. Unfortunately, as discussed in the introduction, this idea is fundamentally limited for a number of reasons:

1. conventional language approaches lead us to think sequentially rather than to think parallel;
2. imperative languages usually lack the high level structuring constructs that are needed for parallel programming;
3. the most scalable parallelism works at a fine level of granularity;

4. we will usually not be able to minimise the use of locking;
5. we will usually need to program very defensively, since we do not have any guarantees about the structure of our parallel program;
6. we will need to expend considerable energy dealing with race conditions, memory contention and deadlock etc.

Moreover, as described above, many of the successful ideas in parallelism actually reflect functional programming concepts at some level. Encapsulation and isolation of both task and memory is key to achieving good parallel performance. The functional programming paradigm naturally lends itself to this.

6 Conclusions

This paper has briefly covered the key problems associated with parallel programming, and shown how functional programming technology can help with many of them. Naturally, there are still many problems and difficulties that remain to be overcome and the paper has both barely scratched the surface of the topic and been deliberately provocative. However, by eliminating uncontrolled side-effects functional programming dramatically simplifies the problem of writing good parallel programs. Functional programming may not be the only thing that works, but it does seem to be one of the most promising.

Acknowledgements

This work has been generously supported by the EU Framework 6/7 projects SCIEnce (RII3-CT-2005-026133) and ADVANCE (IST-2010-248828), and by the UK's Engineering and Physical Sciences Research Council (Islay, EP/F 030657 and HPC-GAP, EP/G 055181).

References

1. Hammond, K., Trinder, P.: Parallel Haskell: Lightweight Parallelism for Heavyweight Parallel Programs (2011) (in Preparation)
2. Trinder, P., Hammond, K., Loidl, H.W., Peyton Jones, S.: Algorithm + Strategy = Parallelism. J. of Functional Programming 8(1), 23–60 (1998)
3. Trinder, P.W., Hammond, K., Mattson Jr., J.S., Partridge, A.S., Peyton Jones, S.L.: Gum: a Portable Parallel Implementation of Haskell. In: Proc. PLDI 1996: ACM 1996 Conf. on Prog. Lang. Design and Implementation, pp. 79–88. ACM, New York (1996)
4. Marlow, S., Maier, P., Loidl, H.W., Aswad, M.K., Trinder, P.: Seq no more: better strategies for parallel haskell. In: Proceedings of the Third ACM Haskell Symposium on Haskell, Haskell 2010, pp. 91–102. ACM, New York (2010)
5. Cole, M.: Algorithmic Skeletons: Structure Management of Parallel Computations. In: Research Monographs in Parallel and Distributed Computing. MIT Press, Cambridge (1989)
6. Peyton Jones, S. (ed.): Haskell 98 Language and Libraries: the Revised Report. Cambridge University Press, Cambridge (2003)
7. Armstrong, J.: Erlang. Commun. ACM 53(9), 68–75 (2010)
8. Petricek, T.: Real World Functional Programming With Examples in F# and C#. Manning Publications (2009)

OOT, DO-178C and SPARK

Roderick Chapman and Trevor Jennings

Altran Praxis Limited,
20 Manvers Street
Bath BA1 1PX, UK
{rod.chapman,trevor.jennings}@altran-praxis.com

Abstract. This position paper briefly covers the design of object-oriented programming in SPARK, and goes on to discuss the potential impact that the emerging DO-178C and Ada2012 standards might have on SPARK.

Keywords: Ada, SPARK, DO-178C, Object Oriented Programming, LSP.

1 Introduction

The SPARK[1] language is designed primarily for the comprehensive application of static analysis. The depth of the analyses achievable ranges from data-flow and information-flow analysis, through proof of absence of run-time exceptions, to formal verification of correct functionality of the code against a specification. This paper looks at the underlying design principles of SPARK and considers the aspects of OOT that have been adopted without compromising those principles. We also look to the future and the impact that Ada2012 and DO-178C might have.

2 Static and Dynamic Verification for OO

Static analysis is recognized as a valuable mechanism for verifying software. Industrial experience shows that the use of static analysis during development eliminates classes of errors that can be hard to find during testing [1]. Moreover, these errors can be eliminated by the developer before the code has been compiled or entered into the configuration management system, saving the cost of repeated code review and testing which results from faults that are discovered during dynamic testing.

Static analysis as a technology has a fundamental advantage over dynamic testing. If a program property is shown to hold using static analysis, then the property is guaranteed for all scenarios if the *soundness* of the analysis can be trusted. Testing, on the other hand, may demonstrate the presence of an error, but the correct execution of a test only indicates that the program behaves correctly for the specific set of inputs provided by the test, and within the specific context that the test harness sets up. For all but the simplest systems, exhaustive testing of all possible combinations of input

---

[1] The SPARK programming language is not sponsored by or affiliated with SPARC International Inc. and is not based on the SPARC® architecture.

A. Romanovsky and T. Vardanega (Eds.): Ada-Europe 2011, LNCS 6652, pp. 206–210, 2011.
© Springer-Verlag Berlin Heidelberg 2011

values and program contexts is infeasible. Further, the impact of correcting errors that are found during the testing phases of the lifecycle is generally massive in comparison to those found during development. In spite of these limitations, testing remains at the heart of most software engineering projects, while static analysis remains undervalued.

2.1 Here Comes DO-178C…

DO-178B does require some forms of static analysis. These appear under the "Source Code is Accurate and Consistent" objectives appearing in Table A.5 and section 6.3.4f. The application of these analyses, though, did not permit subsequent testing activities to be reduced or eliminated and perhaps have remained under-valued in the context of DO-178B for some time.

DO-178C "moves the goalposts" significantly. In our understanding of the current draft of the new standard, it *will* allow verification credit to be taken for static analysis activities, and hence subsequent dynamic analyses may be reduced or eliminated. This is most welcome – effectively catching up with the application of static analysis that has been advocated and implemented by SPARK for more than 15 years.

178C offers the prospect of meeting a verification objective by wholly static means, wholly dynamic, or some combination of the two. We presume that the selection of techniques to be used will form part of the Plan for Software Aspects of Certification (PSAC) in a 178C project, and will have to be justified appropriately. We do not ever imagine that dynamic verification will be entirely eliminated – for instance, testing still has its place in several areas:

- To verify environmental assumptions that underpin static analysis.
- To confirm the results of static analysis under experimental conditions.
- To verify behaviours that lie beyond that mathematical model of whatever static analysis tools have been used. For example – covert channels such as timing and power consumption for security.
- To verify *system* level behaviour and the interaction of software components with other systems, hardware devices, and the outside world.
- To validate that system behaviour really does meet top-level requirements.

Nevertheless, static analysis should still play a significant role in DO-178C projects if only to reduce the cost, risk and repetition of subsequent dynamic analyses.

3 OOT in SPARK: 2002 - Present

Following the advent of tagged types in Ada95, a design study was carried out to see if any of Ada's (then) new OO features could be incorporated in SPARK. This eventually led to release 6.1 of the SPARK language definition and Examiner in June 2002. This section briefly describes the language subset that resulted from this work and persists to this day.

The basic design goal was, in line with the existing design of SPARK, to favour static verification and *soundness* of that verification at all costs over dynamic language features. In short, anything that defied static verification was eliminated.

3.1 Constructors and Finalizers

The model of object creation and destruction in SPARK is explicit. A SPARK object is created simply via its declaration, and its lifetime is statically determined by the scope in which it is declared. The declaration defines its type (and class) statically. The object may be initialized either as part of its declaration, or via an explicit call to an initializing subprogram. Data flow analysis techniques ensure that the object is always initialized prior to first use.

Object finalization is also explicit in SPARK. A finalizer operation must be called explicitly prior to the exit of the object's scope if some finalization action is required.

3.2 Abstraction

Abstraction involves the identification of the abstract features of a class - these are the key features that define each object of the class. SPARK supports abstraction via its abstract data types that define both the abstract data fields for members of the class and the abstract operations for the class.

3.3 Encapsulation

Encapsulation involves the hiding of implementation detail from clients of the class. SPARK supports encapsulation via packages in the same way as Ada. The package specification provides the visible interface for the class. The package body encapsulates the entire implementation of the class, which is hidden from clients of the class. SPARK language rules verify that the implementation conforms to the contracts that define its visible semantics.

3.4 Hierarchy and Inheritance

In OOT the concepts of hierarchy and inheritance are closely coupled. In order to create a hierarchy of related classes, a subclass can be created that is based on a more abstract superclass. The subclass automatically inherits all the visible attributes and operations of the superclass and in addition, the subclass may override certain inherited operations with specialist implementations, and may also add further attributes and operations that are appropriate for its own use.

The creation of hierarchies and the application of single-level inheritance are both supported within SPARK via tagged types and public child packages.

A further characteristic of the SPARK inheritance model is that it enforces statically the Liskov/Wing substitution principle (LSP) [2]. This principle essentially requires that where a subclass operation overrides an operation in the superclass then the subclass operation will conform to all pre- and post-conditions of the superclass operation. In this context, conformance implies that the subclass operation requires at most the pre-conditions of the superclass operation, and promises at least the post-conditions of the superclass operation.

Support for the Liskov substitution principle in SPARK is based on explicit pre- and post-condition contracts that may be applied to any operation, allowing formal verification of code properties. The use of pre-conditions is a very powerful tool in defining the conditions under which an operation can be used safely. One of the major risks of inheriting operations is misunderstanding of the pre-conditions associated with the use of the operation, and not abiding with those pre-conditions in the context of a subclass. SPARK protects against this since the preconditions are stated explicitly and more importantly, the Examiner will statically analyze the program to ensure that the operation is only ever invoked within its pre-conditions.

3.5 Polymorphism and Dynamic Dispatching

Polymorphism is a key feature of OOT, however it can undermine certain aspects of static analysis. The conflict seems obvious: how can a tool *statically* analyze a dynamically dispatched call? This issue applies not only to formal verification by a static analysis tool, but also to verification by code review and by test. There is also an impact on other forms of static verification techniques such as schedulability and structural coverage analysis. Secondly, polymorphic programming is almost always associated with the use of general access types in order to build and iterate over heterogeneous data structures. Access types are currently forbidden in SPARK for very good reasons—principally to avoid aliasing—so it is not even clear that allowing classwide types and dispatching would be any use at all without the addition of access types – something that was too horrible to consider at the time.

For these reasons, polymorphism and dynamic dispatching are not directly supported in SPARK at present.

4 OOT in SPARK – Future

Following the Ada2005 and (soon) Ada2012 standards, there are several areas of OOT in SPARK that are now worth re-visiting.

The most significant development concerns the provision of container libraries in Ada2012. The new "Bounded Containers" proposed for Ada2012 provide libraries that are compatible with the overall design of SPARK, and allow for heterogeneous data-structures to be build *without the explicit use of access types or "pointers."* This is a significant breakthrough, since it implies that classwide types and dispatching could be both achievable and useful in SPARK. This would, of course, be complemented by SPARK's existing support for verification of LSP.

5 Open Issues

Some issues with OOT remain open from our point of view. In particular:

5.1 Is Verification of LSP A Mirage?

Many proponents of OOT cite the LSP as "the way" to justify the use of dynamic dispatch in OO programs. While this is superficially attractive, we must remember that the original formulation of LSP was for a particular formalization of OO that may not apply to "real" programming languages like C++, Ada or Java.

Dynamic verification of LSP has been long-established in languages such as Eiffel [3], for example, and (soon) in Ada2012 with its new pre- and post-condition aspect clauses. While this does constitute progress, dynamic checking of contracts is most definitely not "verification" from a formal point of view – it remains just a highly specialized form of testing.

This leaves static verification of LSP. SPARK has shown how this can be done at the cost (some would say) of Draconian language subsetting and discipline. Static verification of LSP remains extremely challenging in other unsubsetted languages, so we look forward to progress in this area.

5.2 Is LSP Actually Useful?

Next question: is it possible to write useful programs that strictly comply with the LSP? Perhaps LSP is too restrictive, and projects will simply ignore such guidance in favour of increased expressive power? Perhaps we should ask the Eiffel community for advice on this topic?

6 Conclusions

The jury may be still out on the use of OOT in high integrity software to some extent, but the advent of Ada2012 and DO-178C does seem to suggest a bright future where both the technical approach and standards will align with useful results. We look forward to results from projects using these new languages and standards.

References

1. Amey, P.: Correctness by Construction: Better can also be Cheaper. CrossTalk Journal (March 2002), PDF on,
   http://www.stsc.hill.af.mil, http://www.sparkada.com
2. Liskov, B., Wing, J.: A Behavioural Notion of Subtyping. ACM Transactions on Programming Languages and Systems 16(6) (November 1994)
3. Meyer, B.: A Touch of Class: Learning to Program Well with Objects and Contracts. Springer, Heidelberg (2009) ISBN 978-3-540-92144-8

Position Paper: DO-178C/ED-12C and Object-Orientation for Critical Systems

Dewi Daniels

Abstract. DO-178C/ED-12C, six years in preparation, is expected to be published in 2011. This updated document will provide guidance for the development and verification of safety-related software for avionic systems. As this position paper will describe, DO-178C/ED-12C is good news for Ada.

Keywords: Ada, avionics, DO-178B, DO-178C, safety-critical, safety-related, software.

1 DO-178C

For the past nineteen years, DO-178B/ED-12B [1, 2] has provided guidance on the software aspects of airborne systems and equipment. With over 20,000 certified jet aeroplanes in service worldwide [3], DO-178B/ED-12B has turned out to be an extremely important document. The document is currently being updated to reflect the changes in software technologies since 1992. About 375 individuals have been involved in preparing the updated document. These individuals represent a broad mix of organizations, including certification authorities, airframe manufacturers and equipment suppliers from around the world, so DO-178C will present a consensus of the airborne software community. DO-178C/ED-12C is expected to be published at the end of 2011.

2 Object-Oriented Supplement

I believe that DO-178C/ED-12C will be mostly good news for Ada. The object-oriented technology supplement will provide much-needed guidance on how to use, and verify the use of, the object-oriented features of Ada 95 (and later). I'm really impressed by the excellent job done by the folks in the sub-group that wrote the object-oriented supplement. They had a very good starting point in the FAA Object Oriented Technology in Aviation (OOTiA) Handbook. Nevertheless, I was surprised by what they wrote. I expected a list of rules; for example, "thou shalt not use multiple-inheritance". Instead, they've identified a set of objectives that need to be satisfied. Some of these objectives will be very easy to satisfy if you limit the features that you use, but very difficult (and therefore time-consuming and expensive) to satisfy if you're determined to use every feature in the object-oriented toolbox. Nevertheless, nothing is forbidden.

3 Formal Methods Supplement

The formal methods supplement will, at long last, allow certification credit to be taken for the use of technologies such as SPARK. I get frustrated when people

A. Romanovsky and T. Vardanega (Eds.): Ada-Europe 2011, LNCS 6652, pp. 211–213, 2011.

complain that formal methods are immature and unproven. Formal methods have been around longer than MC/DC, yet no-one complains that MC/DC is immature or unproven.

Dijkstra's seminal book on "A Discipline of Programming" [5] was published in 1976. I was personally involved in conducting program proof of a family of Full Authority Digital Engine Controllers, including one for the Rolls-Royce RB211-535, when I worked for Program Validation Limited in the early 1990s. In 2004, a report funded by the US Department of Homeland Security [6] cited Praxis' Correctness by Construction methodology, which relies heavily on the use of formal methods (including SPARK), as one that can produce software with fewer than 0.1 defects per thousand lines of code. More recently, Airbus has been doing some very interesting work using the Caveat tool [7].

4   Strongly Typed Languages

I regret that we did not push harder to promote strongly typed languages in DO-178C/ED-12C. I remember that, at the Vienna plenary, Professor John Knight was trying to drum up support for DO-178C/ED-12C to recommend the use of strongly typed languages. Nevertheless, this was never a battle that we could have won; the voting rules mean that just a few dissenting voters would have been able to block the proposal.

This is a shame; Andy German's work [8] showed that, on C-130J, Ada (and especially SPARK) programs had a much lower average defect rate than C programs.

DO-178B/ED-12B §4.2c states that "methods and tools should be chosen that provide error prevention in the software development processes". This good advice is not followed up elsewhere in the document. Indeed, it's easier to satisfy the DO-178B/ED-12B objectives using C than it is using Ada (for example, verification of array-bound checks is not an issue in C, since they are not a part of the language definition). The result is that Ada is now little-used in civil avionic software development (C is the most widely used language), while Ada is widely used in the European rail industry (because EN 50128 highly recommends the use of strongly typed languages).

5   In-Service Experience of DO-178B/ED-12B

DO-178B/ED-12B has been a spectacularly successful document. Or have we just been lucky so far? There has not been a single accident in passenger service that has been ascribed to software, although software has been a contributing factor is a very small number of accidents, and has been implicated in a small number of in-flight upsets.

The issues that I know of that have caused problems in service have not been because the software failed to implement the requirements correctly; rather, the software implemented the requirements faithfully, but the requirements specified unsafe or otherwise undesirable behaviour (usually in circumstances that had not been foreseen by the requirements author). An example is the A320 accident in Warsaw in 1993, where a software interlock that had been designed to prevent inadvertent deployment of the engine thrust reversers and ground spoilers in-flight prevented their deployment for 9 seconds after landing in a strong crosswind.

6 Model-Based Supplement

It therefore follows that the most effective way in which software developers can help improve aircraft safety is by using methods and techniques that help ensure that the requirements are the right requirements; and that, in particular, they specify safe behaviour. For this reason, I believe that the model-based supplement could turn out to be one of the most significant DO-178C/ED-12C supplements. Model-based techniques allow common tools and notations to be shared between system engineers and software engineers. Furthermore, they allow for early animation of the requirements, providing the system engineers with early feedback that the software behaviour is as they expected and supports the system safety objectives.

Again, Ada has its part to play in model-based design. The SCADE-to-SPARK code generator that is under development promises to combine the advantages of model-based development, formal methods and Ada.

7 Conclusion

Airborne software has an exceptional safety record. We would like to keep it that way. I believe that Ada has a part to play in ensuring that airliners remain a safe way to travel. I also think that DO-178C/ED-12C will be good for the Ada community.

References

1. RTCA, Inc.: DO-178B: Software Considerations in Airborne Systems and Equipment Certification, Washington (1992)
2. EUROCAE: ED-12B: Software Considerations in Airborne Systems and Equipment Certification, Paris (1992)
3. Boeing Commercial Airplanes: Statistical Summary Of Commercial Jet Airplane Accidents, Worldwide Operations 1959-2009, Seattle (2010)
4. Federal Aviation Administration,
   http://www.faa.gov/aircraft/air_cert/design_approvals/air_software/oot/
5. Dijkstra, E.W.: A Discipline of Programming, Englewood Cliffs (1976)
6. Redwine, S.T., Davis, N. (eds.): Processes to Produce Secure Software. Improving Security across the Software Development Lifecycle (National Cybersecurity Partnership Taskforce Report), Appendix B, pp. 17–47 (2004),
   http://www.cyberpartnership.org/init-soft.html
7. Souyris, J., Wiels, V., Delmas, D., Delseny, H.: Formal Verification of Avionics Software Products. In: Cavalcanti, A., Dams, D.R. (eds.) FM 2009. LNCS, vol. 5850, pp. 532–546. Springer, Heidelberg (2009)
8. German, A.: Software Static Analysis Lessons Learned, CrossTalk (2003)
9. Ladkin, P.B.:
   http://www.rvs.uni-bielefeld.de/publications/Incidents/DOCS/ComAndRep/Warsaw/warsaw-report.html

Object Orientation in Critical Systems: Yes, in Moderation

Position Paper for the DO178C and Object-Orientation for Critical Systems Panel

Jean-Pierre Rosen

Adalog, Issy-les-Moulineaux, France
rosen@adalog.fr, http://www.adalog.com

1 Introduction

DO178C introduces a supplement addressing Object Oriented Technology (OOT) for avionics software. Although OOT is more of a methodological issue than a language issue, and despite the wording that tries to be programming-language agnostic, it is clear that this supplement is the result from a strong push from the C++ and Java communities to make their languages more acceptable for critical systems.

For example, some issues were purposedly not included in the supplement on the ground that they were not related to OOT (like concurrency and function pointers), while others were included despite them not being related to OOT either (dynamic memory management, virtualization), because the latter were absolutely necessary for C++ and Java.

In this position paper, we review the origin of the push for OOD, and claim that a restricted form of OOT is all that is needed in the context of critical systems developed in Ada, in order to grasp the benefits of OOT without the heavy load (or the risks) of certification of full OOT systems.

2 DO178C and OOT

2.1 Why Use OOT in Airborne Systems?

A fundamental feature of DO178C is that the whole process is requirements-driven: every aspect of software should be related to a low-level requirement, which is itself connected to high level requirements. Therefore, the decision of using OOT in airborne systems should be connected to some requirements, and OOTiA[1] had a section on "considerations before making the decision to use OOT". There is no equivalent in DO178C that would address which kind of requirements could lead to choosing OOT for the development of airborne systems.

Beyond the desire of developers to use C++ and Java in avionics (but a desire does not make a proper requirement!), there might also be the push to

A. Romanovsky and T. Vardanega (Eds.): Ada-Europe 2011, LNCS 6652, pp. 214–218, 2011.
© Springer-Verlag Berlin Heidelberg 2011

using UML. Although UML is a notation which claims to be methodologically neutral, it forces in practice an OO approach; for example, the main design diagram is the class diagram. But this simply pushes the question to "why use UML for avionics"?

Of course, proponents of the full OO approach will claim that object orientation promotes encapsulation, contracts, reuse, and diminishes development costs. True, but OOT (or more precisely OO by classification[2]) is not the only way to achieve these goals, especially when using Ada.

OOTiA recognized that the true benefits of OOT in avionics is still an open issue; however, it seems unavoidable, simply because it is the way history is going. And after all: why not?

2.2   The Main Issue with OOT: Testing

A fundamental principle of DO178C is that certification is performed on the whole program; exhaustive testing is therefore (in principle) possible. However, dynamic binding implies that for a given (dispatching) call, full coverage would require testing all the methods for all possible classes in the whole class hierarchy. Since this needs to be done at every level in the call graph, it leads to a combinatorial explosion of paths that can make extensive (also called pessimistic) testing impractical.

DO178C would allow such pessimistic testing; however, it suggests another path that relies on the application of the LSP (Liskov Substitution Principle)[3]: if it can be demonstrated that a using class relies only on some properties of the used class, and that every object in the derivation tree satisfies these properties, then there is no need to test all the combinations of objects. What a nice idea! Unfortunately, relying on the LSP in critical and real-time software is not that easy.

- There has to be some differences between the various classes in the inheritance tree, otherwise it would make no sense to define different classes. The key point is that those differences are deemed "not significant" for the point of view of the using class. Any behaviour considered "not significant", but on which the using class inadvertantly relies, would break the whole proof system.
- All real time aspects have to be part of the "significant" properties, and as such inherited by all descendant classes. Therefore, the WCET expected by the using class has to be the worst of all subclasses too, and similarly for all other real-time properties, like blocking aspects, use of resources, etc. This can imply an excessively pessimistic contract.
- Would you board an airplane, knowing that some combination of the components have never been tested?

For these reasons, we think that relying on the LSP as a replacement for pessimistic testing is not acceptable for the highest (A and B) criticality levels; it can be acceptable for the lower levels, and in any case LSP is a useful concept - as long as it is applied in addition to full testing.

3   How is This Applicable to Ada?

Ada has a rich toolbox, and many (but not all) of the claimed benefits of OOT can be obtained by other means. For each issue, it is the designer's job to assess the need, and choose the most appropriate tool.

The fact that OOT might be an appropriate solution for other languages does not mean that it is necessarily the same for Ada; it can be seen as a real benefit of Ada that the OO technology is available when useful, but not required when the drawbacks exceed the benefits. For example, Ada provides packages for modularity, generics for reuse, tasks for concurrency, without needing OOT.

In our experience, the use of tagged types and inheritance is most valuable when the following three criteria are met:

- There is a need to model various entities as abstract data types, and those types are too different to be considered as simple variations of a single type (otherwise, a discriminated type would be appropriate).
- Although different, the various types share a number of properties, and especially operations where each type has its own way of providing the service (true methods[1]).
- There is a need to maintain an heterogenous data structure, where objects of the various types are kept, and the same method must be invoked on the various objects.

Since true methods are intimately linked to the type they operate on, there is no reason for them to perform redispatching, i.e. dispatching calls to some implementation attached to a different type.

There is however a different kind of operation, when a higher level operation is implemented by a combination of true methods. In other languages, these operations are often defined as methods, although they are not conceptually connected to a single type. In Ada, they are best implemented with class-wide operations, i.e. operations with a parameter of a class-wide type, making all calls to primitive operations of the parameter naturally dispatching.

For Ada, we propose therefore to make a clear separation between true methods where redispatching would be prohibited, and class-wide composition subprograms that would provide higher level services. By organizing critical software along those line, the combinatorial explosion would be limited:

- True methods would need testing only for values of the applicable type, and not for values of the whole inheritance tree; testing would not be different from normal subprograms
- Class-wide operations would require testing for all applicable values - like any other operation. Of course, "all applicable values" would include values from the whole inheritance tree.

---

[1] By "true methods", we mean operations that implement an abstract, elementary operation, where different types have different implementations.

- The places where pessimistic testing is required could be easily identified, and hopefully limited in number. Remember that a critical mass is necessary to get an "explosion" (at least one that challenges the testability of a program).

It can be argued that this paradigm is very limiting - and it would be indeed for application that require extensive use of OOT. However, we are dealing here with critical software. Critical software design implies a lot of restrictions, and restrictions are always limiting, and generally annoying! But that is the recognized price to pay when safety is at stakes.

4   A Profile for Using OOT in Ada for Critical Systems

The above proposed design pattern would need enforcement by tools. This can be provided by external tools, such as AdaControl[4], Gnatcheck[5], or RainCode[6], to name a few.

However, the best solution would be to enforce the restrictions at compile time - as well as some other restrictions that would be deemed useful in this context. Such a set of restrictions could be included in a profile, following the example of the Ravenscar profile for tasking features. This approach was first presented at a workshop held during the SIGAda 2010 conference in Fairfax, where the idea received general acceptance, and some additional restrictions were proposed. This effort is naturally open to anyone interested.

Note that there is no need to wait for Ada2012 to define such a profile - nor to ask for a delay to the new standard for this purpose. Like Ravenscar, the profile could be published as a technical report[2], and if proven useful, proposed for inclusion in the next revision of the Ada standard.

5   Conclusion

The main issue when applying OOT to critical software is the combinatorial explosion of tests implied by dynamic dispatching. The OOT supplement to DO178C tries to counter this by extensive use of formal methods, but it remains to be seen if the use of formal methods can be accepted as a replacement for exhaustive testing in the context of levels A and B software.

Instead, we propose a restrictive design pattern for classes that would make extensive (pessimistic) testing acceptable, by limiting dispatching to a small number of well identified places. This pattern is possible in Ada, because OOP is less pervasive than in other languages, and can therefore be restricted to places where the benefits overcome the drawbacks.

Such a profile could give Ada an advantage over other languages, by allowing easier testing and certification when OOT is used for critical software.

---

[2] Not necessarily an ISO TR, although it would help for wider acceptance by compiler vendors.

References

1. FAA/NASA, Handbook for Object-Oriented Technology in Aviation (2003)
2. Rosen, J.-P.: What Orientation Should Ada Objects Take. Communications of the ACM 35(11)
3. Liskov, B., Wing, J.: A Behavioral Notion of Subtyping. ACM Transactions on Programming Languages and Systems 16(6) (November 1994)
4. http://www.adalog.fr/adacontrol2.htm
5. http://www.adacore.com/home/products/gnatpro/toolsuite/gnatcheck/
6. http://www.raincodechecker.com/adachecker.html

On the Evolution of Unnatural Language

Les Hatton

CISM, Kingston University
http://www.leshatton.org/

Abstract. A search of the web reveals that natural language is considered to be language which a human would consider natural and unnatural language is language a human would consider artificial. This clearly raises interpretation questions and plenty of leeway so I am going to take the latter view here and bend it somewhat to consider programming languages as particularly good examples of unnatural language.

Programming languages are something like 60 years old. Their evolution tells us much about the triumph of creativity over parsimony; the need for diversity and the frequent triumph of politics over common sense or logic. Yet their minimum set of features is defined by the beauty and simplicity of the Böhm-Jacopini theorem [1] and their underlying similarity in information theoretic terms is shown in the theorem proved by myself in [3],[4].

This essay is a reflection on programming languages both old and new, engineering, systems evolution and the role of education.

1 A Little Essential Background

In 1966, two Italian computer scientists Corrado Böhm and Guiseppe Jacopini proved a very important and relatively unsung theorem which essentially demonstrated that every computable function could be implemented in a programming language which contained three control structures which we recognise today as sequence, selection and iteration [1]. This seminal paper also initiated the *structured programming* debate, however from our point of view it sets the minimum a programming language requires to implement every computable function.

Such minimum implementations would be a bit bleak to use in practice so it is interesting therefore to consider how much else computer scientists feel they must add to enhance "expressive ability".

1.1 Standardisation: The Good and the Bad

1966 was a busy year. As far as I can see, the first ANSI (American National Standard) programming language appeared in that year and became known as Fortran 66[1]. It was followed shortly after by ANSI standard COBOL in 1968 and a regular series of new languages over the next decades although these

---

[1] It was also the last year in which the lamentable and now massively overpaid England football team won anything of significance but let's not go there.

A. Romanovsky and T. Vardanega (Eds.): Ada-Europe 2011, LNCS 6652, pp. 219–225, 2011.
© Springer-Verlag Berlin Heidelberg 2011

became subsumed within the ISO (International Standards Organisation) from around 1990, (the C standard was probably the first to jump ship when ANSI C89 became ISO C90 with a simple section renumbering). At the time, standards were incredibly important. Without them, chaos would have ensued and although the promise of complete machine independence was never achieved, if you knew what you were doing, you could retain very high levels of portability with a generally negligible effort to move to another environment. Most of the time, you even got the same answers give or take a couple of significant figures, [5].

Unfortunately, things have struggled a bit since then due to rampant featurism. I've sat on a few national standards bodies in my time and one thing was very clear even in the early stages. No language committee was going to sit still and let other languages steal a march on them with some wicked new features however useless they were or turned out to be. It was a regular topic of conversation at Fortran meetings I attended that "we needed to have pointers because C had them". In fact pointers and notably dynamic memory spread across all languages very quickly, (although with odd and non empirically supported restrictions in some, as was the case in Ada 83 for example). As it turns out, almost nothing to do with programming languages is empirically supported. We are not a critical discipline and therefore we are not a scientific one either in the Popperian sense but more of this later.

This really took off with the widespread adoption of object orientation from around 1990 in spite of a complete lack of any supporting evidence. Language committees literally fell over themselves in the rush to add OO features, however inappropriate it might have been. Languages blew up like food addicts at a free hamburger stall. Just have a look at the following if you don't believe me.

Language	Size 1	Size 2	Increase factor
Ada	270Kb zipped HTML (1983)	1093Kb (1995)	4
C	191 pages (1990)	401 pages (1999)	2
C++	808 pages (1999)	1370 pages (2010 draft)	1.7
Fortran	134 pages (1978)	354 pages (1990)	2.5

This whole process whereby languages have evolved into each others' spaces has always seemed odd to me and must surely be driven by the simple need to attract more market share. With hindsight, it would have been much simpler to provide languages fit for a particular purpose and more emphatically encourage heterogeneous systems where the strengths of different languages combine together to provide the best application - Ada for real-time and high-integrity, C for systems work, Fortran for mathematical computation, Perl for pattern recognition and so on. This of course has happened quite naturally to a certain extent. The GNAT translator is a hybrid of Ada95 and gcc which is itself written in C; GNAT will be run on an operating system written in C (Linux) or Windows (C++); Java compilers are written in Java and Java run-time environments in C; Perl translators are written in C; there are Python translators written in (at least) Java, C and Python, and so on. So heterogeneity has occurred naturally but individual languages have become leviathans in the process. Perhaps this is itself unstoppable.

In the period 1990 - present day, the landscape has changed dramatically. I have a copy of the ACM SIGPLAN notices of March 1993 on the History of Programming Languages, (Volume 28(3)). It gives short introductions to: Ada, Algol 68, C, C++, CLU, Concurrent Pascal, Formac, Forth, Icon, Lisp, Pascal, Prolog and Smalltalk.

In 2010, students at my university offered projects in the following languages, C, C#, C++, Java, Perl, PHP, MySQL, XML, HTML, XHTML, VB.Net on XP, of which Java, PHP and MySQL dominated. Just look how little this has in common with the prior SIGPLAN list.

1.2   Validation and Compilers

One very important area in which Ada has done particularly well is in the provision of compiler testing. Until April 2000 or so, it was common for ISO languages to be validated against the validation suites which were available. In the 1990s it was possible to check standardisation of C or Fortran compilers against information provided by national bodies like NIST in the USA. Since then compiler validation has become a distant dream for many languages and the Ada community should be congratulated on keeping them publicly available.

A propos of nothing in particular, I downloaded and measured the size of the Ada validation suite as shown below. Comparing these against two other validation suites which I happen to have licences for, (C90 and Fortran 77), reveals.

Language	Validation suite (LOC)	Validation lines / Standard pages
Ada 95	355,498 (.ADA) + 253,748 (.A)	1,070
C 90	298,867 (.c) + 40,176 (.h)	1,800
Fortran 77	108,842 (.f)	820

These numbers were calculated in the case of Ada by

```
% find . -name '*.ADA' -exec wc -l {} \; \
    | awk '{sum += $1;}END{print sum;}'
% find . -name '*.A' -exec wc -l {} \; \
    | awk '{sum += $1;}END{print sum;}'
```

It is interesting to reflect on the above densities of validation lines to standard pages. Although rather approximate, I will note in passing that Ada validation might perhaps be made more extensive given the size of the Ada 95 standard.

To summarise here, standardisation initially served a very valuable function providing a level of portability which had not hitherto existed. Unfortunately, the need to avoid breaking old code, (backwards compatibility), makes the international standards process highly asymmetric whereby it is generally much easier to introduce new features of unknown value in a standard revision than it is to remove existing features of known problematic behaviour. Consequently the standards get bigger and bigger and considerable effort is needed to trim them back to a level of parsimony and precision appropriate to their use in high-integrity systems. This is not a process which can be continued indefinitely and some languages, for example, C, will struggle unless the thicket of unconstrained creativity can be cut back somewhat. Historically of course, the only alternative has been to start again with yet another new language, the evidence of which surrounds us.

2   Education and Programming Skills

In tandem with the growth and complexity of traditional programming language standards, CS education has changed dramatically. We now live in a world where classic programming such as is found in the study of compilers and data structures has been largely supplanted with concepts such as "mash-ups" in non-standardised languages and exotic development environments for systems such as those found in mobile phones. Such environments mix graphical methods with more traditional coding skills in a frequently very complex and, at least to my ageing eyes, arbitrary manner. As a result there has been a dramatic shift in the centre of gravity of skill sets which can make it very difficult to find competent developers in languages such as Ada and Fortran. Worse, they tend not to be taught widely in universities which almost entirely focus on a single language - the flavour of the last few years being Java. Whether this will be the case in the near future is impossible to tell as new paradigms come and go amongst the hardy-annuals of Ada, Fortran, C and C++.

Marrying a decline in traditional programming skills with increasing complexity in those languages requiring such skills will become a significant gap to fill. There is every sign that Cloud Computing demands, rapid development environments such as Ruby on Rails and the general evolution of web applications will increase rather than decrease the size of this gap. It almost seems to me that two completely different programming paradigms have evolved side by side.

1. The traditional life-cycle languages which involve system design, specification, implementation and validation. It is hard to conceive of a high-integrity system being built in any other way.
2. The "throw sub-systems at each other and see what works" life-cycle, so prevalent in web development.

It remains to be seen how easily people will move between these two very different paradigms. It may be that I am simply getting old but I find it relatively difficult to build web technologies because I tend to approach them too analytically and my experience is not such a benefit. I suspect the converse is also true - the rigour and discipline of specifying and building a system on which peoples lives may depend would not I feel come easily to a Ruby on Rails developer. If we were to explicitly separate them and prepare people in different ways, then that would be perfectly satisfactory according to the demands of each. However, if we continue to prepare the vast majority of CS students at university for the latter of the two, the former will be starved.

3   Underlying Linguistic Similarity

Amidst this blizzard of languages and technologies, it is very reasonable to ask if there are any common denominators. Clearly some languages have great staying power even though they regularly morph into other forms. Fortran is a wonderful example with something like 50 years of sustained use, although 1960s Fortran has very little in common with Fortran 2008, formally approved in late 2010.

Surprisingly however, considering the enormous differences which exist between different applications and different implementations, there appears to be a beautiful form of clockwork underlying this massive externally forced complexity.

In 2009, I proved a theorem [3], [4], which shows that for any system of N components each containing t_i tokens such that the total number of tokens is given by

$$T = \sum_{i=1}^{N} t_i \tag{1}$$

then the probability p_i of a component of t_i tokens appearing is overwhelmingly likely to obey a power-law in the alphabet a_i of *unique* tokens used

$$p_i \sim a_i^{-\beta} \tag{2}$$

where β is a constant, under the constraints that the total size of the system and the total amount of Shannon information in the system is conserved. The theorem combines arguments from statistical physics with standard properties of Shannon's information theory, as can be found for example in [2].

Note that this is completely language independent - it makes no assumptions about the implementation language. In this sense, a token of a programming language is either a *fixed* token a_f, (for example keywords like **if else begin end procedure** or operators like $+ \; ++ \; -$) or a *variable* token a_v, (for example identifier names or constants).

Given that in smaller components, the number of fixed tokens tends to predominate (there is a fixed token startup overhead of implementing anything in a programming language) and in larger components, variable tokens predominate, the theorem further predicts that

$$p_i \sim constant \tag{3}$$

for smaller components merging asymptotically into the power-law described in (2).

Investigating this experimentally has taken some time because of the need to write a universal token parser able to distinguish between fixed and variable

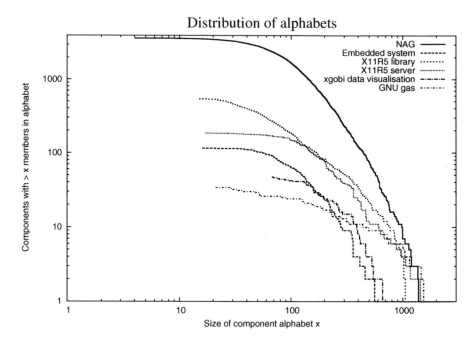

Fig. 1. Examples of disparate systems in different languages which appear to follow the behaviour predicted by (2) and (3). To date, no systems have been found which depart from this.

tokens for a number of languages with enough intelligence to distinguish the start and end of components. This has been done so far for Ada, C, C++, Fortran, Java, Perl and Tcl-Tk. This lexer takes advantage of the standard lexical analysis generator *lex* and the rest is written in C. The results of analysing the distribution of sizes of components across highly disparate systems in several languages is shown in Figure 1. This shape is precisely what is predicted by the development which leads to (2) and (3).

This provides good experimental support for the theorem and suggests that underneath all the complexity of notation, there is a very strong similarity in how we express the information inherent in systems implemented in programming languages.

4   Conclusion

Perhaps then we have come full circle. We started off in 1966 with an underlying simplicity and here almost 50 years later, we appear once again to have an underlying simplicity. However, this does not disguise the fact that the languages themselves have either disappeared or become very complex systems in their own right, presenting a very steep learning challenge to new and even partly experienced engineers.

In parallel with this, changing patterns of education and an apparent and growing dichotomy of development paradigms places further stresses on the ability to produce high quality systems and engineers with the requisite experience. In particular, the modern "mash-up" methods seem strongly in the ascendant.

Will programming languages continue to accrete complexity ? Will the landscape in 30 years time be Ada 2032, C 2038, C++ 2036, Fortran 2040 or will interpreted languages dominate ? Given that these contenders have already had 30 years or more, it would be a brave person to bet against them in spite of the above concerns.

References

1. Boehm, C., Jacopini, G.: Flow Diagrams, Turing machines, and Languages with only Two Formation Rules. Communications of the ACM 9(5), 366–371 (1966)
2. Cherry, C.: On Human Communication. John Wiley Science Editions, Chichester (1963), library of Congress 56-9820
3. Hatton, L.: Power-law distributions of component sizes in general software systems. IEEE Transactions on Software Engineering (July/August 2009)
4. Hatton, L.: Power-laws, persistence and the distribution of information in software systems (January 2010), http://www.leshatton.org/variations_2010.html
5. Hatton, L., Wright, A., Smith, S., Parkes, G., Bennett, P., Laws, R.: Sks: A large scale exercise in fortran 77 portability. Software, Practice and Experience 18(4), 301–329 (1988)

Author Index